THE WORLD'S GREATEST

CIVIL AIRCRAFT

AN ILLUSTRATED HISTORY

THE WORLD'S GREATEST
CIVIL AIRCRAFT
AN ILLUSTRATED HISTORY

Paul E. Eden

amber
BOOKS

Published by
Amber Books Ltd
74–77 White Lion Street
London
N1 9PF
United Kingdom
www.amberbooks.co.uk
Appstore: itunes.com/apps/amberbooksltd
Facebook: www.facebook.com/amberbooks
Twitter: @amberbooks

ISBN: 978-1-78274-245-6

Project Editor: Michael Spilling
Picture Research: Terry Forshaw
Design: Andrew Easton

Printed in China

Contents

Introduction

In a little over 100 years, commercial aircraft have developed from the frail wood and fabric machines of the 1910s, capable of carrying little more than a passenger or packet of mail, into one of the most efficient means of long-range transportation ever designed.

Commercial aircraft are used to fly passengers and freight in order to generate revenue for their operators. When Wilbur Wright took the first passenger aloft on 14 May 1908 the seed for all subsequent airline operations was sown. The first cargo, two packages of silk, was flown between Dayton and Columbus, Ohio, on 7 November 1910, although a major driver of non-passenger operations was mail – Henri Pequet flew 6500 letters across the Jumna River from Allahabad to Naini Junction, India, on 18 February 1911, completing the first official airmail flight.

Delivering mail by air reduced delivery times dramatically and airmail took on particular importance for the U.S.airline industry and for Lufthansa, the German state airline.

The Concorde programme remains among the most significant engineering achievements ever. It produced an airliner of immense performance but flawed economics – it served only British Airways and Air France.

Germany exerted considerable influence in South America after World War I, doing much to establish the earliest commercial operations in the region. Lufthansa also expended considerable effort facilitating airmail routes from Europe to Latin America, driving the development of high-performance seaplanes and overwater navigation techniques.

The very first commercial operators were limited by the capability of their aircraft, but soon the manufacturers began building purpose-designed airliners, with enclosed passenger cabins, space for baggage and increasingly sophisticated navigation and communications systems. Some aircraft builders quickly saw that reliability and safety were the most important factors in creating a successful airliner and Junkers was first to crystallize this thinking into a single airframe – the F13. The first all-metal airliner, the F13 set the standard for others to follow and established Junkers as a major force in commercial aircraft design until shortly before World War II, when a new paradigm emerged from Boeing – the

Trans World Airlines was instrumental in the development process that created the Douglas DC-3, shown here, via the DC-1 and DC-2. The DC-3 was the most important commercial aircraft of the immediate pre-World War II period and helped establish Douglas as the pre-eminent airliner manufacturer into the early 1950s.

Model 247. Boeing sold relatively few of the Model 247, but it represented the next major advance in airliner design, introducing many of the features considered standard today. Built in metal, with a comfortable, heated and ventilated cabin, the aircraft featured retractable landing gear and two engines, each powerful enough to maintain altitude should the other fail.

Boeing's wartime preoccupation with bomber construction allowed Douglas to become the undisputed leader in commercial aviation in the immediate aftermath of World War II, but it fell to Great Britain's de Havilland to take the next developmental stride. Britain and Germany had both flown jet fighters in combat during the later years of the war and now de Havilland applied jet technology to commercial aviation, producing the Comet.

The world's first jet airliner, the Comet's somewhat conservative design nevertheless allowed it to outperform every piston-engined aircraft, but a series of accidents stymied the programme. While de Havilland was fixing its aircraft, Boeing came up with a truly modern jet airliner, the Model 707, truly the template for commercial jet transport. The U.S. planemaker quickly established a market leadership that only Airbus has been able to challenge and then only in recent years.

Passengers quickly became accustomed to flying large distances on swept-wing jet-powered aircraft, but the piston engine still reigned on shorter routes. While Lockheed and the UK's Vickers created successful turboprops for these sectors, the travelling public and airlines began to demand aircraft comparable to those on the long-haul services. Soon Douglas and Boeing were following in the wake of the Caravelle from French company Sud-Est to produce their own short-haul jets. Douglas took the lead with its DC-9, but Boeing fought back with the 737, still the world's best-selling jetliner.

With the sheer number of aircraft movements at overcrowded airports threatening to jam the air transport system, Boeing recognized that aircraft of much higher capacity were needed. While Europe wasted money on the technically superb but commercially flawed Concorde, Boeing created the first widebody and began the next major evolution in airliner technology – the 747 'Jumbo Jet' remains in production more than four decades later.

The commercial aircraft market remained Boeing's plaything until the late 1960s, when a threat to its dominance at last took shape. Western Europe's major aircraft manufacturers had joined forces to create Airbus Industrie and its first product, the short/medium-haul A300 widebody, caught Boeing napping. Since then the two have become the major commercial aircraft rivals.

Airbus continues to challenge the 737 with its A320 family, while the makers trade blows in the medium and long-haul markets with the 767, 777 and 787, and A330 and A350 XWB. Boeing's 747-8, the latest and most advanced 'Jumbo', falls short of the massive passenger capacity of the double-deck A380 'Super Jumbo', but neither has sold particularly well. Now both manufacturers are promising double-digit fuel burn improvements with new models for the near future, mirroring on a grand scale the similar battles of the regional jet market between Canada's Bombardier and Brazil's Embraer. The world of commercial aircraft has never before been so technologically advanced, nor so demanding.

The Golden Age

Severely restricted by terms drawn up by the Allied powers in the Treaty of Versailles after World War I, Germany's aircraft industry moved its manufacturing facilities and best people abroad. By this means it dominated commercial aircraft production with advanced designs, including the Junkers F13 and Dornier Wal, both of which found ready markets around the world. Fokker rose to produce the most worthy competitor to German ascendency, with a series of aircraft that included the excellent F.VII-3m. Fokker also established manufacturing facilities in the US, where its trimotors sold well, but ultimately spurred the development of thoroughly modern Boeing and Douglas airliners. So the Douglas DC-3 took the airlines onto a war footing and although Douglas and Lockheed vied for supremacy with their beautiful piston engined airliners of the 1950s, the age of the jet – in which Boeing would reign supreme – had dawned.

Facing page: The turboprop, harnessing the power, simplicity and relatively light weight of a jet with propeller efficiency, promised economical long-range operations in the post-piston world. In the event, passengers demanded pure-jet speeds over long ranges, but manufacturers, including Vickers, with the Viscount (here flying for British European Airways), found a ready market for shorter-ranged turboprop airliners.

Junkers F13 (1919)

Frequently described by aviation historians as the first modern airliner, the Junkers F13 set the precedent for metal, enclosed-cabin commercial aircraft. Remarkably reliable for its era, the versatile F13 sold well around the world, operating on wheel, float and ski landing gear.

In 1910, Professor Hugo Junkers patented his first aircraft idea of an unusual design that might today be described as a flying wing. The wing was to be of all-metal construction and although the idea remained little more than a concept, Junkers used metal in several subsequent military designs.

In particular, his use of cantilever – attached to the fuselage at their roots and without bracing struts – wings with corrugated Duralumin skinning was advanced for its time and when it became clear that World War I was

drawing to a close, Junkers set his designers to work-up a prototype for an airliner of similar construction. Some sources claim that he gave the order for development of what became the Junkers J13 on Armistice Day.

Built as a single-engined low-wing monoplane with enclosed accommodation for four passengers and a crew of two in open cockpits, the J13 flew for the first time on 25 June 1919. It was the world's first purpose-designed metal airliner and, powered by a Mercedes D.IIIa inline engine, followed its initial flight with a second that same

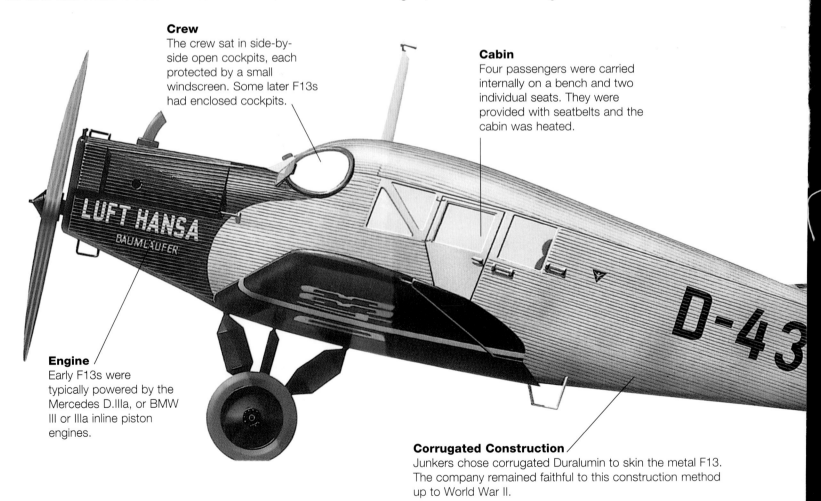

Crew
The crew sat in side-by-side open cockpits, each protected by a small windscreen. Some later F13s had enclosed cockpits.

Cabin
Four passengers were carried internally on a bench and two individual seats. They were provided with seatbelts and the cabin was heated.

Engine
Early F13s were typically powered by the Mercedes D.IIIa, or BMW III or IIIa inline piston engines.

Corrugated Construction
Junkers chose corrugated Duralumin to skin the metal F13. The company remained faithful to this construction method up to World War II.

Established in 1926, Deutsche Luft Hansa took many of its early F13s from Junkers-Luftverkehr, the manufacturer's own airline, which was subsumed into the national carrier.

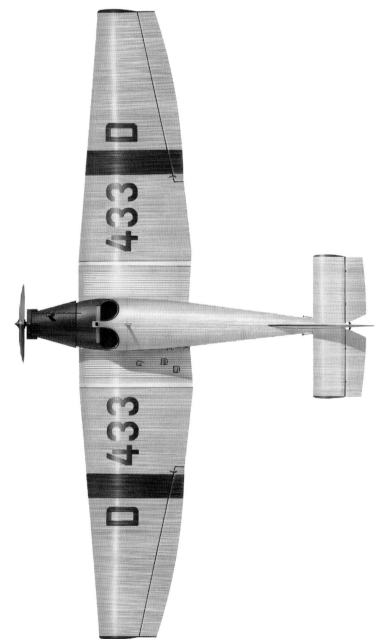

Fin and Rudder

Early F13s featured this short, sharply-swept fin and distinctively-shaped rudder. Later aircraft had a larger fin and revised rudder.

Junkers F13

This F13 has the taller fin of later aircraft. Note also the unusual shape of the cabin door.

day, this time carrying six people, sufficient fuel for three hours in the air and ballast equivalent to baggage.

Junkers immediately put the aircraft into production as the F13, offered with a wide variety of engine types. Sales were no doubt encouraged by Junkers choosing the type to comprise the majority of the fleet of its own airline, Junkers-Luftverkehr. By the time it merged with Aero Lloyd to form Deutsche Luft Hansa in January 1926, the Junkers airline had taken 60 F13s.

Worldwide Service

Junkers production was disrupted in 1921/22 when the nations victorious in World War I attempted to manage aircraft production in Germany under an Allied Disarmament Commission ruling. The manufacturer circumvented the restriction by moving F13 production to Danzig, which at that time fell outside Germany. As if the F13's proven reliability and performance were not enough, Junkers encouraged Europe's airlines to operate the type by offering aircraft for next to nothing as it strove to be involved in the region's major airline groupings.

Airlines from 16 European countries were amalgamated into the Europa-Union in 1925, all of them equipped with F13s. But Junkers was not content with European domination and set about establishing air routes in the Middle East, when Junkers-Luftverkehr began operations in Persia. It also exploited existing German interests in South America and took a hand, through the excellence of the F13, in the creation of several of the continent's major airlines. Aside from the attributes that made the F13 so attractive to European operators, those in South America

Specification

Type:	open cockpit, enclosed cabin airliner
Dimensions:	(early aircraft) wing span 14.47m (47ft 5¾in), length 9.59m (31ft 5in), height 3.50m (11ft 5¾in)
Loaded weight:	1640kg (3620lb)
Powerplant:	one 185hp BMW IIIa six-cylinder inline piston engine
Maximum speed:	173km/h (107mph)
Range:	1400km (870 miles)
Service ceiling:	5000m (16,400ft)
Crew:	2
Passengers:	4

appreciated its ready adaptability to float landing gear. Large stretches of water were often more easily located and employed as landing and take-off strips than areas of flat, obstacle-free land in the rugged, inhospitable terrain of countries like Brazil.

As an alternative to wheels or floats, the F13 flew equally well on skis and thus attracted Canadian bush operators looking to exploit the aircraft's reliability and strength in arduous operations to remote settlements. Canada's preponderance of water made floats an essential requirement, but during its harsh winters the alternatives of wheels and skis allowed operations to continue from snow and ice.

F13 Evolution

A variety of modifications improved the basic F13 over the course of production, which delivered 345 aircraft over the 12 years from 1919. Little came of a scheme for the Larsen Corporation to build F13s for the North American market, although of the eight Junkers-Larsen JL-6 aircraft produced, the majority served U.S. airmail routes and at least one was delivered to Colombia.

The F13 airframe changed little, but most notably the fin was modified from its original sharply-swept shallow form to a deeper, more conventional configuration. A wide variety of engines was successfully mated to the airframe, including radials and inlines from British, German, French and U.S. manufacturers. The world's last commercial F13 was retired in Brazil in 1951.

Several F13s entered military service as utility transports, some of them adapted to deliver bombs and provided with defensive armament. The Luftwaffe operated a number as radio/navigation trainers and the South American F13 fleet was widely used in conflicts throughout the region.

Floatplane Versatility

Suitable airfield facilities were sparsely separated or even non-existent in many parts of the world during the formative years of commercial aviation. Lakes, rivers and even the sea were often in plentiful supply, however, so that floatplane and flying-boat services were commonplace. Airlines were therefore especially taken with the F13's easy transition to float alighting gear, albeit with penalties in terms of drag and weight and therefore performance. Other than the obvious addition of floats, little modification was required to the basic F13 airframe. Nevertheless, the floats could have a detrimental effect on directional control so that some F13 floatplanes gained a taller rudder that extended below the fuselage underside.

Hungarian airline Aero Express operated a number of F13 floatplanes, including H-MACA, 'MACC, 'MACE and H-MACF, as well as the 'MACB shown here. Among the carrier's bases was a seaplane station on the Danube at Budapest.

Dornier Wal (1922)

Like Junkers, Dornier became well known for its exceptional metal commercial aircraft. The Wal excelled in an era when flying-boat transport was the norm. It remained viable into the later 1930s, thanks to its development potential, and became the cornerstone of Luft Hansa's mail service to South America.

The restrictions on German aircraft manufacturing written into the Treaty of Versailles achieved little more than driving the country's most ambitious aviation company owners and designers out of the country. Establishing factories in Italy, Sweden and Switzerland, these manufacturers worked hard to produce world-class designs that became the cornerstone of much of the European airline network, performed important pioneering work in South America and laid the foundations for Germany's dominance in military aircraft at the beginning of World War II.

Claudius Dornier was a designer of particular talent, especially with aircraft of metal construction, having worked with Zeppelin from 1910 and soon been given his own seaplane development arm of the company, Zeppelin-Lindau. A brief series of flying-boat prototypes followed, along with a number of smaller military designs, before Dornier began working on civil aircraft in 1919. The six-seat Gs I airliner flying boat of that year was destroyed by the Allies in 1920 since it contravened regulations. When the nine-seat Gs II was also outlawed, Zeppelin-

Engines
The Do R4 had four engines, mounted back-to-back as push-pull pairs, either side of the wing centreline position.

Cockpit
The Super Wal's cockpit was moved aft and offset to port, compared to the open forward cockpit of the Do J.

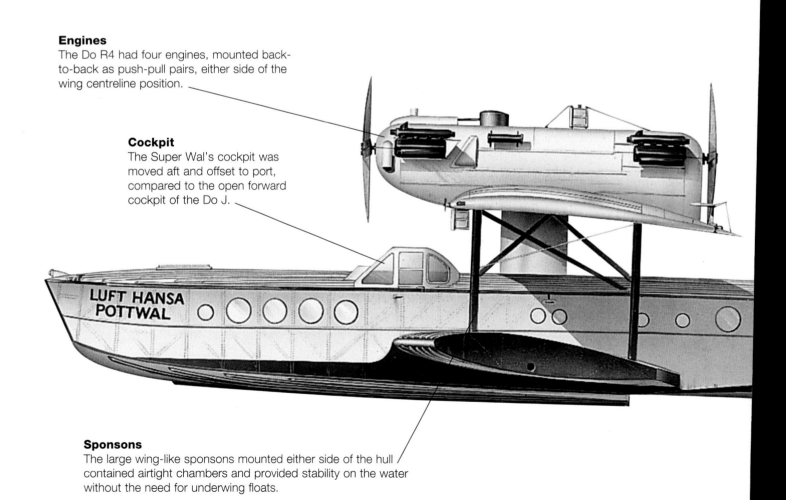

LUFT HANSA
POTTWAL

Sponsons
The large wing-like sponsons mounted either side of the hull contained airtight chambers and provided stability on the water without the need for underwing floats.

Lindau became Dornier Metallbauten, which set up an Italian subsidiary to develop the Gs II.

Wal Emerges

Known as the Wal, the Gs II prototype flew for the first time on 6 November 1922. Constructed primarily of metal, it had a wide hull with broad-chord sponsons, or Stummel, that conferred stability on the water. The wings were mounted on struts above the fuselage and the twin-engined powerplant was mounted on their centreline in a push-pull configuration.

The aircraft was an immediate success with airlines in Europe and South America, demonstrating great development potential in terms of passenger capacity

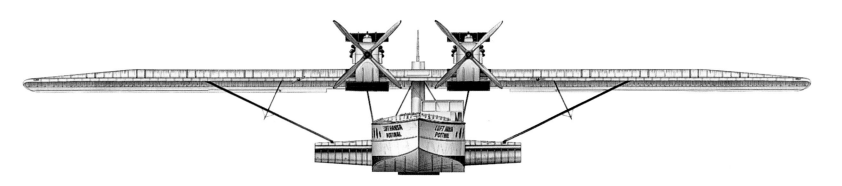

Luft Hansa took seven Do R4s, of which D-1337 *Pottwal* was powered by Napier Lion inline engines rather than the standard Jupiter.

Passenger Cabins
Super Wal passengers sat in two cabins fore and aft of the sponson area.

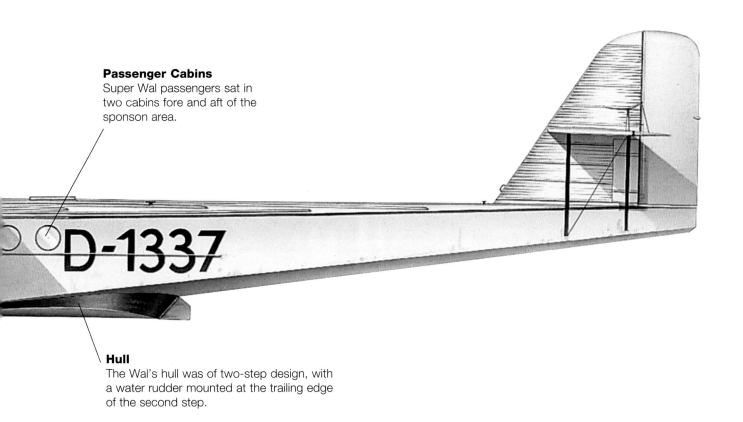

Hull
The Wal's hull was of two-step design, with a water rudder mounted at the trailing edge of the second step.

Dornier Wal

and being inherently suitable for up-engining. Wals were built in Italy for Dornier and under licence in Japan, the Netherlands, Spain and Switzerland, before Dornier set up a production line at Friedrichshafen, Germany, in 1933.

Under the basic designation Do J, several Wal variants emerged, mostly varying in powerplant and including the so-called 8 tonnen- and 10 tonnen-Wal used by Lufthansa (Luft Hansa's name from 1933). The type was also of interest to the military, and Italian production

Wolfgang von Gronau used Do J D-2053 on a round-the-world flight in 1932. The aircraft was named Grönland Wal (Greenland Whale) for the expedition.

included machines powered by the 360hp Rolls-Royce eagle engine for the Spanish navy. Such was their performance that these aircraft set a number of world records in 1925. Two Wals were also purchased for Roald Amundsen's 1925 journey to the North Pole, their crews flying them far north onto the polar ice cap.

Super Wal

The Do J accommodated its pilots in an open cockpit at the bow, with internal space for a navigator and radio operator behind. Aft of them, the hull could be filled with a mix of cargo, mail and passengers, capacity for the latter depending on the quantity of the former, but 12 passengers was a typical load.

Seeking to exploit the Wal's potential to the full, Dornier flew the Do R2 Super Wal for the first time in September 1926. With a longer wing span and hull, the R2 had two cabins for a total of 19 passengers, power coming from a pair of 650hp Rolls-Royce Condor engines. Yet more development was possible, however, and in 1927 the Do

Specification (Do R4 Super Wal)

Type:	four-engined transport flying boat
Dimensions:	wing span 28.60m (93ft 10in), length 24.60m (80ft 8in), height 6.00m (19ft 8in)
Loaded weight:	14,000kg (30,864lb)
Powerplant:	four 485hp Napier Lion VIII W-12 inline piston engines
Cruising speed:	210km/h (130mph)
Range:	2000km (1243 miles)
Crew:	4
Passengers:	19

R4 Super Wal emerged. Powered by two sets of Bristol Jupiter radial engines licence built in Germany by Siemens, the R4 offered gross weights 33 per cent greater than those of the Do J and was 16 per cent faster.

Military Legacy

Luft Hansa employed the Wal extensively on its transatlantic mail routes to South America, and in 1934 Dornier suggested that a replacement could be designed to satisfy the requirements of both the airline and the Luftwaffe as Germany began to rearm. A militarized variant of the Do J, the Do 15 Militär-Wal had entered service that year and Dornier's proposal for its replacement was also accepted by Lufthansa. The resulting Do 18 entered only limited civilian service, and although it was undoubtedly among the most advanced aircraft of its type, its origins in the Gs II of 1922 were obvious.

Air Mail to South America

Such was the importance of its South American influence that Germany sought the fastest method possible of delivering mail from Berlin to Rio de Janeiro, Brazil. In 1930 a letter typically took 14 days to arrive, a time initially cut by Lufthansa and its Brazilian subsidiary Condor, meeting the ships crossing the Atlantic with seaplanes when they were still out at sea. By this means, 14 days were cut to nine.

Clearly the way ahead lay with a non-stop crossing by air, but since no aircraft was available with the required range, Lufthansa set about establishing ocean refuelling stations. A fleet of aviation support ships was therefore commissioned, pioneered by the 5400-tonne Westfalen.

Mail was first flown westbound using the new system on 3 February 1934. Wals flew the overwater legs, alighting alongside the support ship for refuelling (see below). The vessel lifted the flying boat aboard using a crane, where it was refuelled and sent on its way by steam catapult. On 25 July 1935, the 100th crossing was flown and a third ship ordered, with the ocean crossing itself taking around 13 hours.

The Do 18 replaced the Do J from 1936 and also operated across the North Atlantic, but the latter operation wound down in 1938, while the South American service continued into 1941.

Fokker F.VII and F.VII-3m
(1924)

Ultimately settling on three engines for load-carrying performance and reliability, Fokker sold the F.VII and F.VII-3m series widely across Europe. More importantly, the type penetrated into the U.S. market and formed the basis of several pioneering flights.

Anthony Fokker's military aircraft were among the most formidable scout, or fighter, machines of World War I. After the armistice he developed a commercial aircraft based on the exceptional D.VII scout, this F.I leading to a series of airliners culminating in the F.V. The F.I and II were built in Germany, but Allied restrictions made their continued production impossible and Fokker returned to his native Holland.

Here the F.IV and V designs contributed much to the F.VII, on which design work began in 1923. The single-engined machine appeared in 1924 as a six-seater. Only five were built before the improved eight-seat F.VIIA entered production. Like the earlier machine, it had an immensely strong high-mounted wing that did away with any form of external bracing. Power generally came from a Bristol Jupiter engine licence built in France by Gnome-

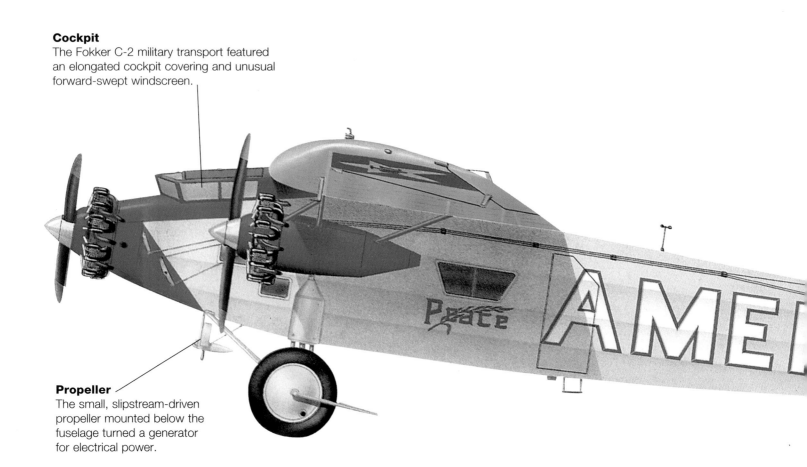

Cockpit
The Fokker C-2 military transport featured an elongated cockpit covering and unusual forward-swept windscreen.

Propeller
The small, slipstream-driven propeller mounted below the fuselage turned a generator for electrical power.

Explorer and pilot Richard E. Byrd and his three-man crew used C-2 NX206 *America* for the first transatlantic mail flight, leaving New York on 29 June 1927. Unable to land in Paris because of poor weather, the crew ditched off Calais on 1 July. The aircraft was destroyed but all four crew survived.

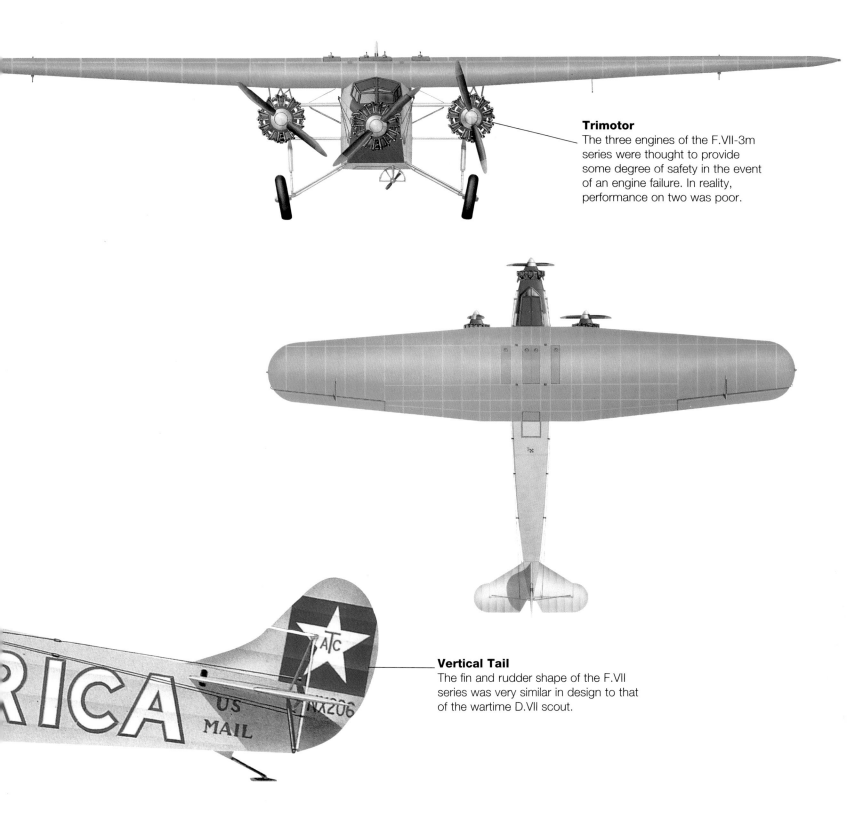

Trimotor
The three engines of the F.VII-3m series were thought to provide some degree of safety in the event of an engine failure. In reality, performance on two was poor.

Vertical Tail
The fin and rudder shape of the F.VII series was very similar in design to that of the wartime D.VII scout.

Fokker F.VII and F.VII-3m

E. Plage & T. Laskiewicz built 19 F.VIIB-3m aircraft under licence in Poland for LOT, the national carrier.

Rhône, providing greater speed and heavier load lifting capability than possessed by the F.VII.

The first F.VIIA flew for the first time on 12 March 1925, powered by a Packard Liberty engine, the choice of U.S. powerplant reflecting the considerable interest that Fokker's designs were generating in North America. Although it achieved a degree of success, the F.VIIA was quickly superseded by the F.VIIA-3m, an aircraft created by combining the F.VIIA airframe with a powerplant of three Wright Whirlwind J-4 engines, most likely as a primary result of U.S. calls for increased commercial aircraft reliability and safety.

Pioneering Fokker

Commander Richard E. Byrd purchased the first F.VIIA-3m after it had taken part in the Ford Reliability Trails

of 1925, using the aircraft on his North Pole expedition as Josephine Ford. Thereafter the type became popular with explorers and pioneers, and this demand combined with airline orders to require licence production in Belgium, Czechoslovakia, France, Italy, Poland and the UK. Fokker also set up a subsidiary, Atlantic Aircraft, to build and develop the aircraft for the U.S. market.

There was still a good deal of development potential in the basic F.VII airframe and this was exploited through the provision of more powerful engines. A variety of powerplants was available to this F.VIIB-3m model, the early aircraft generally boasting Whirlwinds in the 300–330hp class. By increasing the aircraft's wing area, Fokker was able to make the most of the available power and with its new-found weight-lifting capacity the F.VIIB-3m took its place as one of Europe's most important airliners.

Atlantic Aircraft built the F.VIIB-3m as the F.9, from which it developed a series of models including the C-2 military transport. In Great Britain, Avro took an F.VIIB-3m production licence, modifying the aircraft with Armstrong Siddeley Lynx radial engines and building it as the Model 618 Ten, the name a reference to its 10 seats. Four of a smaller variant known as the Five, seating four passengers and a pilot, and a handful of the slightly enlarged Avro 624 Six followed, the latter with six seats.

Subsequent Designs

The F.VIIB-3m achieved considerable success in airline and military service, flying as a transport and bomber with several air arms and on both sides in the Spanish Civil War. Such was its popularity that Fokker

Specification (F.VII-3m)

Type:	trimotor airliner
Dimensions:	wing span 21.71m (71ft 3in), length 14.57m (47ft 7in), height 3.90m (12ft 10in)
Loaded weight:	5300kg (11,684lb)
Powerplant:	three 300hp Wright J-6 Whirlwind nine-cylinder radial piston engines
Cruising speed:	178km/h (111mph)
Range:	1200km (746 miles) with additional fuel
Service ceiling:	4400m (14,435ft)
Crew:	2
Passengers:	8 to 10

continued with its established format for subsequent designs, but never again achieved the success it had with the F.VIIB-3m.

Larger than the F.VIIB-3m, the F.VIII twin seated 15 passengers, while the F.IX trimotor took as many as 20. The F.XII evolved directly from the F.VIIB-3m, with Pratt & Whitney Wasp engines and seats for up to 16 passengers, and itself spawned the larger still F.XVIII. The F.XX was an altogether more modern aircraft with retractable undercarriage, but it retained the now antiquated high-wing, trimotor layout when it first flew in 1933. With Douglas working on the DC-1 and DC-2 in the U.S., the latest Fokker was still way behind the times and the subsequent F.XXII and F.XXXVI, although four-engined and significantly larger than their forebears, were hopelessly outclassed.

Fokker had nevertheless continued his military work in the Netherlands and this kept the company in business until its facilities were destroyed or otherwise broken up in the early stages of World War II.

Transpacific Trimotor

Australian Charles Kingsford-Smith, who had flown in combat during World War I, continued to fly commercially after the Armistice. In 1928 he embarked on a campaign to complete the first crossing of the Pacific by air, arriving in the U.S. and searching for a suitable aircraft. He fell upon the F.VII-3m, purchasing an aircraft to an intermediate standard between F.VIIA-3m and F.VIIB-3m and naming it Southern Cross.

The machine uniquely had the large wing of the 'B' and lower-powered 200hp Whirlwinds of the 'A'. With his co-pilot, a radio operator and navigator, Kingsford-Smith set out from Oakland, California, on 31 May 1928. Stopping off at Honolulu and Fiji, they arrived in Brisbane, Australia, after 83 hours and 38 minutes in the air, covering 11,890km (7389 miles).

Again flying with co-pilot C.T.P. Ulm, Kingsford-Smith used Southern Cross for a successful first crossing of the Tasman Sea over 10/11 September 1928. The aircraft remains on display in the Kingsford-Smith Memorial building at Brisbane Airport, Queensland, Australia.

Ford Tri-Motor (1926)

A peculiar mix of old and new, the Ford Tri-Motor took the proven three-engined powerplant of the Fokker F.VII-3m and combined it with the all-metal construction that Henry Ford believed was the future for aircraft construction.

In July 1925 Henry Ford held a Reliability Trial for commercial aircraft. The test began at his Dearborn, Michigan, headquarters and required participants to undertake flights in most areas of the USA. Ford was keen to expand into civil aviation and was essentially looking for ideas to equip his own airline. Fokker won the competition with the F.VIIA-3m, rapidly modified for increased reliability by conversion from single-engined F.VIIA to trimotor '3m' standard.

Ford might simply have bought Fokkers, but was convinced that the essentially wooden structure of the F.VIIIA-3m was outdated. In August he bought the Stout Metal Airplane Company and in the following February began airmail operations through Stout Air Transport. Requiring an all-metal trimotor larger than the Fokker, he commissioned Stout to build one. Company founder William 'Bill' Stout had already produced pioneering metal aircraft designs, but the 3-AT he built in response

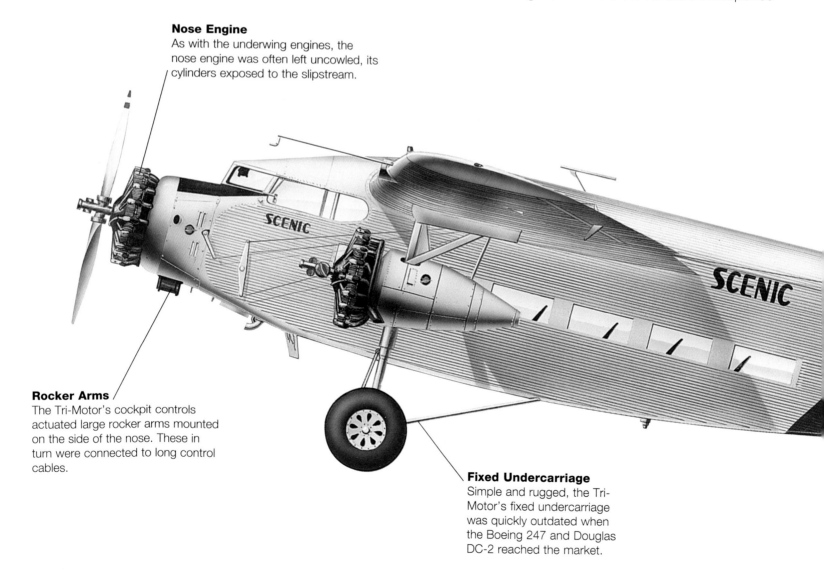

Nose Engine
As with the underwing engines, the nose engine was often left uncowled, its cylinders exposed to the slipstream.

Rocker Arms
The Tri-Motor's cockpit controls actuated large rocker arms mounted on the side of the nose. These in turn were connected to long control cables.

Fixed Undercarriage
Simple and rugged, the Tri-Motor's fixed undercarriage was quickly outdated when the Boeing 247 and Douglas DC-2 reached the market.

was disappointing. A hangar fire on 17 January 1926 destroyed the aircraft and Ford moved Stout on shortly afterwards. A new design team took over and although it remains unclear as to where the majority of the credit for the 4-AT lies, this first of the successful Ford Tri-Motors completed its initial flight on 11 June. Ironically, 'Bill' Stout was among its first customers.

The 4-AT combined the trimotor configuration of the F.VII-3m, prized for its enhanced safety, with a metal structure and the corrugated metal skinning typical of Junkers. The Alclad sheet used for the aircraft's skin could be made thin and light thanks to the strength and damage-resistance inherent in its corrugations. The original machine had an open cockpit for its crew of two and seated eight passengers in its cabin. It sold reasonably well in a number of variants, but the airlines required a larger machine and the 5-AT emerged in response.

Larger Tri-Motor

Passenger accommodation in the 5-AT increased to 14 and power came from the 450hp Pratt & Whitney Wasp Junior, replacing the 200hp Wright J-4 of the earlier machine. The wing span was also extended and the 5-AT became the most successful of the Fords, accounting for the majority of the line's 199 sales to commercial operators in a variety of configurations.

The Tri-Motor represented an odd mix of contemporary construction techniques and anachronistic design that allowed more modern machines from Boeing and

Nevada-based Scenic Airways used 5-AT-C Tri-Motor N414H on sightseeing tours over the Grand Canyon.

Corrugated Rudder
Unusually for the period, the Tri-Motor's control surfaces were metal-skinned, using the same corrugated material as on the rest of the airframe.

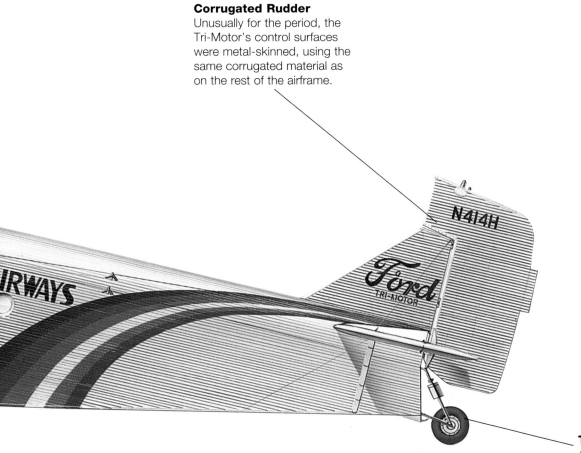

Tailwheel
Among its modern features, the Tri-Motor boasted mainwheel brakes. This allowed the use of a more versatile tailwheel, rather than a tailskid.

Ford Tri-Motor

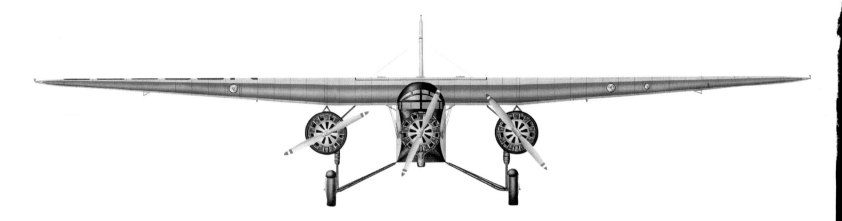

Above is shown the Ford Model 5-AT-B, a variant of the Tri-Motor, featuring three 313kW (420hp) engines and seating for 15 passengers. Forty-two were built.

Douglas to eclipse it very quickly, but it demonstrated a rugged reliability that has allowed a handful of machine to remain airworthy into the 2010s. In its metal structure the Tri-Motor was very advanced and even its control surfaces were metal skinned, when many aircraft of metal construction employed fabric covering for these surfaces.

In the cabin, Tri-Motor passengers stowed their hand luggage in mesh racks mounted along the cabin walls above the windows, or in what in today would be termed overhead bins, located between the wing spars. Unlike that of the F.VII series, the Tri-Motor's wing was mounted within the fuselage structure rather than on top, so that the wing spars encroached on cabin headroom.

The outer engines were suspended some distance below the wings so that the thrust line of their propellers

was parallel to that of the nose engine – this was not the case on the F.VII-3m and had caused British regulators sufficient concern for the Avro Ten to be altered such that there was less disparity between wing and nose thrust lines. The exhaust of the inner engine extended along the fuselage underside, where it passed through a muff, allowing it to heat fresh air that was then passed into the cabin during cold weather. In some aircraft the exhaust carried on along the fuselage underside beyond the cabin, in others it ended below the cockpit.

Byrd Connection

Henry Ford's son Edsel had purchased the F.VIIA-3m that had entered into the 1925 Reliability Trial for Richard E. Byrd's northern Polar flight in 1926. When a flight over the South Pole was planned, Ford supplied a 4-AT-B Tri-Motor for the attempt, powered by Wright Cyclone engines and equipped with auxiliary fuel tanks. The venture came to a successful conclusion over 28/29 November 1929 and the aircraft now resides in the Henry Ford Museum at Dearborn, Michigan.

Specification (Model 5-AT-C)

Type:	all-metal trimotor airliner
Dimensions:	wing span 23.72m (77ft 3in), length 15.32m (30ft 3in), height 3.66m (12ft)
Maximum take-off weight:	6124kg (13,500lb)
Powerplant:	three 420hp seven-cylinder Pratt & Whitney Wasp radial piston engines
Maximum speed:	246km/h (153mph)
Range:	901km (560 miles)
Service ceiling:	5639m (18,500ft)
Crew:	2
Passengers:	13 to 15

Widespread Service

William Stout established Stout Air Transport in 1926, subsequently operating with Ford Tri-Motors as Stout Air Lines, also known as Stout Air Services. The carrier's airmail service continued until 1929, when United Aircraft and Transport Corporation, a Boeing and Pratt & Whitney joint venture, purchased it. Stout's name disappeared from airlines in 1930, but the organization he formed became part of the future United Airlines.

Many other U.S. and South American airlines used the rugged Tri-Motor on pioneering air services, among them American Airlines, Cubana, Panagra and Pan American. Smaller numbers served in Australia, Asia and Europe, and in the 1960s, Aircraft Hydro-Forming attempted to market a modernized 5-AT, designated the Bushmaster 2000. The company had restored and operated a 5-AT for American Airlines and although it flew a Bushmaster prototype in 1966, no production followed.

Dornier Do X (1929)

A triumph of engineering but commercially unviable, the Do X is remembered for its epic transatlantic tour and for being the world's largest aircraft when it first flew in 1929. The aircraft saw only brief airline service with the Italian national carrier.

Resulting from a series of designs for large flying boats produced by Dornier between 1919 and 1926, the Do X was schemed as an airliner capable of flying 100 passengers across the Atlantic in the same comfort that they might expect from an ocean liner. Even by modern standards the aircraft was large, and a full-size wooden mock-up was built to prove its basic design.

Since the Treaty of Versailles had banned Germany from creating aircraft of strategic potential, the Do X was built by Dornier's Altenrhein facility, across the Bodensee, or Lake

Engines
An auxiliary wing connected the six pairs of engines. The flight engineer accessed the motors inflight via the aircraft's thick wing.

Upper Deck
As well as the cockpit, navigator's station and engine room, the upper deck accommodated the radio operator.

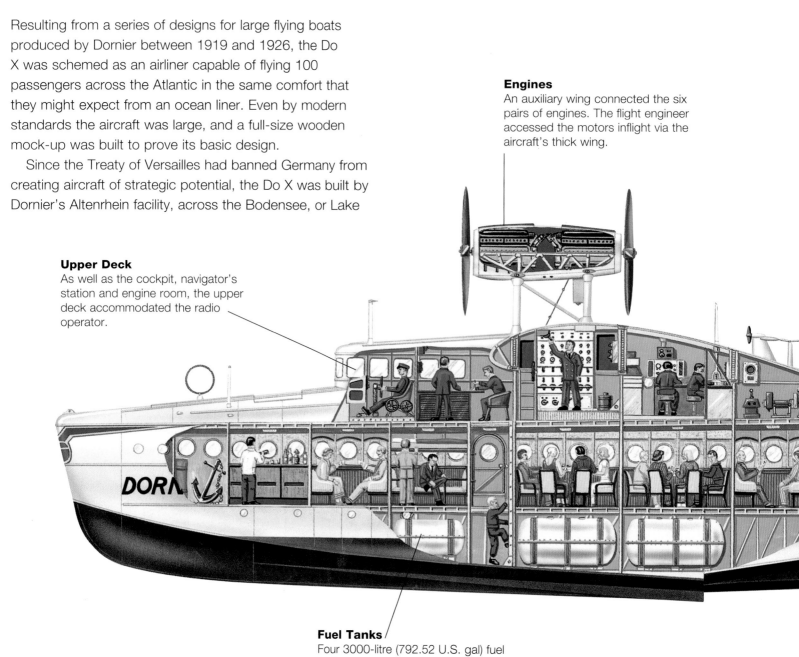

Fuel Tanks
Four 3000-litre (792.52 U.S. gal) fuel tanks were mounted on the hull's lower deck. Passenger baggage was also stored at this level.

Constance, in Switzerland. Styled not unlike a large Wal, with Dornier's distinctive non-tapered, broad chord wing and sponson design, the Do X had a tall hull with a main passenger deck and crew facilities above.

The two pilots and the navigator worked on the aircraft's flight deck, controlling the machine via a device akin to a ship's wheel. There were no throttles in the cockpit, since

a flight engineer, ensconced in an engine room aft of the cockpit, managed all 12 of the aircraft's engines. Excellent crew cooperation and communication was necessary for accurate power control, while it is a reflection of the comparative unreliability of contemporary aeroengines and the demands of powering the Do X that the engineer was expected to service the engines in flight.

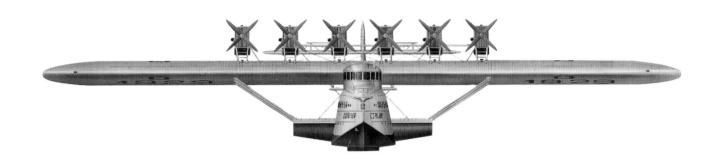

This Luft Hansa Do X aircraft flew the type's tour of the Americas, returning to Berlin in 1932 for a further series of publicity flights.

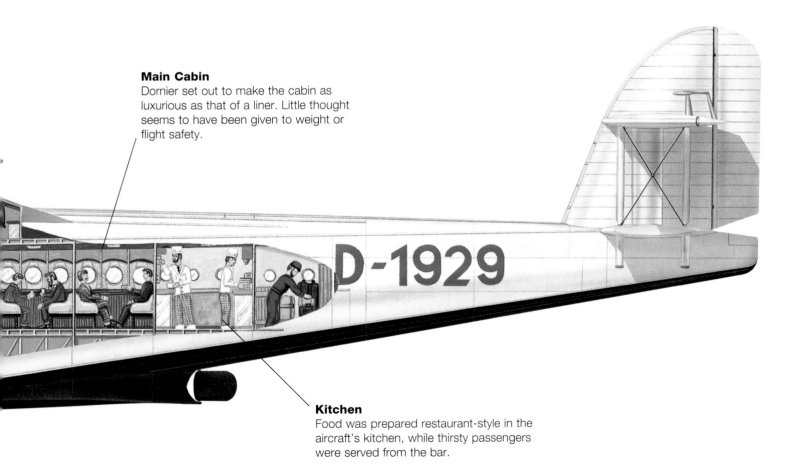

Main Cabin
Dornier set out to make the cabin as luxurious as that of a liner. Little thought seems to have been given to weight or flight safety.

Kitchen
Food was prepared restaurant-style in the aircraft's kitchen, while thirsty passengers were served from the bar.

Dornier Do X

The Do X in its original form, with Jupiter radial engines. Although it flew successfully with this powerplant, it was underpowered for regular operations.

Do X Detail

In its original form the Do X was powered by 12 Siemens-built Bristol Jupiter radials, each of 525hp. Even with all 12 performing well the Do X proved reluctant to fly, however, taking two minutes to 'unstick' from the lake's surface on take-off and almost 20 minutes more to reach an altitude of 600m (1968ft). Soon after its first flight on 12 July 1929 it was therefore re-engined with a dozen 600hp Curtiss Conqueror engines. These provided adequate power under favourable conditions, but cooling was always a problem for the rear engines and the Do X was never entirely free of engine problems.

The powerplant was arranged as six pairs of push-pull engines, connected by a short-span, narrow chord upper wing. As much as 24,600 litres (6499 U.S. gal) of fuel was carried in fuselage and wing leading edge tanks, while a 12hp auxiliary engine was installed for main engine starting and to provide electrical power. The latter was vital, not only for aircraft systems, but also for the luxurious passenger accommodation, which included a bathroom, dining room and smoking room, and individual cabins.

The aircraft's kitchen supplied fresh cooked meals to restaurant standards, while the passengers sat in comfortable dining chairs on rugs, at tables dressed with tablecloths, crockery, glassware and fine cutlery. There were even curtains at the aircraft's porthole windows.

In more than 100 test flights, the Do X proved its flying characteristics and ultimately took off with 169 people on board, including the crew of ten, 150 passengers

Specification

Type:	long-range flying-boat airliner
Dimensions:	wing span 48m (157ft 5¾in), length 40m (131ft 4in), height 10.10m (33ft 1½in)
Maximum take-off weight:	56,000kg (123,459lb)
Powerplant:	six 600hp Curtiss Conqueror V-12 inline piston engines
Maximum speed:	210km/h (130mph)
Range:	2200km (1367 miles)
Service ceiling:	1200m (4100ft)
Flight crew:	5
Passengers:	maximum 150, but planned for 100 on transatlantic services

and, remarkably, nine stowaways. Having flown since 4 August 1929 on Conqueror power, the aircraft was fit for its single real achievement, the transatlantic round trip of 1930–2. Two more Do Xs were built for Italy's SA Navigazione Aerea and fitted with Fiat engines, but they were little used and eventually left to fall into a state of disrepair.

Interestingly, the 'X' of the aircraft's designation had represented 'unknown' and the machine had been something of an unknown proposition. Perhaps a triumph of the possible over the practical, the Do X was a tremendous feat of engineering, but too complex and expensive for successful commercial operations. The German government financed the aircraft's grand tour and even when it returned to Berlin and was donated to Lufthansa, the airline had little interest in it.

The single German Do X never flew commercially with Luft Hansa before passing to Berlin's Museum of Air Transport. It remained there throughout World War II until Allied bombs destroyed it during a raid in 1945.

Transatlantic Tour

On 2 November 1930, the Do X took off from Lake Constance headed for South America. It landed first in Amsterdam, Netherlands, then on to Lisbon Portugal via Calshot, UK. At Lisbon it hit trouble when a fuel tank fire damaged a wing, delaying the onward journey by several weeks while repairs were made.

The aircraft reached Las Palmas in the Canary Islands on 31 January 1931, but on take-off for its next leg the hull suffered damage that required four months to make good. Off again, the Do X reached Villa Cisneros, on the Western Saharan coast, on 1 June, then on to Bolama in Portuguese Guinea by 3 June and out across the South Atlantic to Fernando Noronha, Brazil via the Cape Verde Islands.

The Do X reached South America on 4 June, and then proceeded on a staged flight down to Rio de Janeiro, where it arrived on 20 June. Proceeding back up the coast in stages and through the Caribbean, the aircraft finally reached North America on 22 August, when it landed off Miami. Another three stages saw it land to a tumultuous welcome in New York on 27 August 1931.

The giant Dornier remained a major attraction all though the winter, until departing for the Azores, via Newfoundland, Canada, on 20 May 1932. It reached mainland Europe at Vigo, Spain, on 22 May and continued to Berlin, again via Calshot, arriving in the German capital to public adulation on the 24th.

In all, the trip had covered 35,000km (21,000 miles) in 210.68 flying hours, albeit over more than 18 months. The possibility of transatlantic air travel had been proven, but the Do X had served to demonstrate just how demanding the establishment of regular services to the Americas would be.

Junkers Ju 52/3m (1931)

A natural progression of the Junkers design philosophy, the Ju 52/3m was among the most important European airliners of the immediate pre-war era. After World War II it faded from the scene quickly, however, since spares were difficult to come by and surplus U.S. military transports readily available.

More immediately associated with its wartime roles as a transport and paratroop-carrier, the Junkers Ju 52/3m emerged as a logical development from the single-engined Ju 52 and enjoyed an extremely successful career as an airliner through most of the 1930s. The Ju 52 was a culmination of a line of development that began with the J13 of 1919. It retained the earlier aircraft's tubular metal structure and corrugated skin, as had a series of commercial types in between, including the single-engined G24, the G31 trimotor, the enormous four-engined G38 and the utilitarian W33/34 singles. The Ju 52's ancestry was therefore clear visually and the aircraft retained the

rugged dependability for which the F13 was renowned. The model flew for the first time on 13 October 1930, but only six were built for Sweden's DVS and Canadian Airways. Production quickly switched to the Ju 52/3m, with a Pratt & Whitney Hornet engine mounted on each wing as well as the nose. In this form the aircraft flew for the first time during April 1931 and the first production machines, both to Ju 52/3m standard, went to Lloyd Aereo Boliviano in early 1932.

This initial delivery of Germany's latest airliner to a South American operator was indicative of the importance of the region to the country, as well as German influence on air

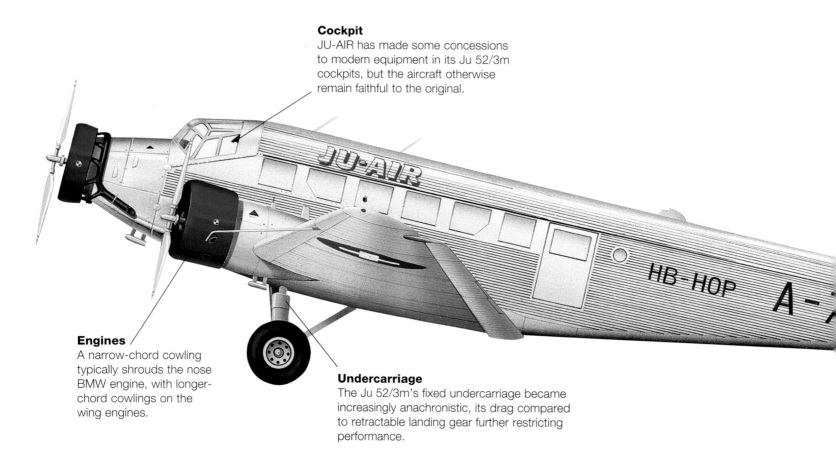

Cockpit
JU-AIR has made some concessions to modern equipment in its Ju 52/3m cockpits, but the aircraft otherwise remain faithful to the original.

Engines
A narrow-chord cowling typically shrouds the nose BMW engine, with longer-chord cowlings on the wing engines.

Undercarriage
The Ju 52/3m's fixed undercarriage became increasingly anachronistic, its drag compared to retractable landing gear further restricting performance.

services throughout the continent. Where the F13 and, later, the W33/34 had traversed the area's typically difficult terrain linking its remote, isolated population centres, the Ju 52/3m arrived to do the same, but with the additional safety of three engines and more modern equipment. As with its forebears, the Ju 52/3m could be fitted with wheel or float landing gear, offering all the flexibility of the earlier machines with much greater load capacity.

Lufthansa Mainstay

Although first deliveries went to Bolivia, the home market was not forgotten and Lufthansa quickly built its own Ju 52/3m fleet, the national carrier and Soviet-German airline Deruluft taking 231 of the type between them. Airlines across Europe also placed orders and Ju 52/3ms were delivered to Britain, where British Airways and Railway Air Services flew the Junkers, Austria, Belgium,

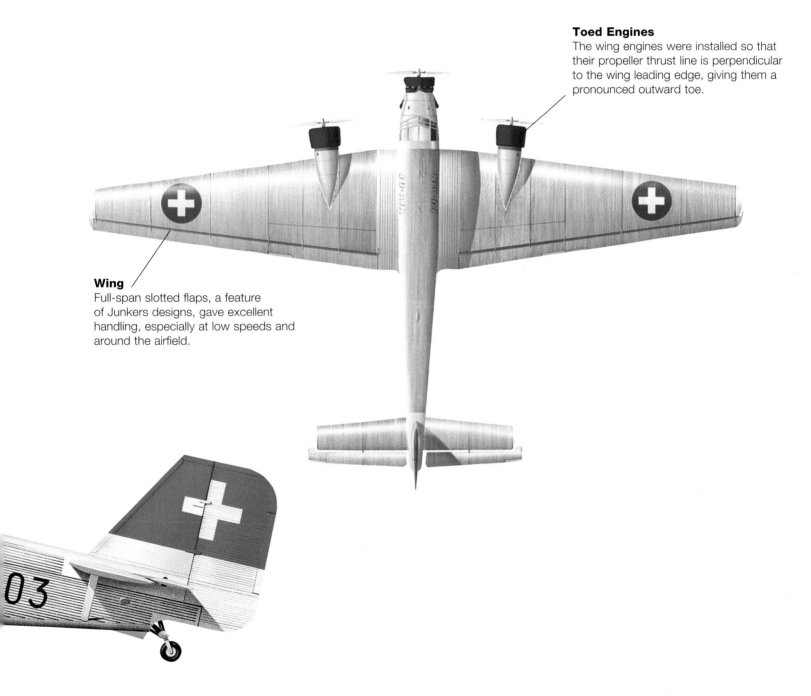

Toed Engines
The wing engines were installed so that their propeller thrust line is perpendicular to the wing leading edge, giving them a pronounced outward toe.

Wing
Full-span slotted flaps, a feature of Junkers designs, gave excellent handling, especially at low speeds and around the airfield.

This aircraft is shown as it appeared shortly after its withdrawal from military service, wearing its Swiss Air Force serial, A-703, and civil registration HB-HOP.

Junkers Ju 52/3m

Czechoslovakia, Denmark, Estonia, Finland, France, Greece, Hungary, Italy, Norway, Poland, Portugal, Romania, Spain and Sweden. Customers further afield came from countries including Australia, China and South Africa, where South African Airways took 15 of the type.

Specification (Ju 52/3m ge)

Type:	all-metal trimotor airliner
Dimensions:	wing span 29.25m (95ft 11in), length 18.90m (62ft), height 6.10m (20ft)
Loaded weight:	9200kg (20,282lb)
Powerplant:	three 600hp BMW 132A-1 radial piston engines
Maximum speed:	290km/h (180mph)
Range:	915km (568 miles)
Service ceiling:	5200m (17,000ft)
Crew:	2
Passengers:	17

This Lufthansa Ju 52/3m was at London's Croydon airport. The airline began Berlin–London services with the type in 1932.

A variety of engines could be chosen for the aircraft and in some cases customers made in-service engine changes, but the BMW-built Hornet powered the majority of commercial and military Ju 52/3ms. Designated as the BMW 132, the engine delivered 660hp in its initial 132A-1 version, as fitted to the early production Ju 52/3ms. Later engine variants could produce more than 800hp, but production increasingly turned towards military needs as the Nazi war machine expanded.

VIP Junkers

Two civilian Ju 52/3ms were taken over for quasi-military purposes in Germany even before the Luftwaffe took over production. Hermann Göring, Reichsminister of Aviation, took D-2527 as his personal aircraft, having it painted red and named Richthofen after the World War I flying ace. Adolf Hitler also used a Ju 52/3m as his personal transport, D-2600 being named Immelmann and ultimately being replaced by a Focke-Wulf Fw 200. The Luftwaffe saw potential in the Ju 52/3m as a transport and a bomber, and it was deployed in both roles with Nationalist forces during the Spanish Civil War. As German forces began their inexorable sweep through Europe, the demand for Ju 52/3m production outstripped Junkers' capacity and captured French industry was put to work building the trimotors in 1941/42. The first French-built machine appeared in June 1942 and after the war the French continued production of the so-called AAC.1 Toucan.

The Toucans flew alongside the CASA 352L, a Ju 52/3m licence built in Spain, to keep the Ju 52/3m in commercial service into the post-war world, even though many hundreds of cheap, more easily maintained U.S. aircraft – essentially C-47/DC-3 airframes – were readily available. Remarkably, in 2014 a single airline remains in operation solely equipped with the Ju 52/3m or its derivatives, Switzerland's JU-AIR flying pleasure flights from its Dübendorf base.

JU-AIR: Alpine Experience

In 1982 the Association of the Friends of the Swiss Air Force established JU-AIR solely to operate the last three airworthy Swiss Air Force Ju 52/3ms, which had been retired the previous year. In 1983 two of the aircraft were registered HB-HOP and HB-HOS, modified for commercial operations and put into revenue service flying passengers on sightseeing tours from Dübendorf. The third machine joined the operation later, as HB-HOT.

A landing accident in 1987 damaged 'HOS, but it flew again in 1988. JU-AIR sent aircraft to Norway in 1989 and Dessau, Germany, ancestral home of Junkers, in 1990. In 1996 the airline painted one of its trimotors in a sponsor's colour scheme for the first time, an option that has subsequently become very popular. A new aircraft joined

the fleet in 1997, a CASA 352L that had previously been on static display at Düsseldorf Airport. HB-HOS suffered another landing accident in 1998, but was soon repaired and on 31 December 1999 JU-AIR launched all four aircraft to welcome in the new millennium.

HB-HOS then set off, on 11 January 2000, for a successful worldwide flight, while JU-AIR celebrated the 70th anniversary of the first flights of 'HOS, 'HOP and 'HOT, in 2009. HB-HOT then made the type's first transatlantic crossing since 1937, for a U.S. tour in 2012, proving just how busy JU-AIR keeps its ageing aircraft, since the fleet has also continued to satisfy a burgeoning demand for Alpine tours and from enthusiasts keen to sample the delights of a 1930s' airliner experience.

Boeing 247 (1933)

Boeing's Model 247 brought retractable undercarriage, modern all-metal construction and a 'clean', aerodynamically efficient airframe to the U.S. airlines for the first time. For just a couple of years during the mid-1930s it was untouchable.

Junkers set the precedent for all-metal commercial aircraft with the F13 of 1919, but it fell to Boeing to take the next major step in airliner evolution with its Model 247 of 1933. In fact, it was with the Model 200 mailplane/freighter that Boeing's innovations were introduced, but the aircraft was of niche appeal and the semi-monocoque metal fuselage construction and semi-retractable main undercarriage technologies that it pioneered were not applied to a passenger carrier until the 247 flew for the first time on 8 February 1933.

Boeing had also produced the B-9 bomber, whose streamlined shape and enclosed engines it combined with the key features of the Monomail to produce North America's first all-metal, streamlined, retractable undercarriage airliner. The aircraft was further streamlined thanks to its cantilever wing, which required no external bracing, and this 'clean' airframe, combined with the power of the 550hp Pratt & Whitney S1D1 Wasp engines, allowed the 247 to maintain a steady climb with one engine out – the possibility of escaping an engine failure was at last a practical reality.

This United Air Lines Model 247D, NC13326, is shown in a typical late-1930s' United colour scheme.

Windscreen
The Model 247D introduced a raked windscreen, replacing the forward-swept screen of the original 247.

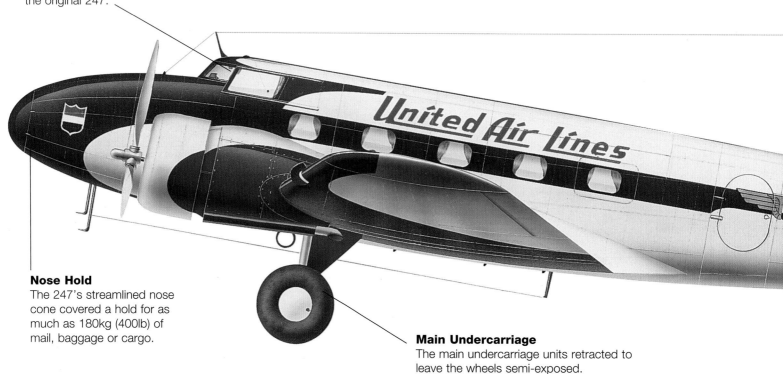

Nose Hold
The 247's streamlined nose cone covered a hold for as much as 180kg (400lb) of mail, baggage or cargo.

Main Undercarriage
The main undercarriage units retracted to leave the wheels semi-exposed.

Passenger Experience

The aircraft was a major advance on the state-of-the-art trimotors then in service, both aerodynamically and in terms of cockpit equipment, the crew benefitting from the latest in radio communications and navigational systems as standard. For passengers it was equally advanced. Although the cabin only seated ten, they were accommodated at 40in (101.6cm) pitch (the distance between one part of a seat and the same part of the seat in front – the modern regulatory minimum is 28in (71cm) pitch). Each seat was adjacent to a window and had a cabin light, while a second lamp was provided for reading. Heating and ventilation were also controlled to maintain comfort.

Less immediately obvious was the passenger benefit derived from the engine-mounting position. The trimotors, including the Ford and F.VII-3m, typically employed high wings with engines strut mounted beneath them, where

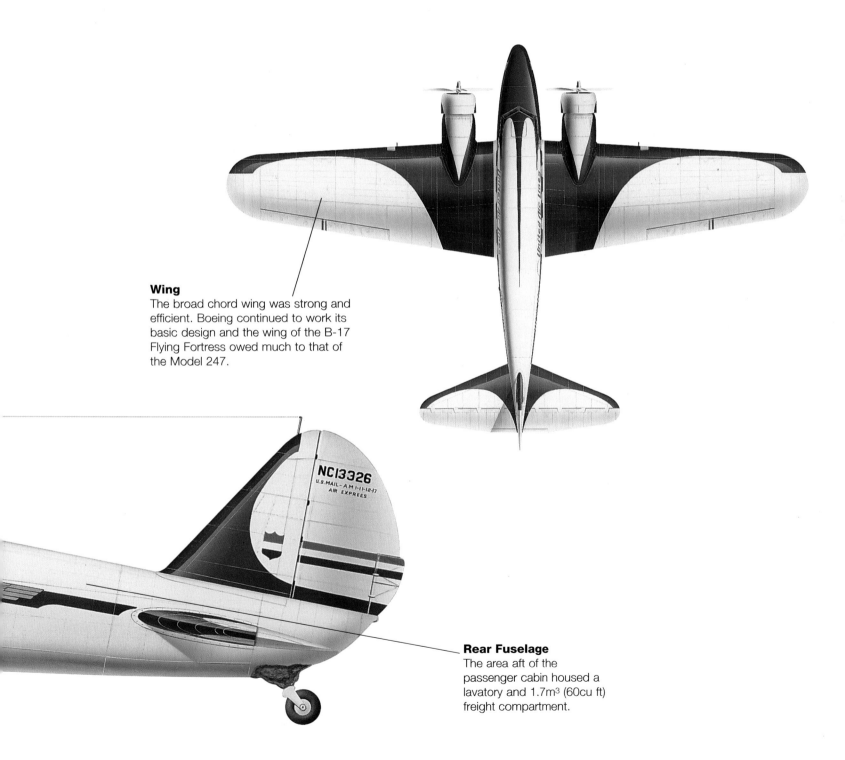

Wing
The broad chord wing was strong and efficient. Boeing continued to work its basic design and the wing of the B-17 Flying Fortress owed much to that of the Model 247.

NC13326
U.S.MAIL-AM 1-11-12-17
AIR EXPRESS

Rear Fuselage
The area aft of the passenger cabin housed a lavatory and 1.7m³ (60cu ft) freight compartment.

they were ideally placed to transmit noise and vibration directly into the cabin. On the Model 247 the engines were mounted in nacelles ahead of the wing, which brought the propeller line forward even of the cockpit and drastically reduced noise in the passenger cabin that was, nevertheless, soundproofed.

Specification (Model 247D)

Type:	all-metal airliner
Dimensions:	wing span 22.60m (74ft 1in), length 15.70m (51ft 5in), height 3.80m (12ft 5in)
Loaded weight:	7621kg (16,770lb)
Powerplant:	two 550hp Pratt & Whitney S1H1-G Wasp radial piton engines
Maximum speed:	304km/h (189mph)
Range:	1400km (870 miles)
Service ceiling:	5000m (16,400ft)
Flight crew:	2
Passengers:	10

Before the PNAHF purchased it in 1966, NC13347 was registered N3977C with Marsh Aircraft in Florida.

Boeing Customer

At the time of the Model 247's first flight, its manufacturer was involved in the airline business as an operator and manufacturer, through the Boeing Air Transport System, comprising Boeing Air Transport, National Air Transport, Pacific Air Transport and Varney Air Lines, and the organization ordered 70 Model 247s even before the first aircraft had been built. In the event, by the time the production line began delivering them, the Boeing Air Transport System had become United Airlines, which accepted 59 initial machines. The 30th was later modified as an executive transport and two more went to Lufthansa.

United returned its first 247 to Boeing soon after delivery in 1933 for a series of performance-improving modifications. After several revised vertical tail configurations had been trialled, Boeing reverted to covering the rudder and elevators with fabric rather than metal. It also replaced the fixed-pitch propellers of the original model with variable-pitch Hamilton Standard units, as well as installing improved engine cowlings and a raked windscreen. Additional fuel capacity and increased maximum take-off weight belied the new Model 247D's improved performance – it cruised at 304km/h (189mph), which was faster than the maximum speed of the 247. Range and service ceiling were also increased.

While the trials aircraft re-entered United service as the Model 247E, the 247D entered production to fulfil the remainder of United's 70-aircraft order. The in-service fleet was then brought up to 247D standard and United enjoyed a brief period during which it offered the fastest coast-to-coast service, at 19.5 hours, compared to the 27 hours typical of the trimotors. The 247D's ascendency was short lived, however, for Douglas was hot on Boeing's heals with an equally advanced design but of much greater capacity. When its DC-3 entered service the Boeing was immediately relegated to second best.

Meritorious 247s

Boeing 247D NC13347 was delivered to United Airlines in 1934 and became one of eight aircraft that passed to the Royal Canadian Air Force (RCAF) before finding its way to a second-line operator. Ultimately modified as a crop-sprayer and cloud-seeder, it flew into the 1950s. In 1966 the Pacific Northwest Aviation Historical Foundation (PNAHF) purchased it in a derelict state and began its airworthy restoration. In late 2014 the aircraft was once again under restoration, with the same owner, albeit renamed as the Museum of Flight, based in Seattle and wearing a blue and white United scheme. Other notable 247s included NR257Y, leased from United and sponsored by Heinz foods and Warner Brothers,

for Roscoe Turner and Clyde Pangborn to enter into the 1934 London–Melbourne MacRobertson Air Race. Some 92 hours 55 minutes and 38 seconds after take-off in the UK, the team arrived at Melbourne, taking second place in the speed trial after a KLM crew in a DC-2 opted to take first in the handicap trial and forfeit their speed result.

Another former United and ex-RCAF aircraft, DZ203 served the British government's Telecommunications Research Establishment for blind landing trials. Its extensive work with specialist equipment paved the way for the instrument landing system technologies still in use today.

Douglas DC-2 and DC-3
(1934)

Through the DC-1 and larger DC-2, Douglas created the epoch making DC-3, a commercial aircraft of such performance that it became the dominant airliner globally prior to World War II and the foundation of the world's resurgent airline fleets after the war.

New U.S. Bureau of Air Commerce regulations in the aftermath of the Fokker F.10 crash that killed football coach Knute Rockne obliged operators of aircraft with wooden structures to make regular and costly inspections for signs of the decomposition that had caused the Fokker's wing to separate in flight. In response, Boeing developed the revolutionary all-metal Model 247, an aircraft of such performance that it quickly garnered airline interest.

Boeing's operation was entwined with that of United Airlines, however, and it refused to make the 247 available to competing carriers until its commitment to United had been satisfied. Over at Trans World Airlines (TWA), vice-

American took 94 DC-3s, retaining the type in service until 1949 and flying 10.5 million passengers with it.

Cabin
Early DC-3s had seats for 21 passengers, later increased to 24. The DST held 16 berths.

Wing
Jack Northrop, whose name lives on in Northrop Grumman, designed the DC-1 wing. The basic structure remained through to the DC-3, proving remarkably resistant to fatigue.

president of Operations Jack Frye decided to look for an alternative. His specification called for 12 passenger seats, a 241km/h (150mph) cruising speed, a maximum speed of at least 298km/h (185mph), landing speed of no more than 105km/h (65mph), service ceiling of at least 21,000ft (6400m) and range of at least 1738km (1080 miles).

Fry envisaged a three-engined aircraft capable of taking off on the power of only two from any of TWA's transcontinental airports. This latter requirement was particularly demanding, since the airline's routes included Albuquerque, New Mexico, where the field was at a performance-sapping altitude of 1510m (4954ft) and temperatures regularly exceeded 32°C (90°F). In today's parlance, such an airport would be regarded as 'hot-and-high', conditions under which neither aerodynamics nor engines tend to work particularly effectively.

Douglas Design

TWA sent its specification to Consolidated, Curtiss, Douglas, General Aviation and Martin on 2 August 1932.

Planform
The DC-3's wing had an unusual planform, American's colour scheme emphasizing its straight trailing edge and swept leading edge.

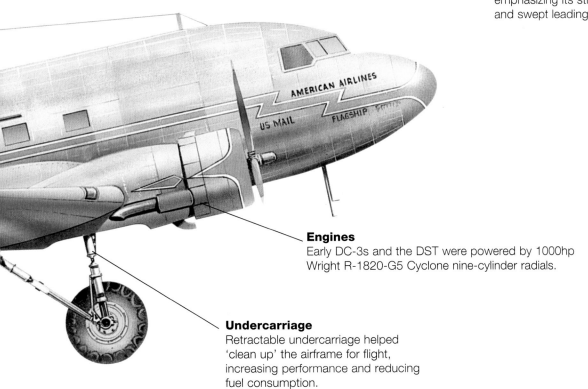

Engines
Early DC-3s and the DST were powered by 1000hp Wright R-1820-G5 Cyclone nine-cylinder radials.

Undercarriage
Retractable undercarriage helped 'clean up' the airframe for flight, increasing performance and reducing fuel consumption.

Just ten days elapsed before Douglas representatives presented their Douglas Commercial 1 (DC-1) design to the airline. It met or exceeded every aspect of the specification, but on two 690hp Wright SGR-1820-F radials. TWA had also made it clear that a biplane would be acceptable and that while the primary structure must be in metal, wood could also be used. In both cases Douglas

Specification (DC-3)

Type:	all-metal twin-engined airliner
Dimensions:	wing span 28.96m (95ft), length 19.65m (64ft 6in), height 5.16m (16ft 11in)
Maximum take-off weight:	12,701kg (28,000lb)
Powerplant:	two 1050hp Pratt & Whitney R-1830-SIC3G radial piston engines
Maximum cruising speed:	274km/h (170mph)
Range:	1650km (1025 miles)
Service ceiling:	7070m (23,200ft)
Crew:	2
Passengers:	24

European DC-3 operators included Finnair, which operated this aircraft for many years after the war. It later appeared on the U.S. register as N58NA.

was also at odds, since it offered only the all-metal DC-1 monoplane and considerable wrangling between airline and manufacturer followed before the aircraft flew for the first time on 1 July 1933.

The airline had signed up for 60 airframes, but as the DC-1 systematically proved capable of delivering everything TWA could ask for, including flying the entire Winslow, Arizona, to Albuquerque route on one engine, the airline opted to change its purchasing strategy to an initial 20 of the longer, 14-passenger DC-2. With a fuselage 0.61m (2ft) longer than that of the DC-1 and powered by 710hp Wright SGR-1820-F3 Cyclones, the DC-2 including all the advanced construction technologies of the earlier machine, as well as its retractable undercarriage, combining them with provision for new levels of passenger comfort.

The airline was adamant that its passengers must travel in comfort and safety if it was to compete with transcontinental rail services and the DC-2's cabin was optimzed with rubber-mounted reclining seats to neutralize vibration, a buffet and a rear lavatory. As with the Boeing 247, every seat had its own window.

Into Service

The DC-2 first took to the air on 11 May 1934 and TWA flew its first service with it on the 18th; the Douglas soon began to demonstrate its superiority over the Boeing. Eastbound transcontinental services could be accomplished in 16 hours 20 minutes, westbound in 18 hours, and airlines began knocking on Douglas' door. Soon DC-2s were flying with the majority of the major U.S. airlines and finding a ready market abroad. Then a KLM-Royal Dutch Airlines aircraft, assembled under licence in the Netherlands by Fokker, came second overall in the MacRobertson Air Race – beating a Boeing 247D into third until the Dutch crew decided to take first in the handicap section – securing the DC-2's domination.

Meanwhile, in June 1934 changes to the regulations governing U.S. commercial flying were introduced. Manufacturers were forced to dissociate their finances from those of the airlines and with the carriers free to buy where they wanted, Douglas was ascendant. While the DC-2 sold like hot cakes, American Airlines needed a modern aircraft for its sleeper service from Los Angeles to Dallas. Douglas responded with a redesigned DC-2, named Douglas Sleeper Transport (DST). Its fuselage was longer and wider than that of its forebear, its wings longer and modified in shape, its empennage larger and its undercarriage stronger.

It flew for the first time on 17 December 1935 and although successful as the DST, its potential as a regular airliner, equipped with 21 passenger seats, was already being exploited by Douglas, which had begun working on the DC-3 even before the DST had flown. The first DC-3 completed its initial flight on 16 August 1936 and went to American Airlines on delivery on the 18th. Soon the type came to dominate the airliner market more or less globally and 803 were built, before World War II forced the switch of production to the closely related C-47 military transport, of which more than 10,000 were built.

Airliner for the World

Douglas exported DC-3s worldwide prior to World War II, airlines from countries as far apart as China, the UK and Canada appreciating the aircraft's economics and reliability. It allowed safer, more efficient operations on existing routes, but also expansion. The aircraft's reputation made it a natural choice for new operators, among them Trans-Canada Air Lines, which had flown its first service on 1 September 1937 with a Lockheed 10A Electra, but soon added DC-3s to its fleet. After the war the DC-3 flew on, although many had been forced into military service and not all survived. The dawning of peace brought a surplus of wartime C-47s and a plethora of new airlines sprang up based on this easily affordable windfall of airframes, while the major carriers also benefitted from the cheap and readily available means to rebuild their fleets.

Lockheed Super Electra and Lodestar (1937)

Lockheed produced airliners of dazzling performance with its Model 14 Super Electra and Model 18 Lodestar, but they were ultimately too late on the scene and too expensive to operate and failed to even dent the Douglas dominance.

Allan Loughead (pronounced Lockheed) formed the Loughead Aircraft Manufacturing Co in 1916, but struggled to become established as a mainstream manufacturer. In December 1926 Loughead renamed the company Lockheed Aircraft Co and found success with the Jack Northrop-designed Vega six-seater. The Air Express, Sirius and Orion followed, all of them single-engined, high-speed civilian types and all prevented from passenger carriage when changing U.S. regulations forbade single-engined aircraft from carrying passengers at night or over terrain where an emergency landing was impossible.

Lockheed was unable to respond with a new design before failing in April 1932. Purchased by a group of

NX18973 was among the executive Super Electras. Lockheed built it for Howard Hughes for use in a round-the-world flight in 1938.

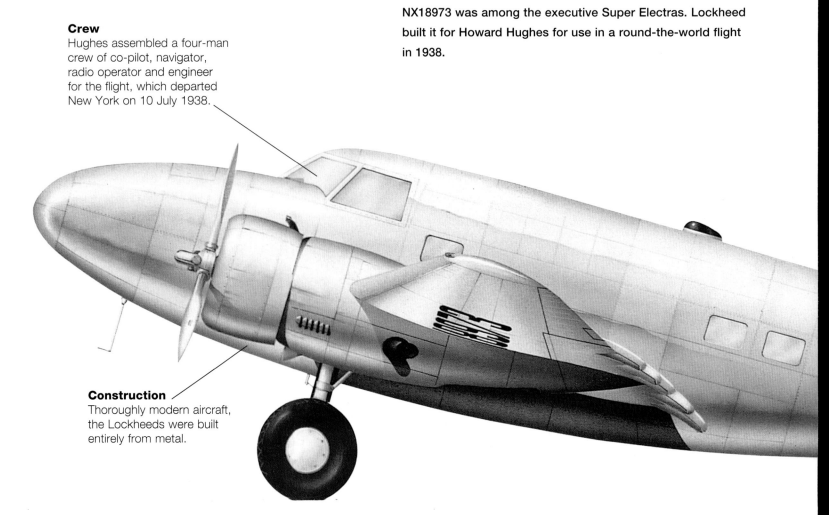

Crew
Hughes assembled a four-man crew of co-pilot, navigator, radio operator and engineer for the flight, which departed New York on 10 July 1938.

Construction
Thoroughly modern aircraft, the Lockheeds were built entirely from metal.

Just 91 hours 14 minutes and 10 seconds after take-off, NX18973 arrived safely back at its airport of departure, New York's Floyd Bennett Field.

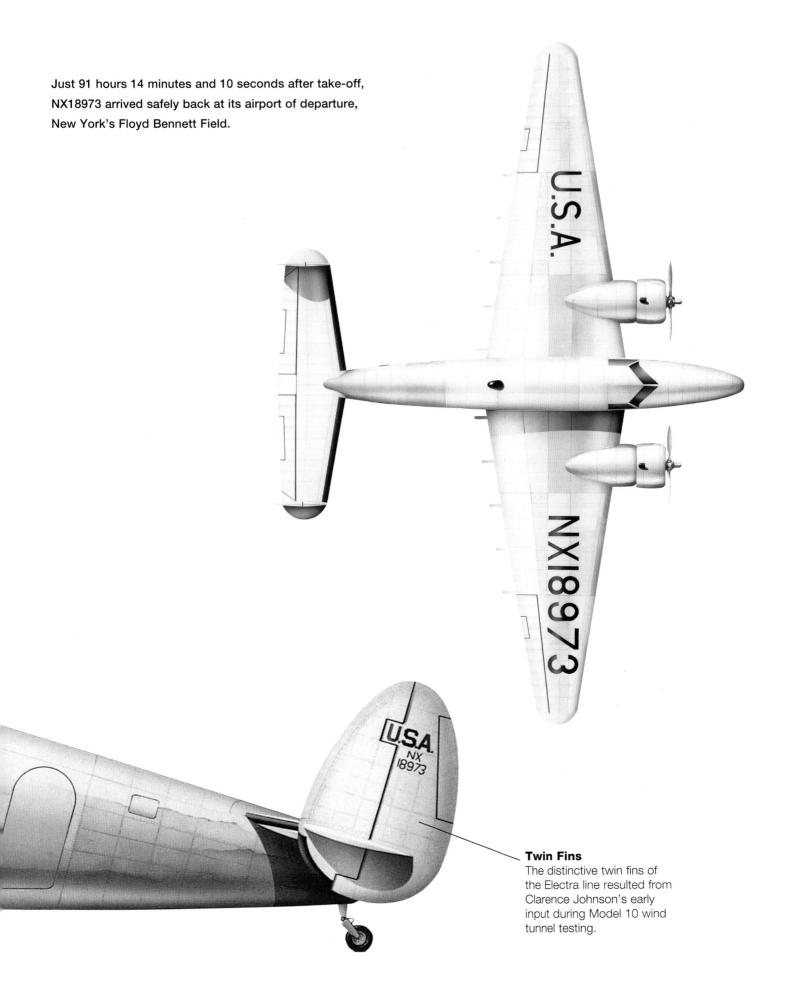

Twin Fins
The distinctive twin fins of the Electra line resulted from Clarence Johnson's early input during Model 10 wind tunnel testing.

Lockheed Super Electra and Lodestar

The Electra's greatest legacy to aerospace is undoubtedly its introduction of the gifted Clarence 'Kelly' Johnson to Lockheed. He became a key designer and engineer at the company, especially on its military high-speed and stealth programmes.

experienced investors, it employed talented designer Hall L. Hibbard and set him to work on a high-speed twin, designed to seat 10 passengers and powered by 450hp Pratt & Whitney Wasp Junior engines. Known as the Lockheed 10 Electra, the aircraft flew for the first time on 23 February 1934 after considerable input from a young designer called Clarence L. Johnson, whose genius would become inextricably linked with Lockheed, right through to the emergence of military stealth aircraft.

The Electra cruised at 306km/h (190mph), maintaining Lockheed's reputation for producing fast airliners. It achieved reasonable sales success around the world, with 148 aircraft produced by the time production ended

in July 1941. It also formed the basis of the six-seat Model 12 Electra Junior, following a U.S. Bureau of Air Commerce suggestion that a high-speed feederliner, delivering passengers from small airfields into larger airports, would find a ready market.

In the event that market failed to materialize, but Lockheed had envisioned an alternative use of the Model 12 as a 'flying office', or business aircraft and most of the 130 built served corporations or individuals in this role.

Super Electra

Lockheed had specialized in small capacity, somewhat niche aircraft, renowned for their performance but not competing in the same marketplace as the big Douglas airliners. Hibbard and Johnson had scaled the Model 10 down to produce the Electra Junior, but scaling it up to create a DC-3 rival was not an option, so that the Model 14 Super Electra was an entirely new design of similar configuration. It flew for the first time on 29 July 1937, with accommodation for 14 passengers in a deep fuselage. Power came from two 875hp Pratt & Whitney S1E-G Hornet engines and the aircraft was fast, cruising at more than 363km/h (225mph). Northwest Airlines took the first Super Electras, while the type also picked up customers overseas where, in fact, it ultimately sold better than at home. Passengers were delighted with the Model 14's high speed and comfortable cabin, but three crashes in 15 months dented their confidence in the Lockheed. The airlines were also less than thrilled, since it was an expensive aircraft to operate and Lockheed set about reducing seat-mile costs by stretching the fuselage to fit more seats into the cabin.

Thus the 18-passenger Model 18 Lodestar flew for the first time on 2 February 1940. With the Electra name dropped to avoid any suggestion that this was new

Specification (Model 18)

Type:	Lodestar 18-seat airliner
Dimensions:	wing span 19.96m (65ft 6in), length 15.19m (49ft 10in), height 3.60m (11ft 10in)
Loaded weight:	7938kg (17,500lb)
Powerplant:	two 875hp Pratt & Whitney S1E2-G Hornet radial piston engines
Maximum speed:	428km/h (266mph)
Range:	4025km (2500 miles)
Service ceiling:	7740m (25,400ft)
Crew:	2
Passengers:	18

machine was derived from the aircraft type involved in the Super Electra accidents, the Lodestar nevertheless struggled to find U.S. airline customers.

Once again though, overseas carriers were keen to buy the type, but the DC-3 was in such widespread service and so well respected in the U.S. market that it had become almost the industry standard. Even with its operating costs spread over 18 seats rather than 14, there was no way in for the Lodestar. Fortunately for Lockheed, the Super Electra and Lodestar lent

themselves to wartime production as the Hudson and Ventura, respectively. Many hundreds of both aircraft were built and several survived to enter the civilian market after the war. Along with the remains of the commercial fleet, these airframes became popular choices for executive use, especially given their high performance. Specialized conversions soon began to emerge, including the Learstar, based on the Lodestar and designed by William P. Lear, who later designed the world-famous Learjet.

In Service Abroad

KLM was a major supporter of Lockheed, taking 11 Super Electras, including PJ-AIT, for its East Indies operation KNILM (Koninklijke Nederlandsch-Indische Luchtvaart Maatschappij, or Royal Dutch Indies Airways). Model 14s also went to British Airways (which had also taken Model 12s), and operators in Romania, Ireland, France and Poland.

Trans-Canada Air Lines placed the largest order for the Lockheed-produced Model 14, acquiring 16, but Japan

Air Transport was the type's primary operator, buying ten from Lockheed and 20 built under licence by Tachikawa. The Lodestar also proved attractive to Trans-Canada, which took 12, but the model's primary customer was South African Airways, with a fleet of 21. British Airways, Air Afrique, Air France and operators in Latin America also bought Lodestars, but between them, the Super Electra and its larger sibling were destined never to achieve the penetration of the Douglas twins.

Boeing 314 Clipper (1938)

Boeing's magnificent Model 314 Clipper allowed Pan American Airways to spread its wings across the Atlantic and Pacific Oceans. Built to the extent of just 12 examples, the magnificent flying boat's career was truncated by World War II and the dawn of the truly long-range landplane.

Pan American Airways (PAA) began operations on 19 October 1927, operating an airmail service between Key West, Florida and Havana, Cuba using a Fairchild FC-2 floatplane. Both the international nature of the route and choice of seaplane were significant factors in the airline's subsequent extension, since under the entrepreneurial leadership of Juan Trippe, it focussed on routes into the Caribbean, and Central and South America.

Through direct operations and subsidiaries, PAA eventually reached the foot of Chile and although the F.VIIb/3m formed the backbone of its fleet, the continent's deficit of suitable landing grounds and abundance of water meant that floatplanes and flying boats were also widely used. The eight-seat Sikorsky S-38 became the primary equipment on Caribbean routes, before the larger S-40 came on line in 1931 as the first of the airline's so-called

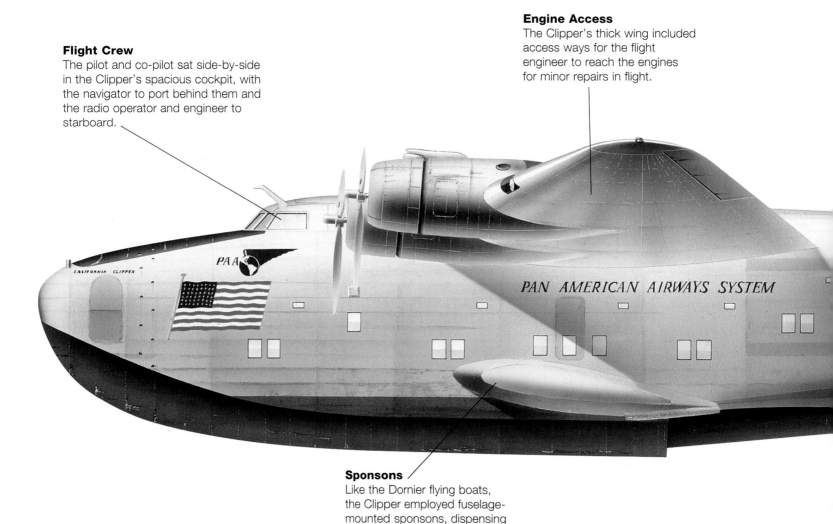

Flight Crew
The pilot and co-pilot sat side-by-side in the Clipper's spacious cockpit, with the navigator to port behind them and the radio operator and engineer to starboard.

Engine Access
The Clipper's thick wing included access ways for the flight engineer to reach the engines for minor repairs in flight.

Sponsons
Like the Dornier flying boats, the Clipper employed fuselage-mounted sponsons, dispensing with the need for wingtip floats.

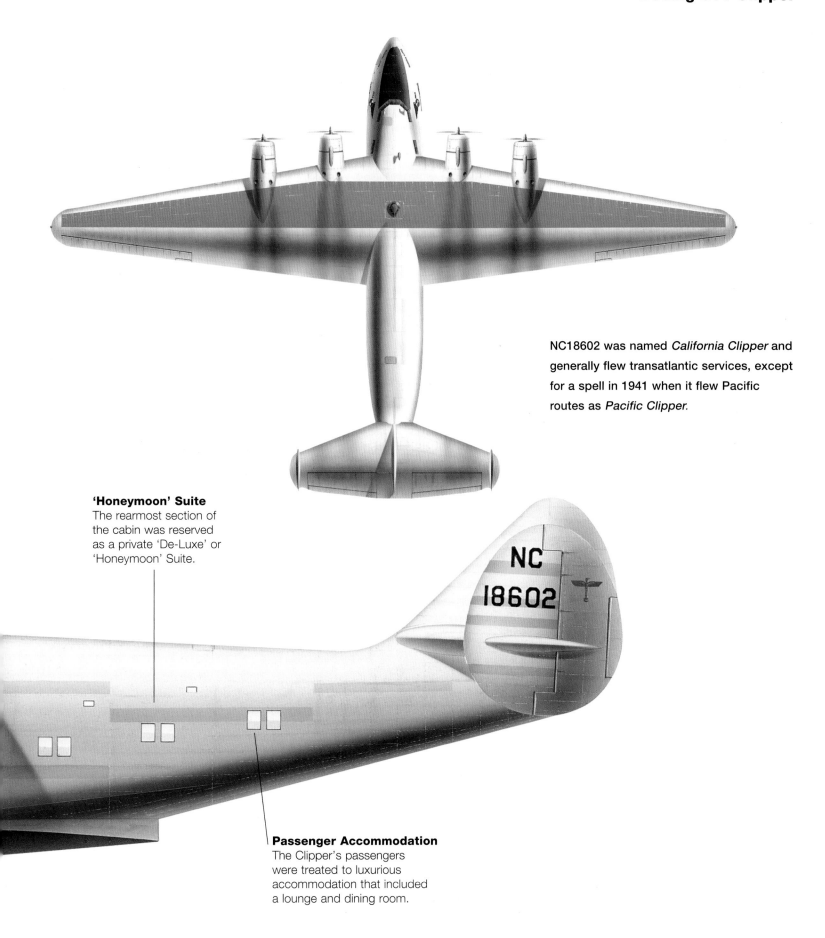

NC18602 was named *California Clipper* and generally flew transatlantic services, except for a spell in 1941 when it flew Pacific routes as *Pacific Clipper*.

'Honeymoon' Suite
The rearmost section of the cabin was reserved as a private 'De-Luxe' or 'Honeymoon' Suite.

Passenger Accommodation
The Clipper's passengers were treated to luxurious accommodation that included a lounge and dining room.

Boeing 314 Clipper

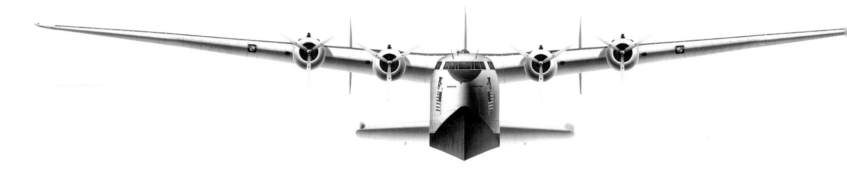

The Clipper's offered the ultimate in passenger comfort for transoceanic travel, but their service was cut short by the onset of World War II.

'Clippers'. By now PAA was the dominant U.S. carrier serving international routes to the south, but it also had ambitions for the Atlantic and Pacific. Joint transatlantic operations with British Overseas Airways Corporation (BOAC) were considered, but the UK airline had no suitable aircraft for such a route.

Frustrated, Trippe turned instead to the Pacific, PAA launching its initial San Francisco–Manila mail service on 22 November 1935. The Martin M-130 'China Clipper', a 41-seat flying boat, was chosen as the route's equipment, the same type operating the service with passengers for the first time on 21 October 1936.

Boeing's Clipper

Meanwhile, Boeing designer Wellwood Beall believed he had a design that could rival the Martin and Sikorsky

'boats in PAA service. His intention was that the machine should have transatlantic range, using as its basis the engines, tailplanes and wings of Boeing's XB-15 bomber. He hung this collection of ready-made items onto a large hull offering accommodation for as many as 74 passengers, or 34 in berths.

Boeing presented the design to PAA during February 1936 and on 21 June it received an order for six, plus six options. Designated as the Model 314 Clipper, the big Boeing flew for the first time off Puget Sound, Washington, on 7 June 1938. It was equipped with a short, almost vestigial fin and large rudder which, between them, proved wholly inadequate for directional control, obliging test pilot Eddie Allen to keep the aircraft straight using differential power from its Wright R-2600 Double Cyclone engines.

A twin-tail configuration was subsequently trialled, again with unsatisfactory results, before Boeing arrived at an arrangement of a central fin, and two endplate fins and rudders at the tip of each tailplane. With handling satisfactory, Civil Aeronautics Authority certification and first delivery came in January 1939; by 16 June, all six were in PAA's hands. Two Clippers were assigned the San Francisco–Hong Kong route and the remainder earmarked for transatlantic work, route-proving trials beginning on 3 March.

Meanwhile, PAA converted the six options, but specified revisions, including more powerful engines and changes to the accommodation to suit three additional passengers. Boeing designated this developed variant as the Model 314A and PAA subsequently brought its earlier aircraft up to the same standard.

On 20 May 1939, PAA flew its first scheduled transatlantic airmail service between New York and Marseille, France, while a second Clipper launched for Hawaii. On 28 June, the Clipper operated its first passenger service, between New York and Lisbon,

Specification (Model 314A Clipper)

Type:	transoceanic flying-boat airliner
Dimensions:	wing span 32.85m (152ft), length 32.30m (106ft), height 8.40m (27ft 7in)
Gross weight:	38,000kg (84,000lb)
Powerplant:	four 1600hp Wright GR-2600 Twin Cyclone 14-cylinder radial piston engines
Cruising speed:	296km/h (184mph)
Range:	8369km (5200 miles)
Service ceiling:	4085m (13,400ft)
Flight crew:	5
Passengers:	74

Portugal and its first North Atlantic service on 8 July, from New York to Southampton, UK.

The undoubted potential of the Clipper on PAA's routes was checked by the outbreak of war, although the airline was able to switch its flying-boat operation primarily to government contract work. Three of the new-build Model 314As were delivered to BOAC in 1941 for use on essential transatlantic routes and the Clippers became trusted long-range transports for President

Franklin D. Roosevelt and Prime Minister Winston Churchill. Those Clippers that survived the war were retired from PAA's service in 1946, while the British 'boats returned to the U.S. in 1947. All passed to second-line operators and none remained airworthy for very long. Their demise signalled the end of the long-range flying boat era as landplanes with sufficient range to operate between airports became more widely available.

Clipper Convention

All 12 Clippers were given individual names, PAA's aircraft as follows: Honolulu Clipper (NC18601), California Clipper (NC18602, illustrated), Yankee Clipper (NC18603), Atlantic Clipper (NC18604), Dixie Clipper (NC18605), American Clipper (NC18606), Pacific Clipper (NC18609), Anzac Clipper (NC18611) and Cape Town Clipper (NC18612). NC18602 and NC18609 swapped names briefly during 1941 as they were exchanged between Pacific and Atlantic services. NC18603 was the only Clipper involved in a fatal accident, when it

crashed during landing on the Tagus River, Lisbon on 22 February 1942, with the loss of 24 of the 39 passengers and crew on board.

Both NC18601 and NC18612 were deliberately sunk after suffering problems at sea, the former in U.S. Navy service, two Clippers having been impressed into naval service and three into U.S. Army Air Corps service during World War II. The BOAC Clippers were named Bristol (G-AGBZ/NC18607), Berwick (G-AGCA/NC18608) and Bangor (G-AGCB/NC18610).

Boeing 307 Stratoliner (1938)

Adding a brand-new fuselage to major components of the B-17 bomber, Boeing produced the world's first pressurized airliner. It proved tremendously successful in service, but with the outbreak of World War II production was curtailed at just ten airframes.

Douglas may have put paid to the Boeing 247D's further sales prospects, but Boeing was not content to be beaten. Instead, it looked to the next generation of airliner, realizing that cabin pressurization, allowing higher altitudes to be obtained, was the way ahead in terms of passenger comfort and flying efficiency.

Pressurization allows an aircraft to fly at high altitudes where air pressure is reduced, while the pressure inside the cabin is maintained at that of a lower altitude. Passengers and crew experience the physiological

conditions of the 'cabin altitude' rather than the flying altitude, at which they would be very uncomfortable or might not survive at all. Pressurized aircraft must of course supply breathable air to their passengers, since at high altitudes ambient oxygen levels are too low for comfortable breathing, and they must also be heated, since temperatures at altitude are much reduced.

The benefits in overcoming the engineering challenge of pressurizing a large life-sustaining container lie in improved performance, since there is less drag at altitude

Flight Crew
The Stratoliner was the first landplane airliner to introduce a flight engineer. Controlling and monitoring the pressurization system was one of his duties.

Passenger Seating
Four compartments, separated by curtains, were provided for the 33 passengers. A line of nine reclining seats was available for those wishing to sleep.

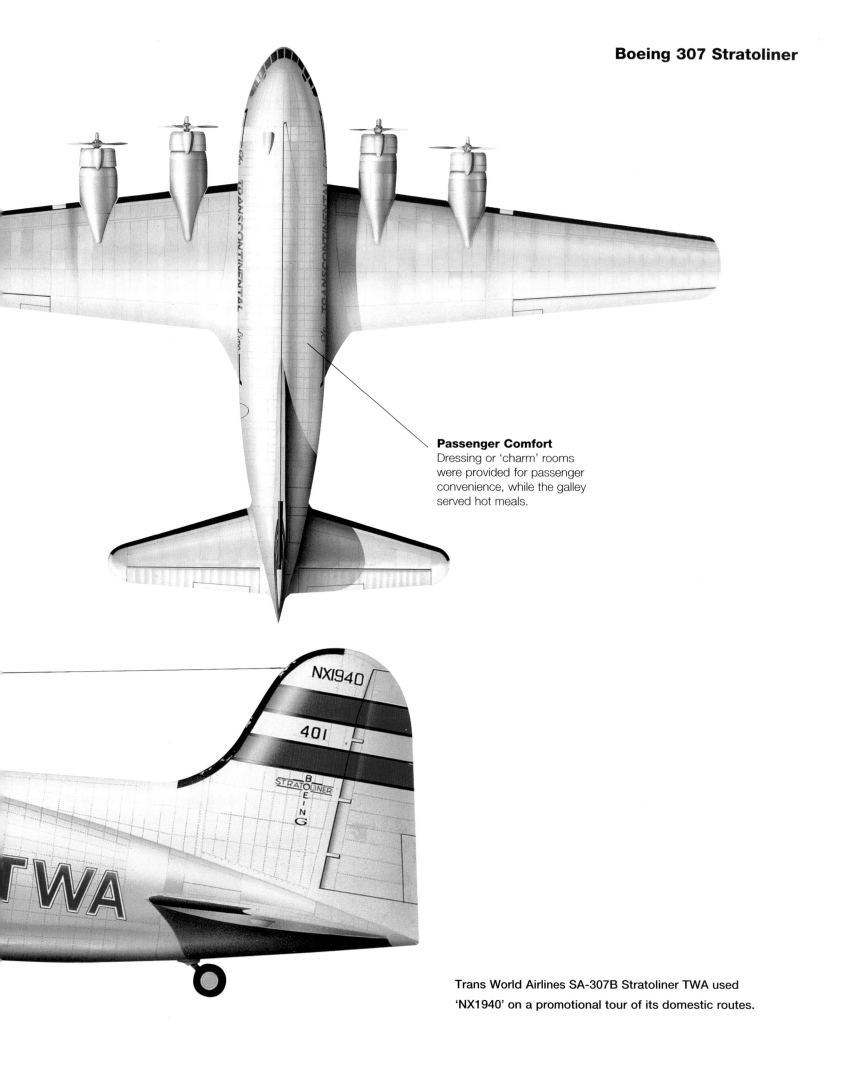

Passenger Comfort
Dressing or 'charm' rooms
were provided for passenger
convenience, while the galley
served hot meals.

NXI940

401

B
STRATOLINER
O
E
I
N
G

TWA

Trans World Airlines SA-307B Stratoliner TWA used
'NX1940' on a promotional tour of its domestic routes.

Boeing 307 Stratoliner

Hughes eventually sold his private Stratoliner and it was converted to serve as a luxury houseboat.

and an aircraft is likely to maintain speed while burning less fuel. If pressurization is sufficient and the aircraft has the altitude capability, it is also possible to 'fly above the weather' for smoother, more comfortable and more direct services.

Stratoliner Engineered

Boeing flew its Model 299 bomber prototype for the first time in July 1935 and company president Claire Egtvedt discussed the type's viability as a pressurized transport aircraft with chief engineer Ed Wells. Model 299 development continued to produce the B-17 Flying Fortress, but Wells concluded that while its empennage, engines and wings could be used as the basis of an airliner, its fuselage was unsuitable for pressurization.

Wells therefore instigated design of a new circular-section fuselage to be pressurized via a supercharger-

driven system. It seated as many as 33 passengers in some comfort and Boeing designated it the S-307 Stratoliner, the name a reference to its high-altitude capabilities. In reality the aircraft's ceiling performance was inadequate to reach the stratosphere, but it could cruise comfortably at 6096m (20,000ft), which kept it above the majority of weather. To this fuselage were attached the wings, Wright Cyclone radials and tail surfaces of the B-17C.

Pan American ordered four aircraft in 1937 and the first of these, also the prototype, made its maiden flight on 31 December 1938. The aircraft was subsequently lost with all onboard, including two KLM representatives, during a demonstration flight. It went into a spin over the Cascade Mountains and although test pilot Julius Barr recovered, the manoeuvre overstressed the airframe and it broke up.

A new and much larger fin and dorsal fillet were designed as a result, subsequently also finding application on the B-17, from the 'E' model onwards. The test programme continued so that certification was granted on 13 March 1940 and PAA soon had its three Stratoliners in service on routes to South America.

TWA

Trans World also wanted the world's first pressurized airliner in its fleet and ordered five slightly modified aircraft known to Boeing as the SA-307B. One of the machines, registered 'NX1940', flew a tour of U.S. domestic routes, publicising the introduction to its network of what TWA termed the '1940 Airliner'. Transcontinental Stratoliner service began in July 1940, one of the aircraft flying Los Angeles–New York in a new record time of 11 hours 45 minutes.

Howard Hughes was also interested in the Model 307, as a platform for an attempt to break his own around-the-world record, established on a Lockheed 14. Boeing informed him that all production was dedicated to PAA

Specification (SA-307B Stratoliner)

Type:	long-range pressurized airliner
Dimensions:	wing span 32.70m (107ft 3in), length 22.70m (74ft 4in), height 6.30m (20ft 9in)
Gross weight:	19,050kg (42,000lb)
Powerplant:	four 1000hp Wright GR-1820 Cyclone radial piston engines
Maximum speed:	396km/h (246mph)
Range:	3846km (2390 miles)
Service ceiling:	7985m (26,200ft)
Flight crew:	3
Passengers:	33 (later 38)

and TWA, but he acquired a controlling share in TWA and had a sixth Stratoliner allocated to his private ownership.

The aircraft was delivered with the original tail configuration and the broad chord engine cowlings fitted to the PAA machines. Eight auxiliary fuel tanks were installed in hopes that the aircraft need stop for fuel only four times during its circumnavigation, but World War II broke out before Hughes could set out and his plans were thwarted. Instead he had the Stratoliner re-equipped as a personal transport.

TWA's five aircraft were impressed for military service and fitted with B-17G wings and engine nacelles after the war. They returned to airline service equipped for 38 passengers and remained with the carrier until 1951. Like the PAA machines, they subsequently became distributed around the world with various second-line operators. One of the former PAA machines ultimately became the personal transport of the president of Haiti and after being abandoned, it was restored by Boeing and now resides with the National Air and Space Museum.

Boeing Business

TWA employed NX19906, registered as 'NX1940' for its '1940 Airliner' national promotional tour. Only 10 Stratoliners were built and TWA flew the majority of them, covering 7.2 million km (4.5 million miles) with the type prior to World War II. Only one complete Stratoliner survives, recovered in a derelict state after use in Haiti and restored to airworthy condition by Boeing in 2001. Named Clipper Flying Cloud, the aircraft was engaged in local flying from Boeing Field International Airport, Washington, on 28 March 2002, when it suffered a main undercarriage problem. The pilot aborted an approach to land so that the flight engineer could extend the offending leg manually.

With the gear down the approach was resumed, but the machine ran out of fuel, forcing the crew to ditch in nearby Puget Sound. There were no casualties and the damaged aircraft was quickly salvaged. It is now displayed in immaculate condition in the Steven F. Udvar-Hazy Center of the National Air and Space Museum.

Douglas DC-4, DC-6 and DC-7 (1938)

After a false start with the DC-4E, Douglas created a series of superb airliners stemming from the DC-4, progressing through the DC-6 and culminating in the DC-7C, arguably the ultimate expression of piston-engined airliner technology.

From its position of dominance with the DC-3, Douglas, like Boeing, realized that the next generation of commercial transport would need to be pressurized and offer increased passenger accommodation. Working with United Air Lines, it produced the DC-4, subsequently designated the DC-4E, a distinctive triple-finned, pressurized aircraft for 52 passengers. It flew for the first time in June 1938, but was immediately disappointing. Complex and difficult to maintain, its performance was also poor and the single

airframe was sold to Japan's Dai Nippon Koku in 1939 without further development.

Douglas had not given up on the idea of a long-range, high-capacity airliner, however, and set about designing a new DC-4. A much simpler aircraft, the DC-4 now did away with pressurization and the ambitious swept wing of the DC-4E. It had a single tall fin and rudder arrangement, and high-aspect ratio wings for efficient cruising. Shorter than the DC-4E, the DC-4 was only three-quarters of the

Merlin Power
Canadair chose the Rolls-Royce Merlin engine for the DC-4M to satisfy the RCAF's desire for greater performance and to avoid the import duty it would have had to pay on U.S. engines.

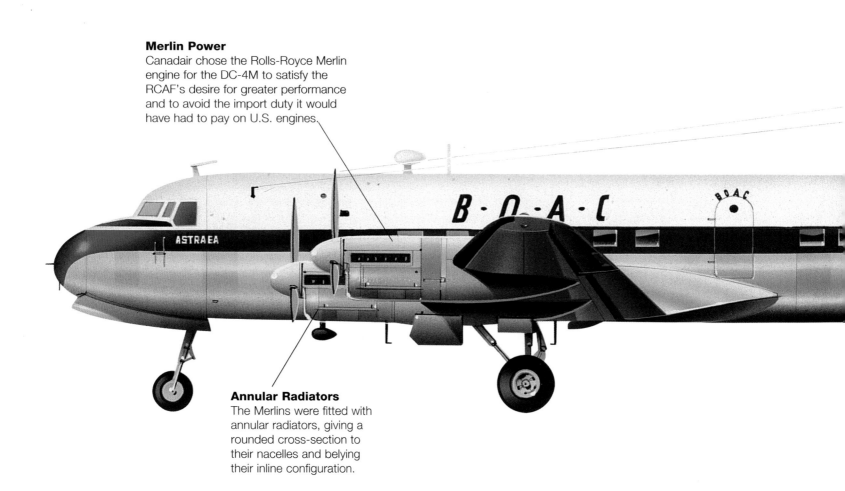

Annular Radiators
The Merlins were fitted with annular radiators, giving a rounded cross-section to their nacelles and belying their inline configuration.

weight of its predecessor and seated 42 passengers. American Airlines, Eastern Airlines and United Air Lines were all interested in the type, but as with the Stratoliner, the outbreak of World War II interfered with the DC-4's development. The first aircraft took its maiden flight on 26 March 1942 as a military C-54 Skymaster. Douglas continued improving the design, but against military contracts, the C-54 completing almost 88,000 Atlantic and Pacific crossings during World War II for the loss of just three aircraft.

This reliability suggested the potential for post-war commercial success and although Douglas sold small numbers of the new-build DC-4-1037 freighter and DC-4-1009 combined cargo/passenger aircraft, the majority of

DC-4 Wing
The DC-4M retained the classic DC-4 wing. The first DC-4M was produced by conversion from a C-54G.

G-ALHX

After the Avro Tudor failed to mature into a workable airliner, BOAC bought 22 C-4M aircraft from Canadair. They initially replaced Avro York landplanes and Short Sandringham flying boats on its route to Hong Kong.

Pressurized Fuselage
Canadair built the DC-4M from scratch, including the pressurized fuselage, which used elements of design work done by Douglas for the DC-6.

Douglas DC-4, DC-6 and DC-7

DC-4s were demilitarized C-54s. These served far and wide, establishing regular transatlantic services for the first time and remaining attractive conversion possibilities into the 1950s. In Canada, Canadair produced 46 DC-4M aircraft, essentially by modifying the C-54 design for Rolls-Royce Merlin power, and the type served Trans-Canada Air Lines, BOAC and the Royal Canadian Air Force.

DC-6

The U.S. Army Air Force (USAAF) was delighted with the C-54 and funded development of a larger, pressurized

Braniff International took delivery of this DC-7C in 1956. It retained the aircraft until 1968, by which time it was well into its jet age, having taken an initial Boeing 707 in 1959.

version. The XC-112A flew for the first time on 15 February 1946 and, under threat in the commercial market from the Boeing 377 Stratocruiser and Lockheed Constellation, both of which were pressurized, Douglas began working it up in parallel as the DC-6. With a 2.06m (6ft 9in) longer fuselage, the new aircraft had standard seating for between 48 and 52 passengers, but could take as many as 86 in a high-density arrangement.

It replaced the 1450hp Pratt & Whitney Twin Wasps of the DC-4 with 2100hp R-2800CA-15 Double Wasps and won an initial order for 50 aircraft from American Airlines. The first American machine completed its maiden flight on 29 June 1949 and services began between New York and Chicago in April 1950. Subsequent variants included the more powerful, 1.52m (5ft) longer DC-6A freighter and convertible DC-6C, suitable for mixed combinations of passengers and freight.

But the DC-6B, first flown on 2 February 1951, was the ultimate variant, built to a total of 288 aircraft by the time production finished in 1958. Similar in length to the DC-6A, the DC-6B's cabin was revised for 64 passengers in standard seating, or 92 in high density. Pan American World Airways had its aircraft revised with increased fuel capacity and greater payload, as well as improved cruising speed, for employment on the carrier's

Specification (DC-7C)

Type:	long-range airliner
Dimensions:	wing span 38.86m (127ft 6in), length 34.21m (112ft 3in), height 9.70m (31ft 10in)
Maximum take-off weight:	64,864kg (143,000lb)
Powerplant:	four 3400hp Wright R-3350-18EA-1 turbo-compound radial piston engines
Maximum speed:	653km/h (405mph)
Range:	7411km (4605 miles)
Service ceiling:	6615m (21,700ft)
Flight crew:	3
Passengers:	105

all-tourist class London-New York service from 1 May 1952. Standard seating on these transatlantic 'Super Six' aircraft was for between 82 and 88 passengers.

DC-7

While the DC-6 effectively challenged the Constellation and Stratocruiser, when Lockheed introduced the Super Constellation, Douglas was again in danger of falling behind. Its counter was the DC-7, produced initially against an American order for 25 and powered by four 3700hp Wright R-3350-18EA-1 turbo-compound radial piston engines. Just 1.02m (3ft 4in) longer than the DC-6B, the DC-7 nevertheless featured an additional row of seats, and evolved into the longer-ranged DC-7B for transatlantic use.

Pan American began flying the DC-7B across the Atlantic on 13 June 1955, but range was marginal westbound and fuel stops frequent. Douglas set out to fix the problem with the DC-7C, which at last brought a modification to the DC-4 wing, adding additional span inboard of the engines to provide extra fuel capacity. More power was also available, so that the fuselage was stretched again and the cabin now took 105 passengers.

Known as the 'Seven Seas', the DC-7C found popularity as one of the ultimate extrapolations of the piston-engined airliner. Neither the Atlantic nor the Pacific offered a challenge to its range and from 11 September 1957 Pan American initiated its 'Great Circle' New York–Seattle route over the pole, but the forthcoming jet age brought an end to the viability of piston-engined airliners.

Skymaster Career

Thomas Braniff founded Braniff Airways on 3 November 1930 and had DC-2 and DC-3 airliners in his fleet by the end of the decade. His airline was typical in taking demilitarized C-54s post-war, including N65145, a former USAAF machine received in November 1945. Braniff flew it until it passed to Los Angeles Air Service in 1954,

then on to Riddle Airlines in 1955. That same year it transferred onto the Canadian register with Wheeler Airlines, spending some time with Mill Aviation in 1956 before returning to Wheeler. It remained with the latter when it was written off after an engine fire during November 1959.

Lockheed Constellation and Super Constellation (1943)

Among the most elegant airliners ever built, the Constellation proved suitable for extensive development. In its ultimate Starliner form it takes its place alongside the DC-7C and Stratocruiser among the greatest piston-engined airliners ever built.

When Howard Hughes and TWA president Jack Frye visited Lockheed on 9 June 1939, they brought with them a daunting airliner specification. It required, among other challenges, four 2200hp engines and range for a non-stop New York–London flight. Boeing and Douglas had passed on the programme, but Lockheed put Hal Hibbard and Clarence 'Kelly' Johnson to work on it. The result was the Model 49, or L-049, Constellation and by the end of 1939, TWA had committed to buy nine.

The design included an unusual curved profile for its long, slender fuselage and a wing scaled up from that of the P-38 Lightning fighter. Designed for high cruising speeds, the sleek aircraft had a triple-fin arrangement and four Wright R-3350 Cyclone radials. It flew for the first time on 9 January 1943 at a time when the USAAF was in desperate need of a high-speed transport aircraft. The TWA order was requisitioned and a further 180 of the military C-69 ordered.

In the event, only 15 of the USAAF's aircraft were completed before VJ-Day brought cancellation of the contract. Another nine were on the production line and having briefly flirted with an all new design, Lockheed bought the 12 surviving USAAF aircraft, all the production

Radar Nose
Many Super Constellations featured an elongated nose, the radome at its tip covering a weather radar.

Tall Nose Undercarriage
The Constellation's stalky nosewheel leg was necessary to maintain wing incidence and keep the propellers clear of the ground.

Speedpack
An optional Speedpak cargo pannier could be carried close up to the underside of the aircraft's centre section. Although compatible with the majority of Constellation variants, it was most commonly associated with the L-649/749.

tooling and incomplete airframes and components. These and the ex-TWA aircraft were refurbished and delivered to TWA as a priority, although by November 1945 Lockheed had taken orders for 89 L-049s from eight customers.

TWA took its first aircraft on 15 November and began route proving on 3 December. But Pan American flew the first L-049 service, on 14 January 1946, between New York and Bermuda, beginning transatlantic service on 4 February. TWA flew New York–Paris for the first time on 7 February and on the 15th it flew the first Los Angeles–

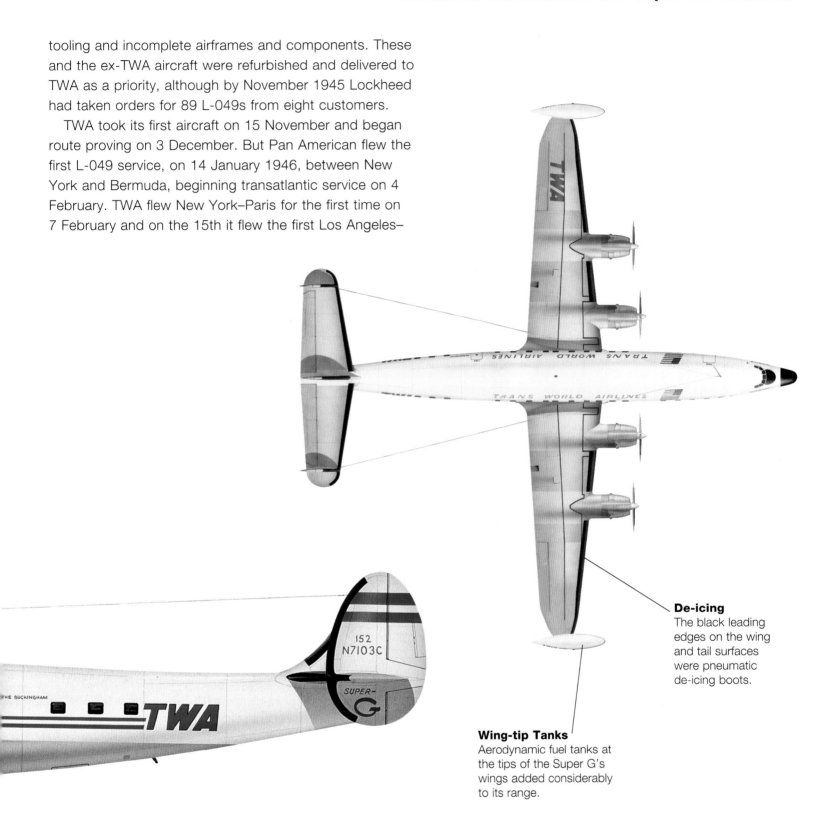

De-icing
The black leading edges on the wing and tail surfaces were pneumatic de-icing boots.

Wing-tip Tanks
Aerodynamic fuel tanks at the tips of the Super G's wings added considerably to its range.

Trans World Airlines was a major Super G operator. Its services included the Ambassador class, which today would be known as a business-class product. Ambassador passengers enjoyed private facilities at airports.

Lockheed Constellation and Super Constellation

New York service, more than five hours faster than was possible with the Stratoliner.

As it proved itself in service, the Constellation began winning orders from the major European airlines, Israel's El Al and other U.S. carriers, although a crash following an electrical fire on a TWA aircraft on 11 July 1946 caused a fleetwide grounding. Now the opportunity was taken to solve ongoing engine problems, by replacing the R-3350 carburettors with fuel injection. The Constellation was flying again by 23 August.

Constellation Evolution

Lockheed had begun working on an improved Constellation a early as May 1945, the airlines –

Specification (L-1049C)

Type:	Constellation (unless otherwise stated) long-range airline
Dimensions:	wing span 37.49m (123ft), length (with radar nose) 35.42m (116ft 2in), height 7.56m (24ft 9in)
Maximum take-off weight:	60,329kg (133,000lb)
Powerplant:	four 3250hp Wright R-3350-972TC18DA-1 18-cylinder turbo-compound radial piston engines
Maximum speed:	602km/h (374mph)
Operational range:	6470km (4020 miles)
Service ceiling:	7071m (23,200ft)
Flight crew:	3 to 5

The Super Constellation prototype was rebuilt from the original L-049. It flew for the first time in its original configuration in 1943 and was withdrawn in 1957.

especially Eastern Air Lines (EAL) – calling for higher cruising speeds, greater payload and improved economy. It satisfied these apparently contradictory requirements with a 50 per cent redesign to produce the L-649. With uprated engines, the new model flew for the first time on 19 October 1946, but only 14 were built, all for EAL.

Production switched to the L-749, which boasted a 1609km (1000-mile) range advantage over the L-649, for non-stop eastbound transatlantic flights, although westerly crossings, into the prevailing headwind, still required a fuel stop. Air France took the first L-749s and the type sold well enough for Lockheed to promote the L-749A version from 1949, featuring increased weights and beefed-up structure. South African Airways received the first new-build L-749A in 1950, but modification of existing L-749s to the new standard was already underway elsewhere.

Super Constellation

In 1949, Lockheed began modifying the original L-049 as the L-1049 Super Constellation prototype. The fuselage was stretched, the empennage enlarged, fuel capacity increased and more powerful 2700hp R-3350-CA1 turbo-supercharged engines fitted. The aircraft flew again on 13 October 1950. Equipped for between 71 and 99 passengers, production Super Constellations began emerging from the factory on 1 August 1951 and the type entered service with EAL on 15 December.

While the L-1049A and B were military variants, the L-1049C was built for the civilian market with new-technology 3250hp R-3350-972TC18DA-1 turbo-compound engines. KLM began L-1049C operations in August 1953, while four of the L-1049D freighter were built for Seaboard & Western, followed by a small number of improved L-1049E airliners.

Super G and Starliner

The major stride in Constellation development was the L-1049G, however, marketed as the Super G. With yet more power and higher weights, it could be fitted with 2271-litre (600 U.S. gal) wing tip fuel tanks for more reliable eastbound transatlantic schedules. First flown on 12 December 1954, the Super G entered service with Northwest in January 1955. The L-1049H convertible freighter was the only commercial Super G variant, although the L-1049G continued to sell well even with the jet age just around the corner. In fact, Douglas had continued to extract extreme performance from its piston-airliner range and in response to the DC-7C, Lockheed developed the L-1649A Starliner. It was the first major departure from the basic L-049 configuration, featuring an all-new wing, but reverting to turbo-compound engines after a failed dalliance with turboprops.

Originally known as Super Star Constellation, the L-1649A had become the Starliner by the time of its initial flight on 11 October 1956. Several airlines signed up for deliveries in small numbers and the first Air France machine flew Los Angeles–Paris non-stop on its 9 July 1957 delivery flight.

The DC-7C and L-1649C operators began exchanging records and competing over the established long-range routes, extracting the most from these highly developed machines, but TWA was typical of most in gradually withdrawing its Starliners in favour of jet equipment. Its flew its final Starliner passenger service in 1963 and last domestic freight service in 1967.

Second-line Service

Constellations of all variants found extensive second-line use after withdrawal by their mainline operators. L-749A PH-TFD was delivered to KLM and re-registered PH-LDD in 1954. It served the Dutch flag carrier until 1960 and in 1963 went to Compañía Aeronáutica Uruguaya SA (CAUSA), which flew a handful of the type. Registered CX-BCS, the aircraft was withdrawn from use in 1968 and broken up in 1972.

Boeing 377 Stratocruiser
(1947)

Boeing's Stratocruiser rightfully takes its place alongside the DC-7C and the Starliner as the most advanced piston-engined airliners ever. It was a complex machine that in many ways heralded the era of jets that was just around the corner and ultimately limited its useful first-line career to little more than a decade.

Boeing had been unfortunate in seeing its Stratoliner and Clipper, both excellent designs, maturing in service just as World War II curtailed airline operations and re-focused aircraft production activities on military expansion. But it had established a precedent for taking the best of its military technology and applying it to the civilian market – the B-9 design informed the Model 247, the B-17 lent major components to the Stratoliner and the XB-15 to the Clipper.

Next Boeing took the wings, engines, empennage and undercarriage, and two-thirds of the fuselage of the B-29 Superfortress, as the basis of the XC-97 transport

prototype for the USAAF. A bulbous upper section was designed to replace the upper third of the bomber's fuselage, producing an inverted figure '8' cross section that provided for enormous space below the main deck and a voluminous main cabin.

The design had obvious potential and the USAAF initially took three XC-97 prototypes, six YC-97 pre-production aircraft, three YC-97A machines with elements of the B-50 bomber and a single YC-97B, equipped for 80 passengers in a luxurious interior fit. The YC-97As employed the aluminium alloy 75ST used in the B-50 development of the

Cockpit Glazing
The unusual un-stepped cockpit arrangement gave the crew excellent visibility, which some pilots claimed as compensation for the Stratocruiser's difficult handling.

'Coronet' Cabin
BOAC originally configured its transatlantic Stratocruiser's in 'Coronet' configuration with 67 passengers on the upper deck and 14 below.

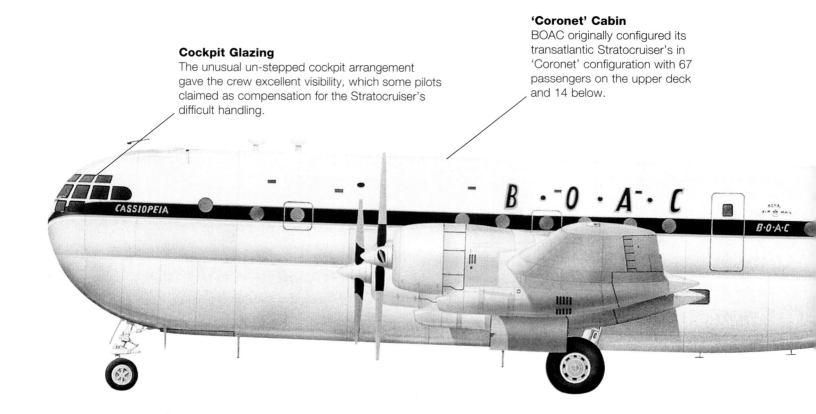

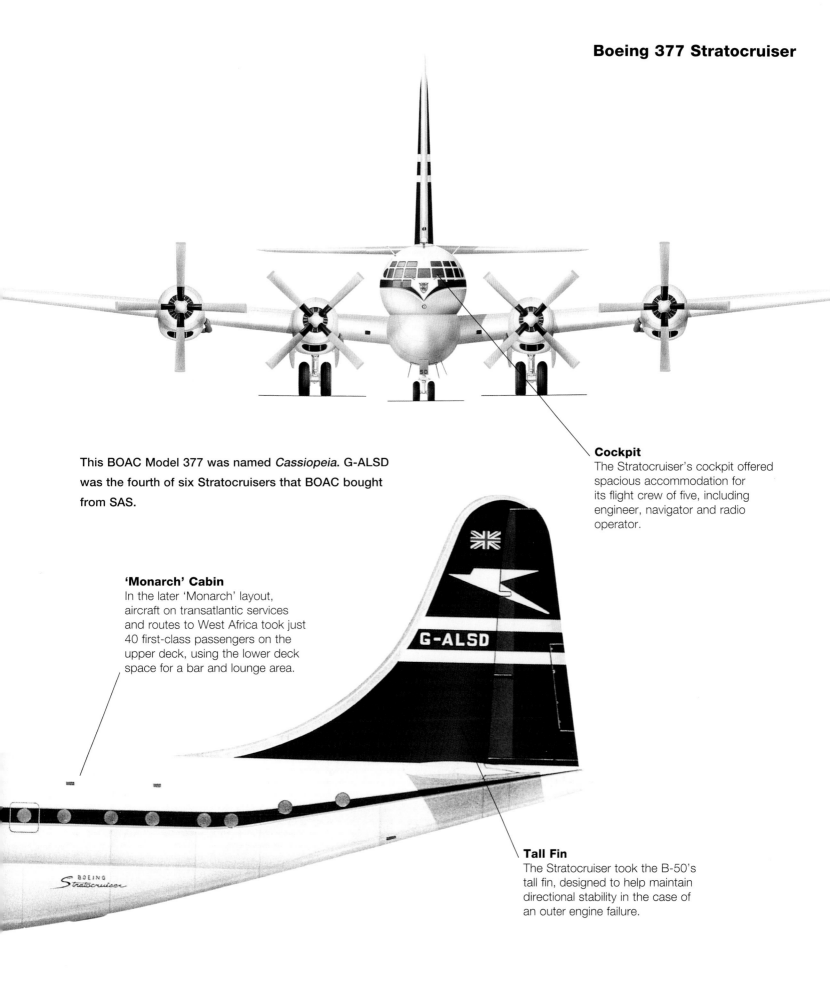

This BOAC Model 377 was named *Cassiopeia*. G-ALSD was the fourth of six Stratocruisers that BOAC bought from SAS.

Cockpit
The Stratocruiser's cockpit offered spacious accommodation for its flight crew of five, including engineer, navigator and radio operator.

'Monarch' Cabin
In the later 'Monarch' layout, aircraft on transatlantic services and routes to West Africa took just 40 first-class passengers on the upper deck, using the lower deck space for a bar and lounge area.

Tall Fin
The Stratocruiser took the B-50's tall fin, designed to help maintain directional stability in the case of an outer engine failure.

Boeing 377 Stratocruiser

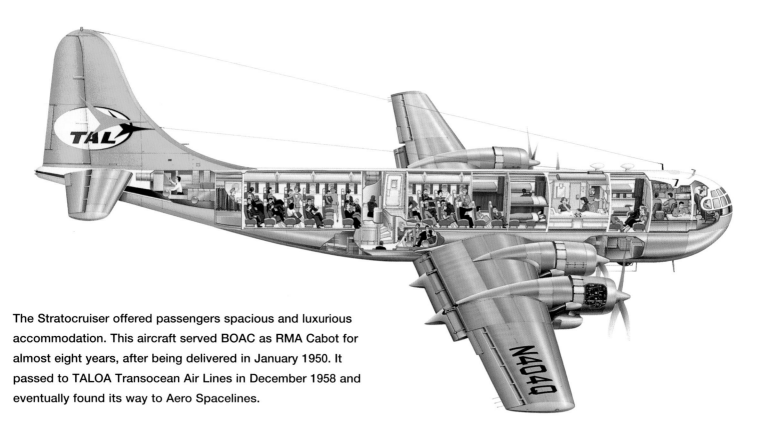

The Stratocruiser offered passengers spacious and luxurious accommodation. This aircraft served BOAC as RMA Cabot for almost eight years, after being delivered in January 1950. It passed to TALOA Transocean Air Lines in December 1958 and eventually found its way to Aero Spacelines.

B-29, as well the latter's taller fin and engines. The YC-97B was to all intents and purposes a military airliner and the Model 377 Stratocruiser prototype progressed up the production line immediately behind it.

Complex Design

With its five-man flight crew, twin decks, turbo-compound engines, cabin pressurization and heated,

Specification

Type:	long-range airliner
Dimensions:	wing span 43m (141ft 3in), length 33.65m (110ft 4in), height 11.66m (38ft 3in)
Normal take-off weight:	76,195kg (145,800lb)
Powerplant:	four 3500hp Pratt & Whitney R-4360 Wasp Major 28-cylinder, four-row turbo-supercharged radial piston engines
Maximum speed:	603km/h (375mph)
Range:	7360km (4600 miles)
Service ceiling:	more than 9760m (32,000ft)
Flight crew:	5
Passengers:	typically 67 passengers on the upper deck and 14 below

pressurized cargo hold, the Model 377 was a technically advanced, complex aircraft, even compared to the latest Douglas and Lockheed propliners. It was always going to challenge airline maintenance departments and therefore be costly to operate, but it had a high passenger capacity and the space for carriers to offer luxury travel over long ranges – although certificated range was initially deficient for comfortable Atlantic crossings.

The XC-97 took off for the first time in November 1944, Boeing having announced the Model 377 a week earlier. Pan American was first with an order for 20 aircraft. The prototype made its initial flight on 8 July 1947 and entered Pan American service on 24 October 1950, although the initial production aircraft had flown its first route, between San Francisco and Honolulu, on 1 April 1949. The airline subsequently added 1519 litres (410 U.S. gal) to the fuel capacities of its Stratocruisers, enabling them to cover the New York–London–Paris route with ease. The type began replacing Pan American's Constellations over the Atlantic from 2 June 1949.

Other carriers, including American Overseas Airlines (AOA), which bought eight Stratocruisers, Northwest (10), United (seven) and BOAC (six), added handfuls of orders to Pan American's 20, but sales remained disappointing. There was money to be made with the

Stratocruiser on luxury services, but it was a challenging aircraft to fly and operate, and the latest incarnations of the DC-6 and 7, and Super Constellation, kept the pressure on Boeing. A series of accidents, two of them fatal, also marred the type's record and from the total run of just 56 machines, six were destroyed in only a decade of first-line service.

The aircraft's Hamilton Standard propellers were prone to fatigue failure and a primary cause of problems, accounting for two fatal accidents and as many as a dozen further incidents. Aircraft fitted with Curtiss Electrics propellers suffered no such problems. Engine reliability was also an issue, especially the spark plugs, engineers struggling to keep all 56 firing, while cylinder life was initially very brief and oil consumption erratic.

Nevertheless, Pan American and BOAC both used the Stratocruiser successfully and expanded their fleets. The U.S. carrier bought AOA and its six Model 377s in 1950, while BOAC bought a further aircraft from Pan American, four from SAS (Scandinavian Airlines System) and six from United. BOAC used the Stratocruiser on its primary routes for a decade from 1949 on transatlantic routes as well as schedules to West Africa.

Its final services were flown for West African Airways and Ghana Airways, by which time the fleet was already being sold, mostly back to Boeing for onward sale to second-line operators. Similar fates befell the majority of Stratocruisers as the 1950s drew to a close and several aircraft eventually found new careers as stock for the unusual Guppy and Super Guppy conversions.

Stratocruiser Prototype

Boeing flew NX90700, the Stratocruiser prototype, for the first time in 1947. Its test duties over, the machine was refurbished and delivered to Pan American on 24 September 1950, re-registered as N1022V. All the carrier's Stratocruisers were given 'Clipper' names and N1022V became Clipper Nightingale. It served for a decade or so, before Pan American sold it and Clipper Nightingale

reappeared with Venezuelan cargo carrier Rutas Aereas Nacionales SA (RANSA) as Carlos and registered YV-C-ERI. It flew alongside Curtiss C-46 Commando and Douglas DC-6 freighters from 1961, but was broken up in 1969. RANSA also operated three other Stratocruisers, including ex-N1036V Clipper Washington, which it lost in an incident and broke up during 1968.

🇬🇧 **Vickers Viscount** (1948)

Given the Comet's disastrous early career, the Vickers Viscount introduced the world to sustained turbine-engined commercial operations. The aircraft became a favourite with passengers for its smooth ride and large cabin windows, and remains the UK's most widely produced airliner type.

Great Britain's fist airline had been established in 1916 and its aircraft industry began producing commercial aircraft from early 1919, but these had typically been tailored closely to British requirements and exports had been few. This situation continued right up to the outbreak of World War II, no British manufacturer having achieved the global market penetration of Douglas, Dornier, Fokker or Junkers.

As early as 1942, however, the UK government began to think around the needs of post-war commercial flying. It appointed John Moore-Brabazon, 1st Baron Brabazon

of Tara, a pioneering British aviator and former Minister of Aircraft Production, to lead a committee for the definition of aircraft requirements. The so-called Brabazon Committee arrived at a range of conclusions, some of greater prescience than others.

Among the better suggestions was the Brabazon Type II, which described a short-haul airliner for European routes and broke down as the piston-powered Type IIA and turbine-powered Type IIB. The former produced the Airspeed Ambassador, all 20 of which went to British European Airways (BEA), while the Armstrong Whitworth

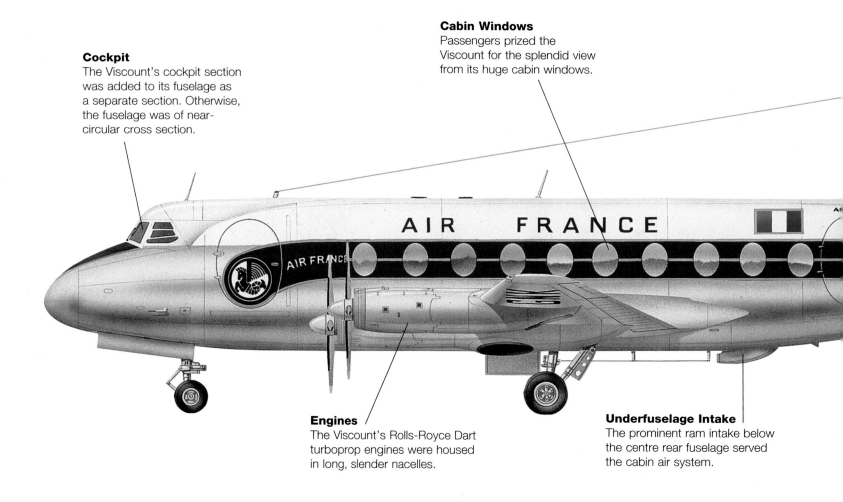

Cabin Windows
Passengers prized the Viscount for the splendid view from its huge cabin windows.

Cockpit
The Viscount's cockpit section was added to its fuselage as a separate section. Otherwise, the fuselage was of near-circular cross section.

AIR FRANCE

AIR FRANCE

Engines
The Viscount's Rolls-Royce Dart turboprop engines were housed in long, slender nacelles.

Underfuselage Intake
The prominent ram intake below the centre rear fuselage served the cabin air system.

Vickers designated the Air France Viscount V.708. The airline took 12 between May 1953 and August 1954, operating them until 1961 when they passed to Air Inter.

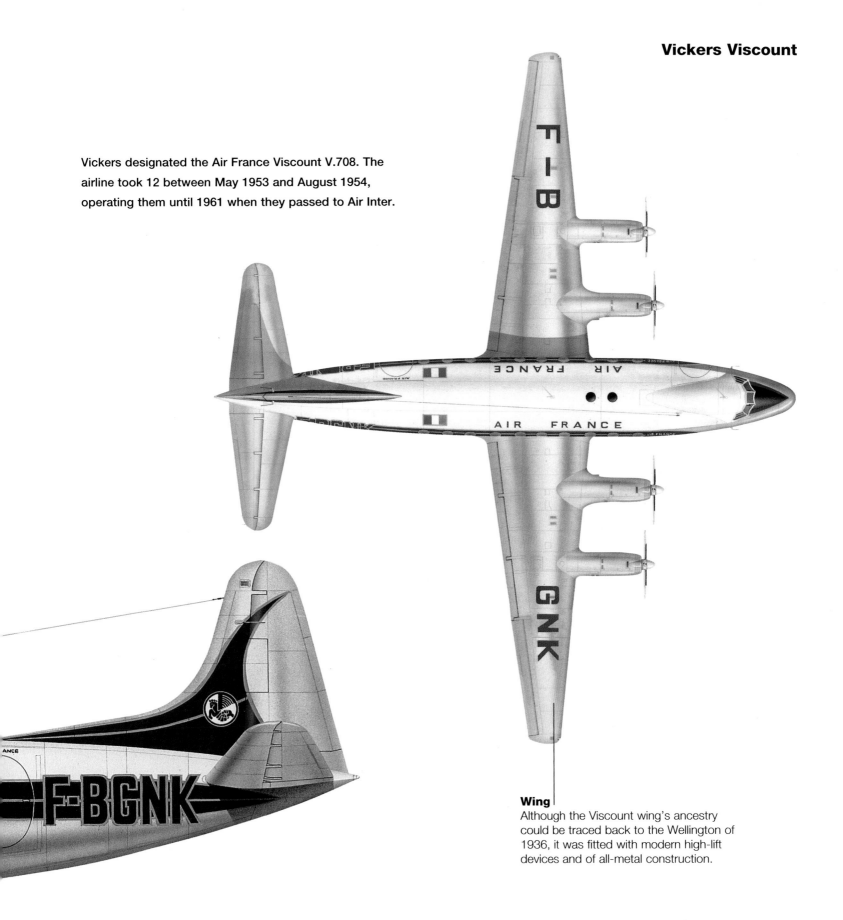

Wing
Although the Viscount wing's ancestry could be traced back to the Wellington of 1936, it was fitted with modern high-lift devices and of all-metal construction.

Vickers Viscount

The Viscount's sharply dihedralled tailplanes and sloping nose profile were particularly evident from the front.

Apollo and Vickers VC2 (Vickers Commercial 2) were proposed against the latter.

Vickers Advantage

In October 1944, Vickers had taken a government order for three 'Wellington Transport Aircraft' based on its successful Wellington bomber. The company developed it into the VC1 Viking, in the class of the DC-3 but by no means as successful. It had therefore been working on a Viking replacement for sometime when the Type IIB specification was published in April 1946. The requirement detailed a 24-seater with a 1000-mile range, but chief designer G.R. Edwards believed

this passenger capacity too small and led his team in producing a 32-seat airliner.

The machine's wing was based on that of the Wellington, but incorporated stressed skin construction, where the aircraft's skin has a load-carrying role and the underlying structure can therefore be made less substantial. Power was to come from four turboprops in long, narrow nacelles. The new turboprop technology promised to combine something of the performance advantages of the turbojet with the relative economy of the piston engine/propeller combination.

The Ministry of Supply ordered two Armstrong Siddeley Mamba-powered VC2s in March 1946, with the expectation that Vickers would fund a third. By now the aircraft had gained the Vickers' type number 609 and been given the very British name, Viceroy. The rather more conservative 900hp Rolls-Royce Dart RDa.1 turboprop was selected for the third Viceroy. In fact, considerable experience had already been gained with the Dart, and Edwards decided to abandon the Mamba in favour of the Rolls-Royce engine on all three machines, which now became V.630s. The aircraft's name also changed, to Viscount, after India gained independence in August 1947. Another very British choice of appellation, it was hardly ideal for the export market.

The V.630 flew for the first time on 16 July 1948, almost a year before the Apollo, and while the Armstrong Whitworth aircraft was beset by unsolvable engine problems, the Viscount flew superbly. When the more powerful 1400hp RDa.3 was offered, Edwards suggested that 32 seats was inadequate and even though BEA had committed to the Ambassador on 22 September 1948, he elicited interest from the airline in a stretched

Specification (V.810 Viscount)	
Type:	short/medium-range airliner
Dimensions:	wing span 28.56m (93ft 8½in), length 26.11m (85ft 8in), height 8.15m (26ft 9in)
Loaded weight:	32,885kg (72,500lb)
Powerplant:	four 1990ehp Rolls-Royce Dart RDa.7 turboprops
Continuous cruising speed:	565km/h (351mph)
Range:	2832km (1760 miles)
Service ceiling:	7620m (25,000ft)
Flight crew:	2
Passengers:	75

Viscount. The second V.630 was diverted for jet engine testing, so that it fell to the first aircraft to begin a month of scheduled operations on 27 July 1950.

There were no reliability issues and passengers were thrilled with the experience. BEA committed to 20 stretched aircraft on 3 August 1950 and the V.700 first flew on 28 August 1950, having used several components from the cancelled third machine. BEA eventually took 26 of a slightly revised 53-seat V.701 variant, the type entering service on 18 April 1953.

There followed a series of variants offering greater capacity, higher weights and longer ranges, and the Dart always proved capable of development to keep pace. Significantly for Vickers, it broke into the U.S. market with a 60-aircraft order for Capital Airlines. And when the original customers moved on to new equipment and put their used Viscounts up for sale, they were quickly taken up thanks to their fine performance and high passenger appeal.

Towards the end of the Viscount's career and long after the last of the 444 aircraft built had come off the production line, a Freightmaster conversion was introduced, keeping surviving airframes commercially viable into the late 1990s.

Viscount Customers

British Midland was typical of the Viscount's many operators. It took its first aircraft in 1966, around two years after production had ceased and the last new-build aircraft delivered to the Civil Aviation Administration of China (CAAC). In all, it flew 20 airframes over a 20-year period, retiring the last in 1988. As well as BEA, other original customers included Air France, Continental Airlines, Egyptian Airlines, Northeast (which took 10 of the aircraft intended for Capital after the airline collapsed and was purchased by United) and New Zealand National Airways. The aircraft delivered to Capital entered widespread service, some plying Aloha Airlines' inter-island routes and services to the mainland.

⊞ De Havilland DH.106 Comet (1949)

It fell to Britain's de Havilland to first exploit pure-jet technology in a commercial application. The revolutionary Comet transformed airliner performance, but a series of accidents tarnished its reputation and the UK's early lead over the U.S. jets vanished.

With pressurized four-engined piston airlines achieving near-transatlantic ranges, the next great step in commercial aviation was the exploitation of jet technology. Jet propulsion promised higher cruising altitudes, well above the weather, high speeds and quiet, vibration free journeys. Given the capabilities of the Constellation, DC-6 and Stratocruiser, it seemed inevitable that the world's first jetliner would come from a design team at Lockheed, Douglas or Boeing, but instead it came from de Havilland in the UK.

De Havilland's success was founded on its pre-war range of light aircraft, the ubiquitous Tiger Moth trainer and a variety of airliners, the majority biplanes, but culminating in the graceful, all-wood Albatross of 1938. The unusual construction methods pioneered in the Albatross were used in the wartime Mosquito, a multi-role warplane of incredible performance, while de Havilland also extended its capabilities to include the Vampire, Britain's second operational jet fighter.

The Comet was a very clean aircraft, designed to create the minimum of drag for efficient operations and high-speed cruising.

Stretched Fuselage
The Comet 4B's long fuselage housed a cabin for around 100 passengers, although Dan-Air installed as many as 119 seats in its second-hand machines.

Cabin Windows
The cabin windows and apertures for the air direction finding antennae (responsible for the Comet 1 break-ups in square-edged form) were oval in the redesigned Comets.

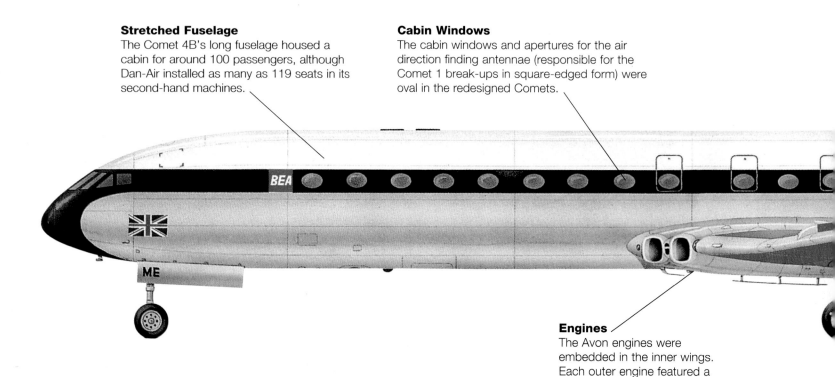

Engines
The Avon engines were embedded in the inner wings. Each outer engine featured a thrust reverse system.

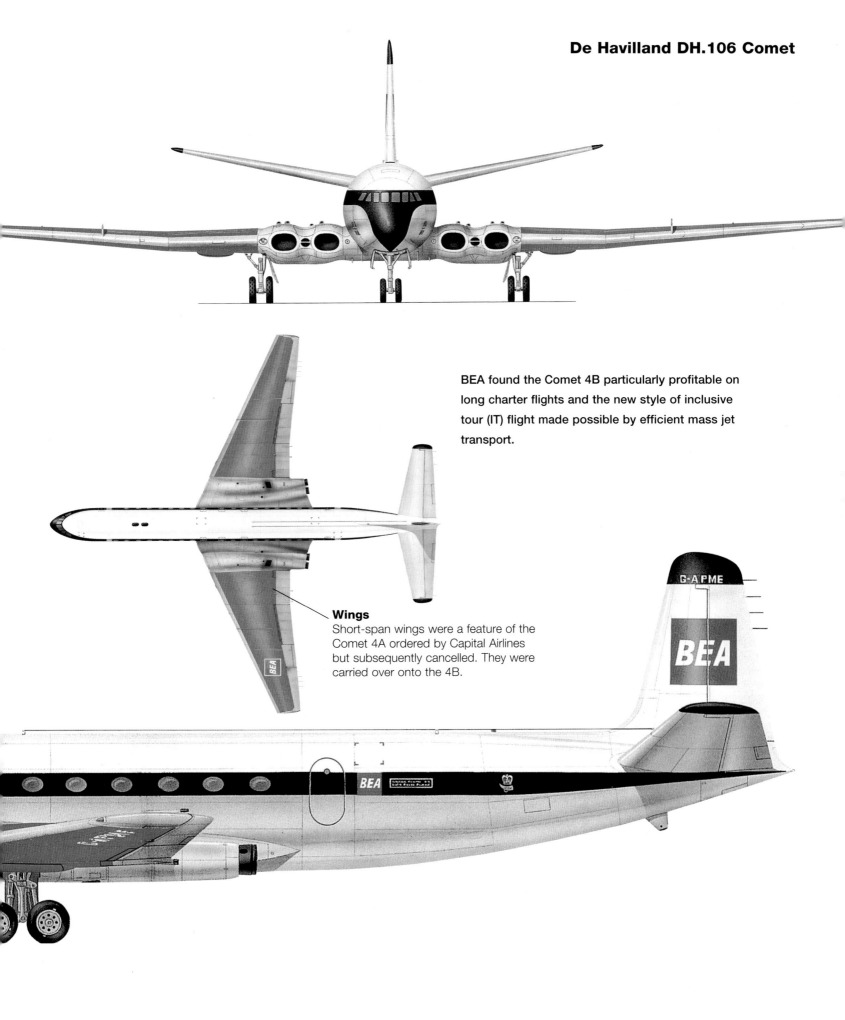

BEA found the Comet 4B particularly profitable on long charter flights and the new style of inclusive tour (IT) flight made possible by efficient mass jet transport.

Wings
Short-span wings were a feature of the Comet 4A ordered by Capital Airlines but subsequently cancelled. They were carried over onto the 4B.

De Havilland DH.106 Comet

Middle East Airlines flew a mixed fleet of Comet 4Bs and 4Cs, as here. It lost three Comets and a pair of Caravelles in an Israeli attack on Beirut International Airport in 1968.

The company therefore had a basis of expertise and it was this that attracted the interest of the Brabazon Committee for its Type IV requirement. This called for a jet transport, which might allow British industry to gain a lead in airliner technology by leap-frogging the advanced piston-engined designs coming out of North America. De Havilland was unusual in having design and production facilities for aircraft and their engines; the Vampire was already flying on the power of the de Havilland Goblin turbojet when the DH.106 jet airliner received company go-ahead in February 1945.

Design Definition

Jet power had been applied to fighters and the German Arado Ar 234 bomber/reconnaissance aircraft during the later stages of World War II. These were all relatively small

aircraft and while designs for large jet bombers were under development, the potential applications for a jet airliner remained somewhat vague in the second half of the 1940s.

BOAC was the initial Comet customer, but was undecided on how such an aircraft should be employed. Consideration was given to a range of possibilities from a short-ranged 14-seat machine to a transatlantic mailplane with luxury accommodation for as few as two passengers, but de Havilland's plan for a more versatile aircraft eventually saw fruition, albeit with the acknowledgement that available jet engines were too thirsty for non-stop transatlantic range to be feasible.

The government's Ministry of Supply ordered a pair of prototypes in September 1946 and BOAC placed the first commercial order, for eight aircraft, down from an earlier requirement for 25, the following January. In December 1947 the aircraft was named the Comet.

De Havilland designed a technically advanced airframe to extract maximum potential from its own Ghost turbojet. Extensive research, on the ground and in flying test beds, had taken place by the time the first prototype took off for its maiden flight on 27 July 1949. Its design was challenging but not entirely revolutionary, as illustrated by the wing, which was extensively swept at the leading edge and less so at the trailing edge, resulting in a very modest sweep overall. The engines were buried in two pairs at the wingroots and the cockpit unstepped, so that the lines of the aircraft's nose were unbroken. Construction made extensive use of Redux, a pioneering metal-to-metal bonding process that de Havilland was first to use on such a grand scale.

Jet power promised much higher cruising altitudes than the piston airliners could reach and the Comet's cabin pressure was twice that of previous machines, for a 2349m (8000ft) cabin pressure at 12,192m (40,000ft). This degree of pressurization, combined with the stresses of high-speed flight on such a large aircraft, led de Havilland to undertake extensive component and whole airframe testing. The work included fuselage pressure testing,

Specification (Comet 4B)

Type:	medium-haul jet airliner
Dimensions:	wing span 32.87m (107ft 10in), length 35.97m (118ft), height 8.69m (28ft 6in)
Maximum take-off weight:	73,483kg (162,000lb)
Powerplant:	four 46.80kN (10,500lb) thrust Rolls-Royce Avon Mk 524 turbojet engines
Maximum cruising speed:	856km/h (532mph)
Range with maximum payload:	5391km (3350 miles)
Service ceiling:	12,000m (39,370ft)
Flight crew:	4
Passengers:	101

during which a large fuselage test section exploded, with damage so extensive that the point of failure was impossible to detect – it was perhaps a portent of problems to come.

Service Debut

On 2 May 1952 the first ever commercial jet service left London for Johannesburg, BOAC operating Comet 1 G-ALYP over the route. The type's great passenger appeal immediately became obvious and other airlines began showing interest, especially as de Havilland continued to develop the aircraft. But then a BOAC Comet crashed on take-off in Rome on 26 October and a Canadian Pacific Airlines jet suffered a similar fate at Karachi on 3 March 1953. The cause of both accidents was pilots employing take-off techniques applicable to piston airliners, but which made the Comet unsafe – the problems were eradicated through improved training.

On 2 May 1953, G-ALYV broke up soon after take-off from Calcutta, its failure attributed to turbulence caused by monsoon conditions, but then G-ALYP broke up after take-off from Rome on 10 January 1954, resulting in a temporary grounding. Modifications were made to the fleet and flying resumed, but another inflight loss, again out of Rome, grounded the Comets for more thorough investigation. The structural failures were traced to a square-cornered antenna aperture on the aircraft's upper fuselage and de Havilland was forced to redesign several aspects of the machine.

It did so, very effectively, producing a series of Comet variants that proved reliable and efficient. But the stigma of those early accidents was difficult to overcome and when the first Comet 4s appeared in BOAC service over the Atlantic on 4 October 1958, the first Boeing 707 schedule was just 22 days away. The Boeing was a more modern, more attractive machine; de Havilland and Great Britain had lost the commercial jet race.

Comet Variants

De Havilland produced a range of Comet versions that extended the type's range and expanded its passenger capacity enormously. The Comet 1A had more fuel and 44 passenger seats, while the Comet 2 had a stretched fuselage and Rolls-Royce Avon turbojet engines, which became standard on subsequent aircraft. First flown on 19 July 1954, the Comet 3 promised a 4345km (2700-mile) range and 76 passenger seats, but its sales prospects were destroyed by the type's grounding.

De Havilland re-entered the market with the ultimate Comet 4 (shown here in MEA service), available as the short-haul Series 4A, 100 passenger/5390km (3350-mile) Series 4B and long-range, high-capacity Series 4C. The 4A was cancelled, while the 4C was the most successful. Used Comet 4s were very popular with second-line operators and their greatest proponent, Britain's Dan-Air, retired its final example in 1980. Interestingly, the Nimrod maritime patrol and reconnaissance aircraft was based on the Comet, the last Nimrod being withdrawn in 2011.

Boeing 707 (1954)

Using its experience with the B-47 and B-52 bombers, Boeing produced a jetliner of far greater ambition than the Comet. Through constant innovation and development, it fought off competition from Convair and Douglas to make jet transport a practical reality.

Boeing managed to elicit very little interest from the airlines or the U.S. military when it proposed a jet-powered development of the Stratocruiser. The company was busy building Model 367/KC-97 tanker/transport variants of the Model 377 airliner, as well as its advanced swept-wing B-47 Stratojet and B-52 Stratofortress jet bombers, and, no stranger to applying military technology to commercial designs, it developed the Model 367-80 using its own money.

The new transport was the 80th design study around producing a jet airliner from the Model 367, hence its 367-80 designation, generally expressed as 'Dash 80'. In fact, although the Dash 80 retained the 'double-bubble' fuselage cross-section of the 367, it was an entirely new aircraft and even the double-bubble was covered in an outer skin for a smooth exterior shape. Boeing swept the aircraft's wing at 35° and used four Pratt & Whitney JT3 turbojets, derived from the B-52's J57 and pod mounted

This is a Ecuatoriana Jet Cargo 707-320C. A former Pan Am 707-321B, Israel's Atasco modified this aircraft as a 707-320C freighter for Ecuatoriana.

Freight Door
The 707 freighters featured a large cargo door in the port forward fuselage.

Engine Nacelles
Distinctive, large-diameter forward cowlings were fitted to the nacelles of the JT3D turbofan engine.

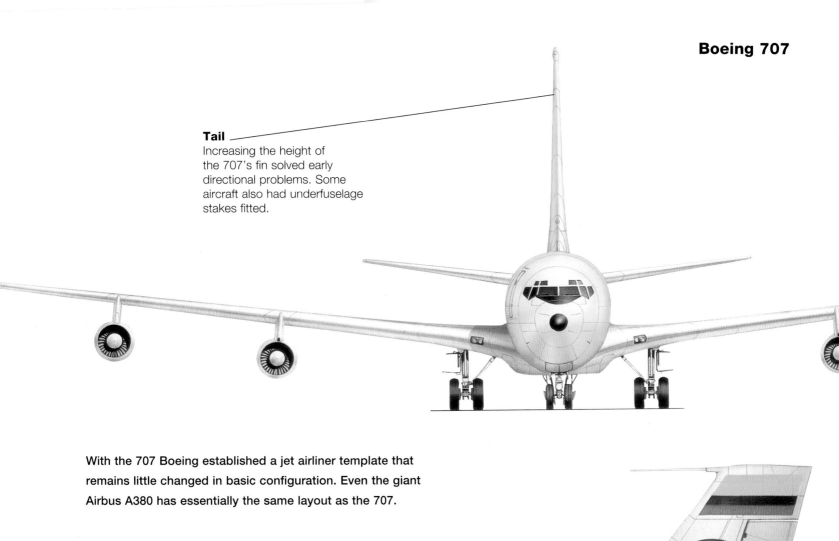

Tail
Increasing the height of
the 707's fin solved early
directional problems. Some
aircraft also had underfuselage
stakes fitted.

With the 707 Boeing established a jet airliner template that
remains little changed in basic configuration. Even the giant
Airbus A380 has essentially the same layout as the 707.

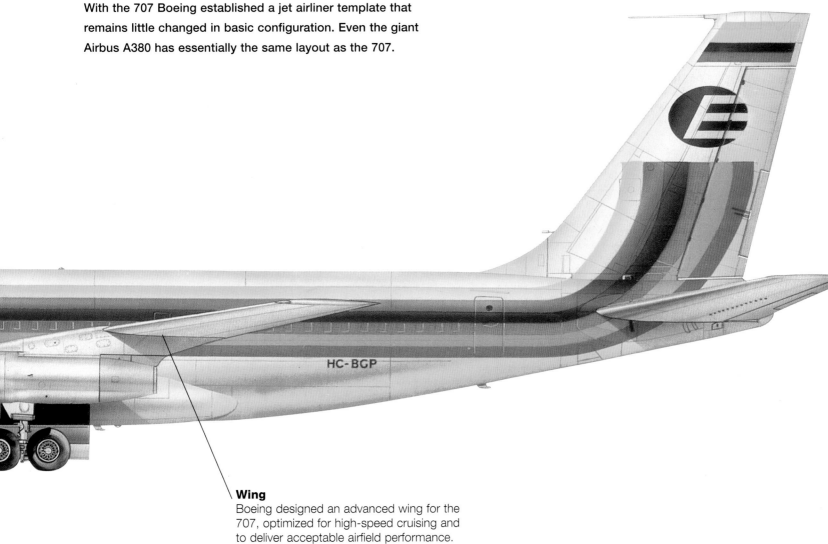

HC-BGP

Wing
Boeing designed an advanced wing for the
707, optimized for high-speed cruising and
to deliver acceptable airfield performance.

Boeing 707

Aer Lingus was among many airlines that operated the 720 from new. This is an early machine, with JT3C turbojet engines.

below and ahead of the wings, to power it. When the aircraft flew for the first time on 15 July 1954, it remained without orders, but the U.S. Air Force was already considering the need for a jet tanker and placed its first order for what would become the KC-135 Stratotanker in September. The 367-80's production future was secure, but Boeing went back to the airlines in hopes of developing a parallel commercial version.

By now, Douglas was offering a larger quad-jet airliner promising much greater range than the 367-80 or the

resurgent de Havilland Comet could reach. The Douglas model's 'longer legs' and wider cabin tempted the airlines. Losing orders to Douglas, Boeing therefore left the market to develop a new, wider fuselage for what became the 707 airliner, leaving the C-135 series of military tankers and transports, already under development as the Model 717, with the original narrow fuselage.

Into Service

The aircraft that Boeing brought back to the airliners offered a cabin 5.08cm (2in) wider than that of the competing DC-8 and given its rival's later start and relative lack of experience with large, swept-wing jet aircraft, Boeing was still able to get its first 707 into service – with Pan Am – in October 1958, five months after the DC-8's maiden flight. The airline had ordered 20 Boeings and 25 DC-8s, beginning transatlantic flights just weeks after BOAC began similar Comet 4 services, although, like the Comet, Pan Am's original 707-121 jets had insufficient range to complete the crossing non-stop unless crews flew them extremely carefully to conserve fuel.

Meanwhile, the more powerful Pratt & Whitney JT4A that Douglas had hoped would power a DC-8 offering comfortable transatlantic range had not materialized in time for the type's service entry. The DC-8-10 therefore entered service on transcontinental routes, giving Boeing the time it needed to produce the truly long-ranged 707-320 Intercontinental. This was the jet the airlines had been waiting for and while Douglas sold more than 600 DC-8s, Boeing sold in excess of 900 707s.

Even though the holy grail of transatlantic range had been achieved, the quest for better fuel efficiency

Specification (707-320B)

Type:	long-range jet airliner
Dimensions:	wing span 44.42m (145ft 9in), length 44.35m (145ft 6in), height 12.93m (42ft 5in)
Maximum take-off weight:	148,325kg (327,000lb)
Powerplant:	four 81kN (18,000lb) thrust Pratt & Whitney JT3D-3 turbofan engines
Maximum cruising speed:	1010km/h (627mph)
Range with maximum payload:	9915km (6160 miles)
Service ceiling:	10,973m (36,000ft)
Flight crew:	4
Passengers:	up to 189 in single-class accommodation

continued as a primary driver of development. When Boeing debuted the larger, 189-seat Intercontinental, it offered only the JT4A as powerplant, but Rolls-Royce subsequently entered the market with the Conway, a bypass turbojet where some of the air entering the engine bypassed its hot core, with less fuel burned.

BOAC specified the Conway for its Intercontinentals, which became 707-400s. Just 37 were built, emphasizing Boing's willingness to modify the basic 707 variants to suit customer needs. Pratt & Whitney responded to the Conway by modifying the JT3C turbojet, removing its first three compressor stages and

installing a wide-diameter, two-stage fan to produce the JT3D. The resulting turbofan powered the majority of 707-300s, which became -300Bs, while applying the same engine to the 707-100 produced the -100B.

Boeing built the 707 in a variety of forms, including the short-fuselage, long-range 707-138 for Qantas and similar 707-200 for Braniff, powered by JT4A-3 turbojets for improved hot-and-high performance on the carrier's South American routes. Variations on the fan-engined -300B included the 707-300C, built in freighter and combi forms, the latter among the last 707s to leave the production line in 1979.

Boeing 720

Typically considered as a short-range 707 development for regional routes, the Boeing 720 actually offered considerable range, at 8433km (5240 miles). It was, however, suited to operations from regional airports, where runways were typically short – major airports globally had been obliged to lengthen runways and modernize to meet the requirements of the new jet airliners.

Shorter and with a modified wing, the 720 was also lower powered, but given its lower weight compared to the 707-100, boasted an improved thrust-to-weight ratio. First flown

on 23 November 1959, the type entered service with United on 5 July 1960. Combining the JT3D with the 720 airframe produced the 720B, of which 79 of the 154 aircraft in the series were built and 10 re-engined.

The 720 offered very different performance to the 707-100, but looked very similar and, keen to avoid confusing its passengers with a new type, American Airlines named its aircraft '707 Astrojet'. A major 720 operator, American took 25 of the type, while several other airlines also bought the regional Boeing in small numbers.

Sud-Aviation Caravelle (1955)

While the UK pioneered jet travel over longer ranges, France saw the potential for short-haul jet sectors. The Caravelle appeared as an exceptional short/medium-haul airliner that set the benchmark for subsequent designs.

There was no shortage of aerospace design talent in post-war France and the country's government proved willing to fund an array of prototypes, many of which never advanced into production. French industry was therefore no stranger to the latest technologies and poised to take a leading role as jet propulsion became a realistic possibility for a number of new applications. Among these, the government's Sécretariat Générale de l'Aviation Commerciale et Civile (SGACC), responsible for French civil aviation, suggested a market for a 55–65 seat jet airliner suitable for short-haul routes.

The Société Nationale de Construction Aéronautiques du Sud-Est (SNCASE, often written as Sud-Est, or Sud)

proposed its Model 200 in response, featuring a series of design proposals, among them the X-210 powered by a rear-mounted triple arrangement of indigenous Société Nationale d'Etudes et Construction de Moteurs d'Aviation (SNECMA) Atar turbojets. A relatively immature design rated at 27kN (6000lb) thrust, the Atar was quickly replaced by the proven Rolls-Royce Avon, the 41kN (9000lb) rating of the British engine allowing Sud to adopt a twin-engined layout.

This Alitalia Caravelle III was later modified to VIN standard and passed to Alitalia's SAM charter outfit. The Italian flag carrier had 21 Caravelles in service during 1965.

Comet Nose
Caravelles prior to the VI shared the forward fuselage and cockpit section of the de Havilland Comet 1.

Cabin Windows
The Caravelle's unusual cabin windows took a rounded triangular shape.

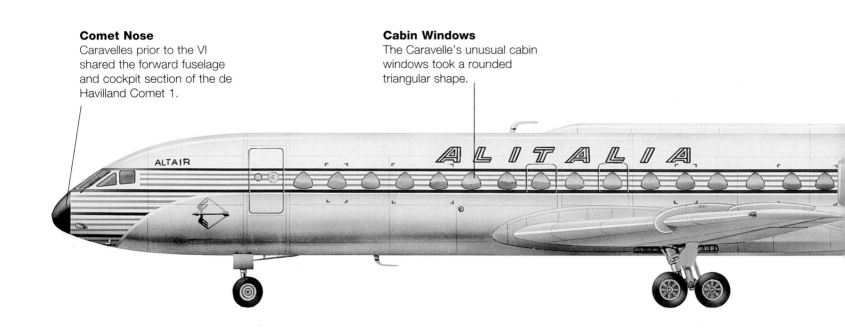

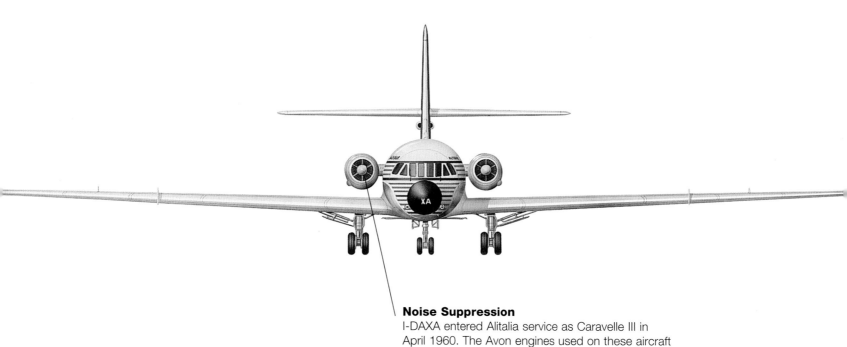

Noise Suppression
I-DAXA entered Alitalia service as Caravelle III in April 1960. The Avon engines used on these aircraft were noisy and suppression technologies were often applied to the nacelles and exhausts.

Sud's decision to develop a short-haul jetliner was both visionary and risky. Conventional wisdom had it that only piston or turboprop engines could deliver cost-effective services over such routes.

Engine Configuration
Setting the Caravelle's engines in pylon-mounted pods either side of the rear fuselage, Sud-Est established a configuration still employed on modern regional jets and business aircraft.

Design Features

Mounting the engines on pylons attached to the aft fuselage left them easily accessible for maintenance and safely separated from the airframe in case of fire or other problems (unlike the Comet, where they were buried in the wing). It also rendered the Caravelle easily re-engined as alternative or more powerful engines became available.

Specification (Caravelle III)

Type:	short/medium-haul jet airliner
Dimensions:	wing span 34.30m (112ft 6⅜in), length 32.01m (105ft ¼in), height 8.72m (78ft 7⅓in)
Maximum take-off weight:	46,000kg (101,411lb)
Powerplant:	two 51kN (11,400lb) thrust Rolls-Royce Avon RA.29/3 Mk 527 turbojet engines
Maximum cruising speed:	805km/h (503mph)
Range with maximum payload:	1845km (1153 miles)
Service ceiling:	12,000m (39,370ft)
Flight crew:	3
Passengers:	65

As well as CJ805 engines, the Caravelle Horizon featured wing and tailplane changes. Its cabin windows were raised to a higher position.

The aircraft's fuselage was cleanly designed, its forward section identical to that of the Comet 1, so that two Comet sections were used to speed production of the first prototypes. The wing was moderately swept and, apart from a pair of prominent fences, extremely clean, since it had no engines to accommodate.

The X-210 gradually morphed into the SE210 Caravelle, a production contract for which the SGACC placed in July 1953. Sud built four prototypes, two for flight test, one for water tank pressure testing and the last for static testing, flying the type for the first time on 27 May 1955. The first prototype had flown in Air France colours and the national carrier ordered 12 aircraft, with the promise of 12 more to come on 3 February 1956.

By April 1958 the Caravelle had received French and U.S. certification, and sales tours of Europe and the Americas began. Scandinavian Airlines ordered six jets with 19 options, but while TWA and United showed interest, no American orders materialized. Deliveries to Air France and SAS began in spring 1959, and the Scandinavians began revenue services, between Copenhagen and Beirut, on 26 April. Powered by Avon RA.29/3 Mk 522 engines, the initial aircraft were designated Series I, or Caravelle I, and Air Algérie and VARIG also took small numbers. Relatively few of the subsequent Caravelle IA, powered by the Avon Mk 522A were built, before the 51kN (11,400lb) thrust Mk 527 allowed Sud-Aviation to offer the improved Caravelle III. (By now the Société Nationale de Construction Aéronautiques du Sud-Ouest had been merged with SNCASE to become Sud-Aviation.)

Improved Caravelles

The Caravelle III flew for the first time in December 1959 and as well as orders for new-build aircraft, attracted interest in the form of upgrades from I and IA standard. Hoping to realize a U.S. order, Sud-Aviation re-engined a Caravelle III with General Electric CJ805-23C turbofans and signed a sales and support contract for the type with Douglas. TWA ordered 20 of this new Caravelle VII, but when Douglas decided to abandon its agreement with Sud-Aviation and develop its own aircraft – the DC-9 – TWA cancelled.

Sud-Aviation nevertheless continued with the CJ805 to produce a stretched Caravelle 10A Horizon. It sold badly, but the Pratt & Whitney JT8D-engined Caravelle 10B, known as the Super B or Super Caravelle, achieved

a great deal more success. Meanwhile, work on Avon-powered developments had continued. The Mk 532R engine powered the Caravelle VI, which also had revised forward fuselage contours for an enlarged cockpit area.

Ironically, it was a modification of this model, the Mk 533-engined VIR, that finally cracked the U.S. market, United Airlines taking 20, each configured for 64 passengers and with first delivery in June 1961. The Caravelle VIR was equipped with thrust reversers, while other United aircraft, equipped with noise-suppression systems, were designated Caravelle VIN. United's Caravelles served until 1970, while several airlines in South America also took the type.

The final Caravelle versions were variations on the Super B theme. The Caravelle 10B1.R combined the airframe changes of the VI with JT8D engines, while the Caravelle 11R was a 10 modified for freight and passengers. Perhaps the ultimate model, the Caravelle 12, was stretched fore and aft of the wing and used 67.50kN (15,000lb) JT8D-9s. Only 12 were completed, for a Caravelle production total of 280. The aircraft had pioneered a new genre of air transport but its sales, compared to those of the U.S. types to come, were disappointing.

Caravelle in Service

Super Caravelle F-BTDA was typical of the Caravelles in finding ready employment as soon as its first-line service was over. French domestic carrier Air Inter made extensive use of the type, installing 128 seats in its Super Caravelles and leasing the last five Caravelle 12s. Other European operators included Alitalia, Sterling, LTU and Iberia, while Jordan's ALIA, Air Afrique and Air Congo also flew Caravelles.

Fokker F27 Friendship and F50 (1955)

Fokker set out to develop a DC-3 successor with its F27 Friendship and enjoyed more success than most manufacturers that attempted to replace the Douglas twin. It convinced regional airlines to abandon the piston engine and later modernized the F27 as the re-engined F50.

Fokker had assembled and distributed Douglas DC-2 airliners after its own range of commercial aircraft had failed to keep up with the latest U.S. developments, and subsequently offered technical support to European DC-3 operators. In the immediate post-war years it sought to rejuvenate its aircraft construction business with a turboprop twin aimed at the DC-3/C-47 replacement market.

Fokker despatched designers to Boeing and Canadair in 1948, to examine the state-of-the-art in airliner design and assess whether Fokker's twin-turboprop concept was workable. This was a time of transition between tried-and-tested piston power and the promising future offered by the gas turbine, whether tethered to a propeller for maximum efficiency, or as a pure jet for speed.

The North American manufacturers were focussed very much on the latest piston engines, while Handley Page in the UK was working on the Herald, an aircraft similar in configuration to the machine proposed by Fokker, but powered by four piston engines. Fokker remained convinced on its choice of powerplant, however, dallying

This Fairchild-built machine was an F-27A, equivalent to the F27-200. Fairchild built several variants mirroring Fokker's models, but also developed versions unique to the U.S. market.

Dart Engines
Rolls-Royce set a precedent for performance and reliability with the Dart, convincing airlines to move away from piston power.

Passenger View
With tall oval windows and a high wing, the F27 series offered passengers an excellent outside view.

Wing
The wing passed across the top of the fuselage, encroaching into the central area of the cabin and restricting overhead space.

Pneumatic De-icing
Pneumatic de-icing boots lined the leading edges of wings and tail, and the propeller blades.

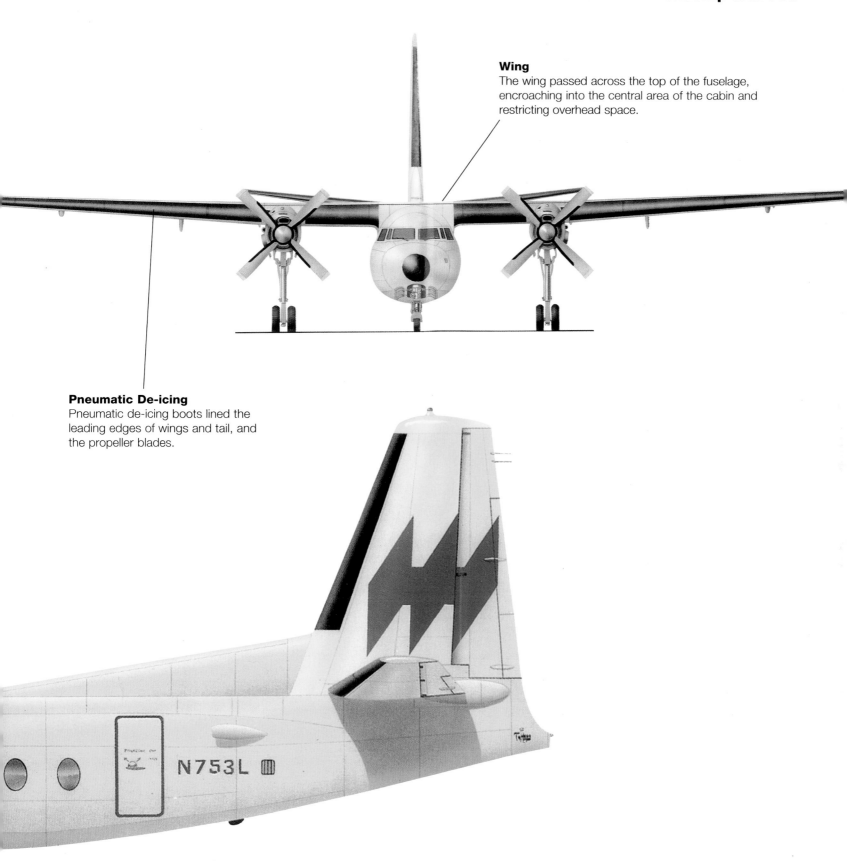

N753L

Hughes Airwest's large network expanded across the western U.S., where the F-27A's hot-and-high performance was especially appreciated.

with the Armstrong Siddeley Mamba, before switching to the Rolls-Royce Dart after Vickers had followed a similar course with the Viscount.

It planned the aircraft's capacity at 32 seats, but soon stretched it for greater capacity, hanging the fuselage under a straight wing of high aspect ratio for maximum cruising efficiency. Known as P.275, the aircraft was designed to use de Havilland's Redux bonding technology, first used extensively on the Comet, in elements of its stressed metallic structure, with fibreglass

Northeast Airlines was typical of the U.S. regional airlines that operated the Fairchild-Hiller developed FH-227.

used elsewhere. In keeping with the latest developments in airliner technology, the P.275 was designed to accommodate a pressurized cabin.

Building the Friendship

By the time the aircraft flew for the first time on 24 November 1955 it had become the F27, subsequently named the Friendship. Fokker had already begun discussing the potential for a licence-production agreement to cover the North American market, courting Fairchild, which remained unconvinced on the choice of powerplant. With the first aircraft performing well in trials, however, a deal was struck on 26 April 1956.

Meanwhile, more powerful Dart 511 engines were installed on the second airframe, which also featured a 0.91m (3ft) fuselage stretch. Airlines had also expressed reservations over turboprop power, but with the Viscount proving so successful, these doubts faded and Fokker began taking orders, initially from Australia's TAA, Aer Lingus and Braathens, but business was slow. Fairchild began marketing the aircraft as the F-27, taking orders for 16 compared to Fokker's eight in 1958.

West Coast flew the type's first commercial service, using an F-27, on 28 September, Aer Lingus flying the initial European routes in December. With the Friendship proving itself useful, orders increased to the extent

Specification (F27-200)

Type:	twin-turboprop regional airliner
Dimensions:	wing span 29m (95ft 2in), length 23.56m (77ft 3½in), height 8.50m (27ft 10½in)
Maximum take-off weight:	20,412kg (45,000lb)
Powerplant:	two 2280eshp Rolls-Royce Dart Mk 536-7R turboprop engines
Cruising speed:	480km/h (298mph)
Range with 44 passengers:	1926km (1197 miles)
Service ceiling:	8990m (29,500ft)
Flight crew:	2
Passengers:	44

that Fokker had to subcontract elements of European production. In the U.S., Fairchild merged with Hiller but F-27 production continued, as did that of the stretched, 52-passenger FH-227 until the line closed in 1973.

Friendship Variants

Responding to calls for increased range, Fokker developed the F27-200 (F27 Mk 200, or Friendship 200) with more fuel and 2020eshp Dart Mk 528 turboprops. The original configuration typically became known as F27-100, while Fokker continued to produce the F27-300 Combiplane, designed to carry mixed loads of freight and passengers in civilian service. The F27-400 was similar but with more power and the F27-500, with 60 seats, the last of the major production versions. Although both the FH-227 and F27-500 were stretched, they were developed separately and optimized for different passenger loads.

Fairchild and Fairchild-Hiller between them produced 173 aircraft, Fokker adding almost 600 more. The Friendship had turned out to be exactly the aircraft the regional airlines needed, but through the 1970s it began to lose its competitive edge as the Dart engine aged. The Dart was noisy, a fact addressed through the provision of hush kits from the early 1980s, but also thirsty compared to more modern engines. Plans for a re-engined F27 fell by the wayside, and although the Dart Mk 551 improved the situation, offering a 10 per cent reduction in fuel burn and available by retrofit to earlier engines, a more convincing solution was required. It appeared in 1985 as the F50 or Fokker 50, an aircraft that looked very much like a Friendship but differed significantly in key areas.

Fokker 50

Fokker announced its intention to produce an F27 successor in 1983, on the 25th anniversary of the Friendship's service entry. Seating 50 passengers (hence its designation, although between 46 and 68 seats is a common configuration in service), the F50 introduced Pratt & Whitney PW120 turboprops driving modern six-bladed propellers, a Honeywell electronic flight instrumentation system (EFIS) 'glass' cockpit and extensive use of composites. Small winglets and the replacement of the F27's popular Viscount-like cabin windows with a larger number of smaller windows were key recognition features.

The new Fokker flew for the first time on 28 December 1985 and Lufthansa CityLine took the first delivery on 7 August 1987. Other customers included Sudan Airways and Germany's DLT. Subsequent developments included the hot-and-high F50-300, while proposals for a stretched F50-400 were abandoned. Fokker fell into financial difficulties while the F50 was in production and although Daimler-Benz Aerospace took a controlling interest in 1993, it subsequently withdrew support and Fokker ceased operations as an aircraft manufacturer in March 1996.

Douglas DC-8 (1958)

Douglas never quite managed to match the success of Boeing's 707 with its DC-8 jetliner. But history records that the DC-8 was the more rugged of the two and it found renown in the later stages of its career as the most capable airliner of the era.

Douglas initially fell foul of unlucky timing with the DC-8, having initially identified that Boeing's 367-80 derived airliner would be too small for non-stop transatlantic operations, but then suffering from its comparative lack of experience with large swept-wing jets and engine unavailability. These factors combined to allow Boeing sufficient time to meet all the airlines' requirements, leaving Douglas permanently in its wake.

There could be no questioning Douglas' pre-eminence in airliner construction into the 1950s. Boeing and Lockheed had produced worthy contenders to its crown, but the DC-4, -6 and -7 series reigned supreme. Keen to retain its lead, the company presented ideas for a transcontinental quad-jet in 1952, but it met with little encouragement and desisted with the concept in 1953.

The airline industry was still adjusting to the possibilities of jet transport in 1955, when the UK government announced that the Comet's problems had been overcome

and BOAC would be embarking on transatlantic services with the Comet 4 in 1958. Pan Am had an immediate requirement to compete and while it ordered 20 707-120 jets as a stopgap, it based its future over the Atlantic on the DC-8, a larger, more powerful aircraft that Douglas promised would fly non-stop services, replacing the 707 which, like the Comet, would need to land and refuel.

Douglas was scheming its aircraft for the Pratt & Whitney JT4A engine and planned for it to be available from 1959, but also had plans for a lighter domestic variant, for which United became launch customer. It claimed that its preferred the DC-8's wider cabin to that of the 707, sending Boeing back to its drawing board, although the Douglas was also a little less expensive.

CargOman operated a single DC-8-55F. The model applied all the aerodynamic and powerplant improvements of the -55 to a dedicated freighter.

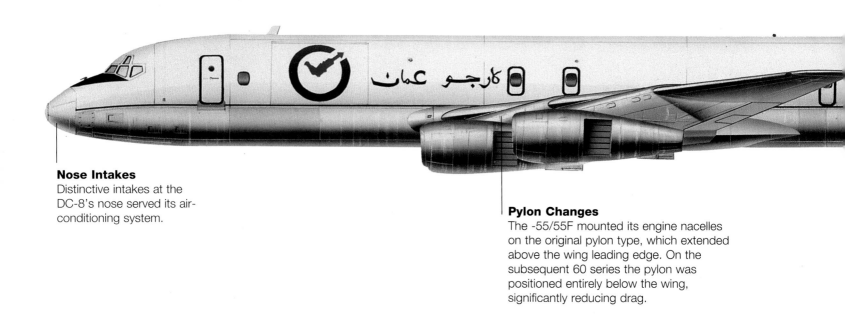

Nose Intakes
Distinctive intakes at the DC-8's nose served its air-conditioning system.

Pylon Changes
The -55/55F mounted its engine nacelles on the original pylon type, which extended above the wing leading edge. On the subsequent 60 series the pylon was positioned entirely below the wing, significantly reducing drag.

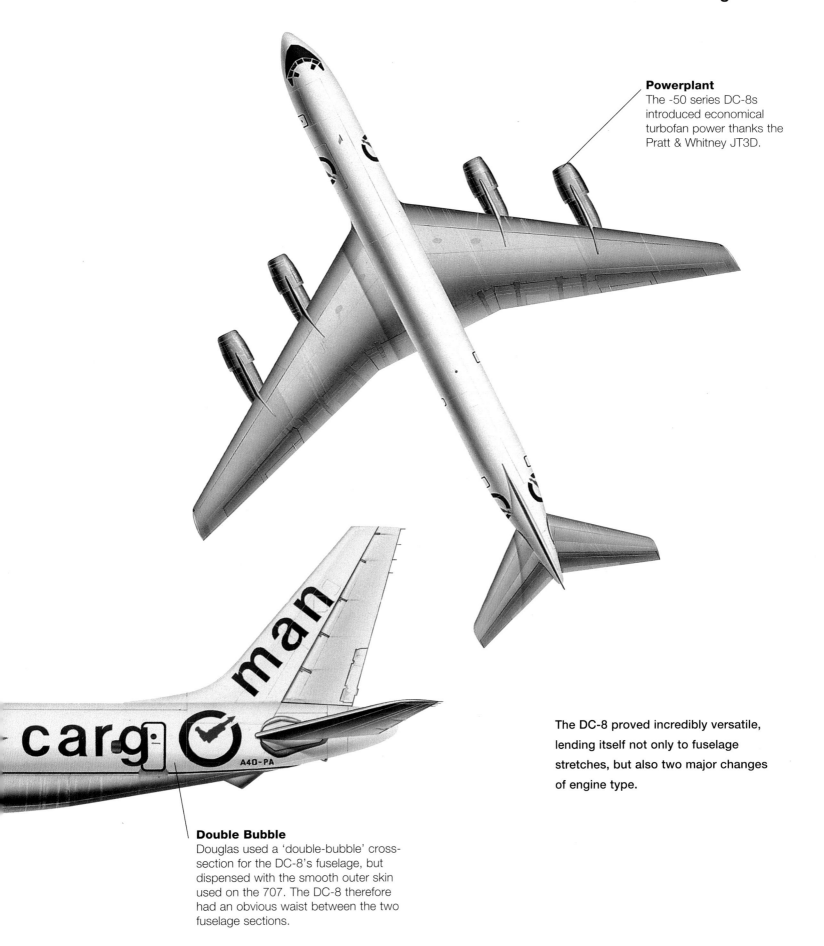

Powerplant
The -50 series DC-8s introduced economical turbofan power thanks the Pratt & Whitney JT3D.

The DC-8 proved incredibly versatile, lending itself not only to fuselage stretches, but also two major changes of engine type.

Double Bubble
Douglas used a 'double-bubble' cross-section for the DC-8's fuselage, but dispensed with the smooth outer skin used on the 707. The DC-8 therefore had an obvious waist between the two fuselage sections.

Douglas DC-8

DC-8s served throughout the world, the Dutch carrier KLM's fleet including this DC-8-33.

The domestic DC-8-10 flew for the first time in May 1958, powered by 61kN (13,500lb) thrust JT3 engines similar to those on the 707-120 but, being a larger aircraft, the DC-8 was underpowered. Douglas sold only 28 and the type entered service in September 1959, by which time Boeing's 707-320 was already flying non-stop transatlantic services. Availability of the intended JT4A engine allowed a heavier DC-8 to be certificated, but Douglas brought the improved domestic DC-8-20 into service before moving on to the even more powerful long-range DC-8-30, which flew its first revenue services in April 1960.

Like the Intercontinental 707, the DC-8-30 used water injection for greater power on take-off, producing clouds of black smoke to add to the immense noise of its engines. Also like the 707, it was offered with the Rolls-Royce

Conway bypass turbojet, delivering greater power with less drama, as the DC-9-40.

Turbofan Revolution

Just as Boeing applied the Pratt & Whitney JT3D turbofan to the 707, so Douglas produced the fan-engined DC-8-50, transforming the type's performance. The -50 could fly non-stop from the U.S. West Coast to London and by refining its aerodynamics, Douglas produced the even more capable DC-8-55, as well as the DC-8F Jet Trader or DC-8-54 convertible, based on the -50 and, subsequently, DC-8-55F.

Jet transport was now well established and passenger numbers sufficient for U.S. airports to begin struggling with the number of aircraft movements. The answer appeared to lay in larger aircraft and Douglas responded by stretching the DC-8-55 to produce the DC-8-61 Super 61, -62 Super 62 and -63 Super 63. Now the DC-8 was at its zenith; the Super 61 was 11.48m (37ft 8in) longer than the -55, the Super 62 just long enough to seat as many passengers as the 707-320 and with more fuel and revised engine pylons for reduced drag. The Super 63 combined the long fuselage of the DC-8-61 with the efficient wing of the -62 to produce unbeatable transcontinental economy. The Super 62 was the longest ranged commercial aircraft of its era.

The Super 61 first flew in March 1966, the last of the new variants, the Super 63CF freighter entering service in June 1968. All the 60 series sold well, but widebody technology was looming and a cash-flow crisis had forced a merger with McDonnell in April 1967. With sales in decline, McDonnell Douglas ceased DC-8 production in 1972.

Resurgence

And there the story might well have ended but for the huge increase in oil prices following the 1973 Arab–Israeli War. Airline expansion slowed as air tickets increased in price, reflecting higher fuel costs. Suddenly the fleets of

Specification (DC-8-71 Super 71)

Type:	medium/long-haul airliner
Dimensions:	wing span 43.36m (142ft 3in), length 57.22m (187ft 5in), height 12.93m (42ft 5in)
Maximum take-off weight:	147,415kg (325,000lb)
Powerplant:	four 108kN (24,000lb) thrust CFM International CFM56-2-1C turbofan engines
Maximum speed:	965km/h (600mph)
Range with maximum passenger load:	7485km (4650 miles)
Flight crew:	4
Passengers:	up to 259 in single-class accommodation

widebodies seemed less attractive and the airlines looked for large-capacity, economical aircraft that were available cheaply and would allow them to operate through the crisis. The DC-8-60s were the very best aircraft available but since production had ended, prices for the few used airframes available began to soar.

There was another snag to DC-8 ownership – noise. New, strict regulations on noise were imminent and the Super 60s would no longer be able to operate out of U.S. airports. An elegant solution was found in re-engining with the new-technology CFM56, produced jointly by General Electric and SNECMA and in dire need of a customer. In 1978, the engine manufacturers created Cammacorp to convert Super 60s with CFM power and 110 had been modified when the programme ended in 1986.

Redesignated as 70-series machines, the resulting aircraft were among the most capable of their type, the Super 72 boasting greater range even than the range-optimized Boeing 747SP. In later life the DC-8 proved not only suitable for re-engining, but also more easily converted than the 707 for freight work. Its structure was inherently more sound and suitable for engineering changes, and in late 2014 a handful of DC-8-60 and -70 aircraft remained in service as freighters.

Passenger Accommodation

Between them, the Boeing 707 and Douglas DC-8 introduced new standards of passenger accommodation, with a recognized class structure for seating used as standard practice. Passenger amenities were also improved, these DC-8 passengers enjoying seat-mounted reading lights and armrest ashtrays.

Hawker Siddeley Trident
(1962)

De Havilland might have cornered the market for a second-generation short/medium-haul jet airliner had it not focussed its design efforts on the needs of one airline. And so it was that the Trident emerged as a fine aircraft, but one ill-suited to the market and that sold in only small numbers.

De Havilland offered its 119 design in response to a July 1956 British European Airways (BEA) requirement for a short/medium-haul jet airliner suitable for operations from short runways and accommodating as many as 100 passengers. It was a specification very similar to that against which Boeing designed the 727, having taken careful note of de Havilland's work, but while the U.S. manufacturer built an aircraft that would appeal to foreign airlines as well as its core domestic market, de Havilland chose to tailor its machine to BEA's needs.

The early de Havilland concept called for a powerplant of four Rolls-Royce Avon turbojets in a design oddly

revised as the DH.120 in an effort to suit BEA's needs and a British Overseas Airways specification for a long-haul airliner, with a single airframe. These disparate requirements were impossible to meet and the DH.120 morphed into the DH.121 trijet.

Power was to come from the Rolls-Royce Medway turbofans, mounted in a configuration specified by BEA. De Havilland joined with Fairey and Hunting to form the Airco company that was to jointly design and

Hawker Siddeley produced the revised Trident 1E in an attempt to interest export customers, of which there remained few.

Trident 1E-140
Northeast Airlines eventually operated four of the last five Trident 1E aircraft built. All four were to 1E-140 standard, with four additional overwing emergency exits and seats for 139 passengers.

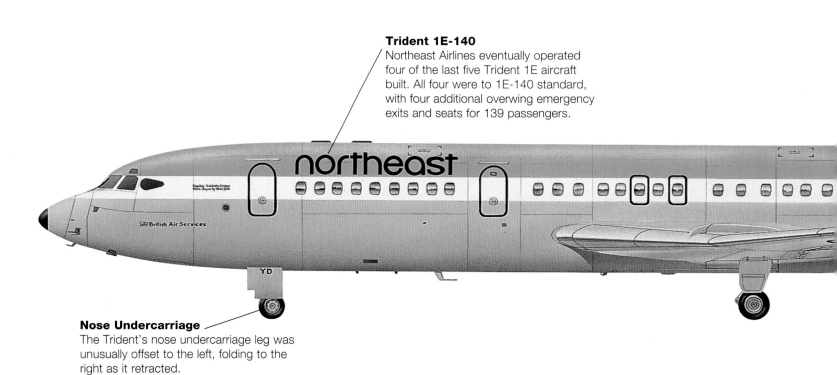

Nose Undercarriage
The Trident's nose undercarriage leg was unusually offset to the left, folding to the right as it retracted.

manufacture the DH.121, whose selection for BEA the British government announced in February 1958. Now BEA revised its specification to include a very short range requirement of just 810 miles (1300km), which effectively ruled out the Medway as the engine of choice. Rolls-Royce therefore cancelled the motor and instead the RB.163, a smaller turbofan more suited to the reduced specification, was chosen.

This short-ranged aircraft satisfied BEA's requirements exactly, but was resolutely unattractive to foreign airlines, which typically flew over longer ranges and with more passengers. Indeed, after BEA signed for 24 aircraft with options on 12 more in August 1959, de Havilland stopped talking to potential export customers altogether and its merger with the giant Hawker Siddeley group, completed

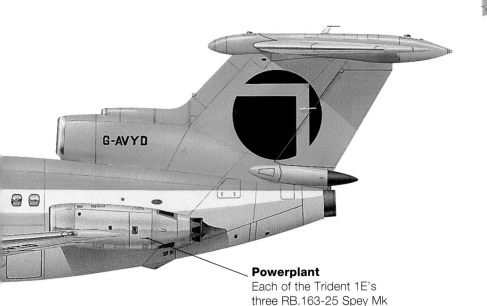

Wing Sweep
Clean and aerodynamically advanced, the Trident's wing was swept at 35°, matching the sweep on the Boeing 707.

Powerplant
Each of the Trident 1E's three RB.163-25 Spey Mk 511-5 engines generated 50.70kN (11,400lb) of thrust.

G-AVYD was one of two Trident 1Es delivered direct to BKS Air Transport, later renamed Northeast Airlines. The carrier took a further pair of similar aircraft from Channel Airways in 1972.

Hawker Siddeley Trident

by May 1960, saw Airco dissolved. De Havilland continued work under its new ownership, developing the DH.121 as an extremely advanced aircraft with challenging aerodynamics, including a clean wing fitted with extensive trailing edge high-lift devices, a drooped leading edge and overwing spoilers. It also included split ailerons for roll control and use as airbrakes.

Soon named Trident, the aircraft's avionics were especially impressive, BEA calling for the capability to achieve fully-automatic blind landings, through a triple-redundant Smith's Flight Control System, the airline, de Havilland, Hawker Siddeley and Smiths performing pioneering work to develop safe operations with the equipment. Unfortunately for its already poor sales

Specification (Trident 2E)

Type:	short/medium-haul airliner
Dimensions:	wing span 29.87m (98ft), length 34.98m (114ft 9in), height 8.23m (27ft)
Maximum take-off weight:	65,318kg (144,000lb)
Powerplant:	three 53.19kN (11,960lb) thrust Rolls-Royce RB.163-25 Spey Mk 512-5W turbofan engines
Cruising speed:	974km/h (605mph)
Range:	3965km (2464 miles)
Service ceiling:	9450m (31,000ft)
Flight crew:	3
Passengers:	139

This aircraft was one of 33 Trident 1Es ordered by the Civil Aviation Administration of China.

prospects, the Trident seated a maximum of only 95 passengers.

Trident Testing

There was no prototype Trident and the initial flight was by BEA's first aircraft on 9 January 1962. The airline placed the jet into full revenue service on 1 April 1964, deliveries continuing into 1966 when the 23rd aircraft was lost to a deep-stall accident – a problem afflicting early T-tailed jets at high angles of attack, where the wing masked the elevators, denying the crew pitch control. Modifications were made to prevent pilots entering deep-stall conditions. The second Trident had undertaken extensive blind-landing trials, leading to the first fully-automatic landing in zero visibility on a scheduled flight on 4 November 1966.

In service, BEA upgraded what became known as the Trident 1 to 1C standard, with more powerful versions of what had become the Spey engine, increased fuel capacity and seating for 109 passengers. Still the Trident was unattractive to export customers, however, and Hawker Siddeley therefore developed the Trident 1E, with yet more power, extended wing span, leading edge slats, more fuel and higher weights, as well as 115 passenger seats.

Export Opportunity

The Trident 1E took a trickle of orders from several customers, Kuwait Airways coming first in the short queue with a requirement for three. Iraqi Airways was first into service with the 1E, and Pakistan International Airlines took four from March 1966. Five more were built without customers, bringing total production to 15, some of this last batch eventually flying in 139-seat configuration with Channel Airways as Trident 1E-140 aircraft.

BEA subsequently took 15 of a revised Trident 1E, designated 2E, for service from 18 April 1968. Others were exported, the major operator becoming the Civil Aviation Administration of China, which ordered 33. The last of the Trident variants was again a BEA-specific aircraft. With capacity for 180 passengers and reduced range, the Trident 3B featured a 23.20kN (5250lb) thrust Rolls-Royce RB.182-86 auxiliary turbojet above its rear fuselage for improved take-off performance or higher-weight operations. The type flew for the first time on 11 December 1969 and the first aircraft from BEA's 26-aircraft order entered service on 1 April 1971.

BEA called its Trident 2s, Trident Two, and Trident 3s, Trident Three for marketing purposes and continued with the latter until 31 December 1985, although Tridents remained operational in China until 1995. A total of 117 aircraft was built, compared to 1832 Boeing 727s.

BEA's Tridents

To its credit, BEA obliged de Havilland to take a major step forwards in airliner safety with its stringent requirements for blind landing capability, although the manufacturer's slavish devotion to other aspects of BEA's operation killed of the Trident's export potential.

Re-engined with 43.80kN (9850lb) thrust Spey Mk 505-5F engines the original aircraft became Trident 1Cs. These were augmented by the extended-range Trident 2E, which allowed BEA to serve routes to the Middle East non-stop from London.

The final Trident 3B suffered wing fatigue problems after modifications to meet BEA's requirements, but subsequent revisions, partly to the original standard, allowed the aircraft to remain in service.

![British flag] Vickers VC10 (1962)

Politics and short sightedness condemned the exceptional VC10 to the status of also-ran. Had the programme attracted the government and airline support it deserved, it might have produced a worthy rival to the long-range Boeing 707 and Douglas DC-8 variants.

By 1952, Britain was the clear leader in jet airliner technology, de Havilland's Comet having ushered in a new era in air transport. Among de Havilland's indigenous rivals, Vickers was also keen to enter the jetliner market and had begun work on a transport using much of the design effort already expended on its Valiant bomber. Although BOAC had encouraged Vickers' efforts, in 1956 the government's Ministry of Supply declared the programme too expensive and cancelled it.

Even without the Comet crashes that had struck de Havilland a mighty blow, it seems likely that this decision

ceded jetliner dominance to the U.S. at a stroke. In any case, BOAC claimed that the Bristol Britannia turboprop would allow it to operate long-haul routes effectively into the mid-1960s, a claim disbelieved by Vickers management, whose scepticism was vindicated when BOAC ordered Boeing 707s in October 1956.

Buoyed by the success of its Viscount and larger Vanguard turboprop airliners, Vickers had nevertheless continued jetliner studies, becoming interested in the rear-engine layout adopted for the Caravelle. Ten days after placing its 707 order, BOAC issued a specification for a

BOAC found the Super VC10 extremely profitable in service, but for a variety of political reasons surrounded the aircraft in negative publicity.

Stretched Fuselage
The Super's longer fuselage allowed its cabin to seat around 139 passengers in mixed classes or 163 in an all-economy layout.

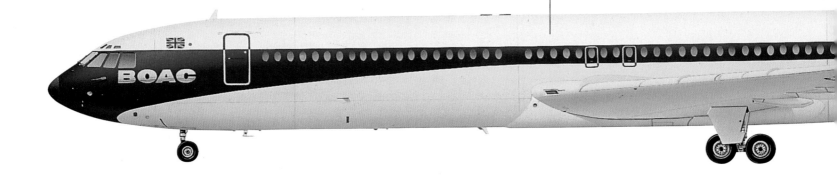

long-range aircraft capable of servicing its African and Australasian routes, where short runways and hot-and-high conditions were prevalent. Like Boeing with the 727, Vickers realized that adopting rear-mounted engines would leave the wing uncluttered for the business of providing maximum lift and optimum cruising capabilities. For its Type 1100 design Vickers chose the Rolls-Royce Conway

and the Vickers Commercial designation VC10. Leading edge slats and large flaps provided plenty of lift for landing and take-off, while the Conways provided an exceptional thrust-to-weight ratio – in service the VC10 was always regarded as something of a hot rod. The tailplane was mounted high on the large fin, well clear of the wings' powerful aerodynamic wake.

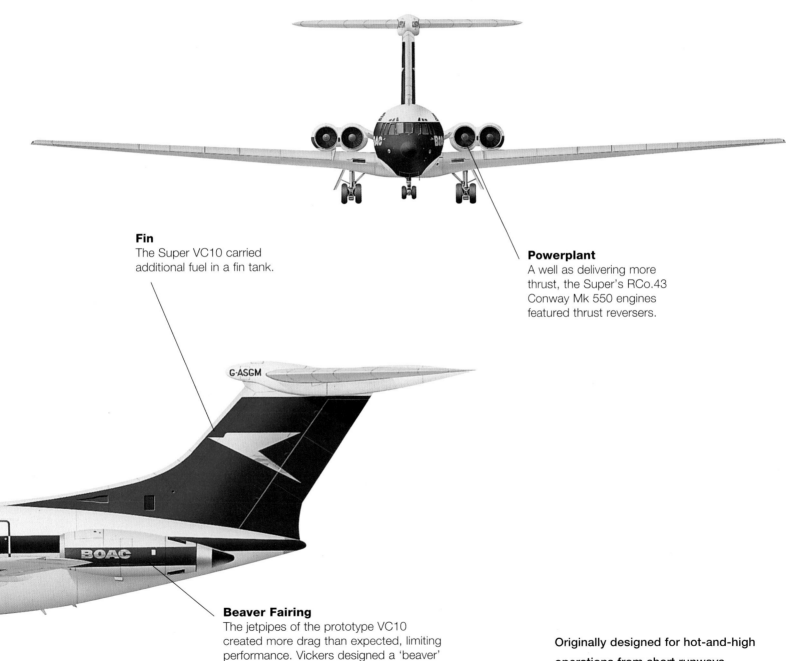

Fin
The Super VC10 carried additional fuel in a fin tank.

Powerplant
A well as delivering more thrust, the Super's RCo.43 Conway Mk 550 engines featured thrust reversers.

Beaver Fairing
The jetpipes of the prototype VC10 created more drag than expected, limiting performance. Vickers designed a 'beaver' fairing, separating each pair of exhausts and immediately solving the problem.

Originally designed for hot-and-high operations from short runways, the VC10 remained a sparkling performer throughout its career. Pilots regarded it as something of a 'hot rod'.

Vickers VC10

It was expected that the VC10 would be more costly than the Boeing 707 to operate, since it had been designed to provide exceptional performance under trying conditions. As with the de Havilland Trident, it seemed that once again Britain's aircraft makers were shooting themselves in the foot by matching their products too closely to the home airlines. BOAC placed an initial

The VC10's extensive high-lift devices were particularly evident on take-off.

order for 45 VC10s, as 35 standard aircraft and ten of a stretched Super VC10 variant, but then changed its requirements to just 12 'standards' and 17 'Supers'.

The cut in orders related to the airline's financial performance, which had been declining. Aircraft orders were reduced and routes cut, but recovery was quick and by 1964 BOAC was back in profit, re-expanding its routes and with insufficient VC10s to serve them. Given its expected higher operating costs, the airline also claimed a government subsidy to support its small VC10 fleet.

The aircraft had flown for the first time on 29 June 1962 and entered scheduled service on 29 April 1964. It quickly impressed on routes into Africa, with immediate passenger appeal thanks to the lack of cabin noise and sparkling performance. On 7 May the first Super VC10 completed the variant's maiden flight and on 22 July the last standard aircraft was delivered. The Super took up to 163 passengers thanks to a 3.90m (13ft) fuselage stretch, featured more powerful Conways to maintain performance and carried more fuel.

Transatlantic Super

Now the VC10 could operate non-stop across the Atlantic and performed its first revenue service, to New

Specification (Super VC10)

Type:	long-haul airliner
Dimensions:	wing span 44.55m (146ft 2in), length 52.32m (171ft 8in), height 12.04m (39ft 6in)
Maximum take-off weight:	151,953kg (335,000lb)
Powerplant:	four 100.10kN (22,500lb) thrust Rolls-Royce RCo.43 Conway Mk 550 bypass turbojet engines
Maximum speed:	935km/h (581mph)
Range with maximum payload:	8690km (5400 miles)
Service ceiling:	11,582m (38,000ft)
Flight crew:	3
Passengers:	up to 163 in single-class accommodation

York, on 1 April 1965. By year-end it was clear that BOAC management had made a series of errors in procurement policy. The Super VC10 was proving far more popular on transatlantic services than the Conway-engined 707-400 and it turned in a far more substantial profit, since its higher load factors, ease of maintenance and better reliability compared to the Boeing far outweighed any additional operating costs. BOAC had too many 707s and far too few VC10s.

The airline was reluctant to acknowledge the VC10's superiority, however, since it was keen to continue receiving the government subsidy and unwilling to admit to its poor decision-making earlier in the development of the aircraft. Its refusal to portray the VC10 in an honest light destroyed the considerable export potential of the Super in particular and with only a handful of aircraft built for other operators, just 40 VC10s were built for commercial customers.

VC10 in Service

BOAC's fleet included standard and Super VC10s, as shown here. Vickers also built a pair of Type 1102 standard aircraft for Ghana Airways with cargo doors and equipped as combis for freight/passenger operations and three similar machines went to British United Airways. Five Type 1154 Super VC10s were also built for East African Airways, again for combi work.

BOAC leased standards to Gulf Air, which also bought ex-BOAC Supers when the British airline began withdrawing its fleet. Nevertheless, some Super VC10s remained with BOAC long enough to survive its merger with BEA, remaining in British Airways service until 1980. The governments of Oman, Qatar and UAE operated executive standards, the Omani aircraft becoming the last VC10 in civilian service when it was retired in 1987.

The VC10 also enjoyed a long and illustrious military career with the Royal Air Force, which took 14 hybrid standard/Super VC10s from 1966 and subsequently added second-hand standard and Super aircraft. It retired the type in 2013.

Aero Spacelines Guppy and Super Guppy (1962)

Aero Spacelines created a series of extraordinary freight carriers based on redundant Stratocruiser and C-97 airframes. Guppies became NASA and Airbus Industrie mainstays and today one Guppy 201 continues to support the space programme.

Unusual requirements are occasionally satisfied by extreme solutions and the Aero Spacelines series of Guppy aircraft is among the most extreme in aviation history. The National Aeronautics and Space Administration (NASA) was established in 1958, with an immediate requirement to move huge components for the Saturn and Apollo programmes between manufacturer facilities, and test and launch sites. Giant equipment built in California, for example, was moved by barge via the Panama Canal and back up to Cape Canaveral, Florida incurring shipping costs, taking time and risking damage at sea.

Aircraft broker Lee Mansdorf and ex-U.S. Air Force

pilot John 'Jack' Conroy between them realized that Boeing Stratocruisers just coming out of service could form the basis for outsize transports capable of moving NASA's unusual loads by air. Mansdorf had purchased Stratocruisers as BOAC, Pan American and Northwest released them from service, and Conroy drew up preliminary plans for a cargo conversion.

NASA showed very little interest when Conroy presented the scheme in 1960 and offered no funding. Conroy therefore joined with Mansdorf to raise sufficient capital to establish Aero Spacelines International (ASI) and begin private development. The company made use of NASA

Hinges
The forward fuselage hinged to port for loading, the entire section moving on two giant hinges faired into the left side of the fuselage.

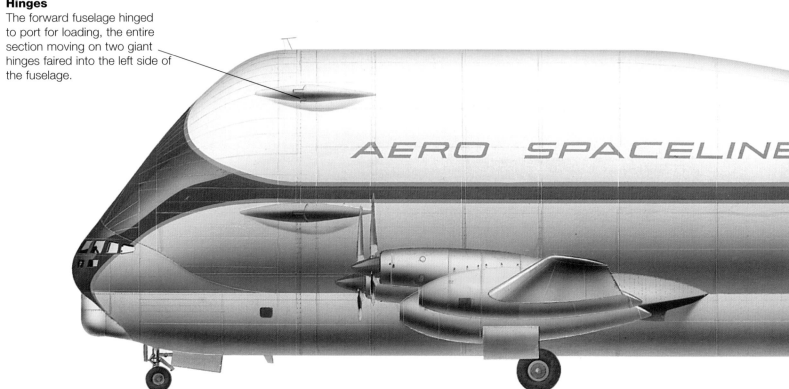

wind tunnel facilities to arrive at the B377G, named Pregnant Guppy by a NASA representative after the initial drawings were revealed. It used the wings, engines, empennage and cockpit of a former Pan Am Stratocruiser, with a 5.08m (16ft 8in) fuselage plug from a BOAC aircraft, combined with a new upper fuselage section of 6.02m (19ft 9in) internal diameter. The rear fuselage and tail could be detached for straight-in loading.

The aircraft first flew on 19 September 1962, behaving very much as a standard Stratocruiser, albeit 8km/h (5mph) slower owing to the drag of the upper fuselage. Now NASA became interested and with certification granted, ASI

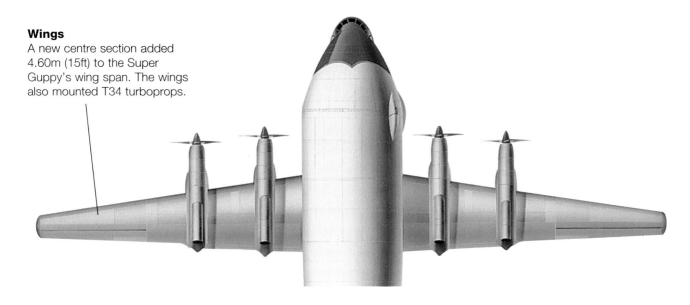

Wings
A new centre section added 4.60m (15ft) to the Super Guppy's wing span. The wings also mounted T34 turboprops.

Outsize Fuselage
Although there are many aircraft with payloads greater than that of the Guppies, few can match their extraordinary cabin volume. The Super Guppy's volume was 1410m³ (49,790cuft).

Empennage
A replacement empennage, or tail section, was designed for the Super Guppy, with a tall square-topped fin and revised tailplanes.

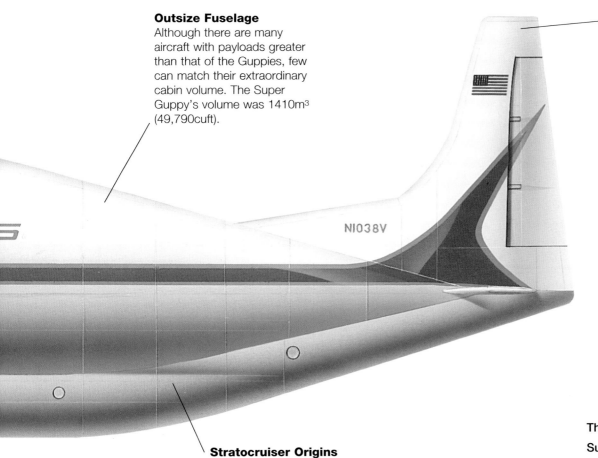

NI038V

Stratocruiser Origins
The Super Guppy's origins in the Stratocruiser were obvious around the cockpit area. It also retained the veteran airliner's lower fuselage.

The Aero Spacelines B-377SG Super Guppy remained on NASA duties until 1991, when it was retired into storage.

took a short-term support contract from summer 1963. Encouraged, ASI bought 25 Stratocruiser and surplus C-97 airframes in preparation for further conversions.

Super Guppy

With the Pregnant Guppy in service, NASA quickly recognized its own need for a larger aircraft and ASI constructed a second machine, 4.57m (15ft) longer

Specification (B377SG Super Guppy)

Type:	outsize cargo transporter
Dimensions:	wing span 47.63m (156ft 4in), length 43.80m (143ft 8in), height 14.78m (48ft 6in)
Loaded weight:	77,111kg (170,000lb)
Powerplant:	four 6900shp Pratt & Whitney T34-PI-WA turboprop engines
Maximum speed:	565km/h (351mph)
Range:	3211km (1995 miles)
Service ceiling:	7620m (25,000ft)
Flight crew:	3 to 4

With its vast forward fuselage hinged to port, a Guppy 201 takes on a load of Airbus components.

in span, 9.40m (30ft 10in) longer and with an internal diameter of 7.77m (25ft 6in); the forward fuselage was hinged for loading. The aircraft was based on the YC-97J turboprop development airframe and retained its Pratt & Whitney T34 engines.

Designated B377SG Super Guppy – it was known very briefly as the Very Pregnant Guppy – the aircraft flew for the first time on 31 August 1965. The only aircraft capable of carrying the third stage of the Saturn V rocket, it was joined on the NASA contract by a second Pregnant Guppy, constructed after Unexcelled had purchased ASI. NASA bought the B377SG in 1978, basing it at the Johnson Space Center, Houston, Texas for Space Shuttle support work.

Mini Guppy

ASI continued theorizing on outsize aircraft under its new ownership, considering a B-52 based Colossal Guppy and the Virtus Space Shuttle transporter, employing paired B-52 fuselages and a straight wing. Neither came to fruition, but at the other end of the scale there seemed to be demand for a more modest cargo carrier. Turning back to the Stratocruiser, therefore, ASI took an ex-Pan Am aircraft and modified it using BOAC and Northwest components to produce the B377MG Mini Guppy.

The new aircraft flew for the first time on 21 May 1967, its fuselage 3m (9ft 10in) shorter than that of the Super Guppy and with an internal diameter of 4.70m (15ft 5in). Once again a swing-tail was fitted and ASI hoped that a Guppy 101 production version would follow, powered by Alison 501-D22C turboprops in place of the Pratt & Whitney R-4360 Wasp Majors of the B377MG. An Alison-powered version flew for the first time on 13 March 1970, but crashed in May, after which both the Pregnant Guppy and Mini Guppy were sold to American Jet Industries.

CL-44-0

The Stratocruiser lay at the heart of all Guppies apart from one, the Conroy CL-44-0 Guppy. Canadair had based its CL-44 transport on the Bristol Britannia and Conroy took an ex-Flying Tigers CL-44DX freighter, removed the upper fuselage and replaced it with a new outsize section. The modified aircraft retained the original's cockpit section and swing tail, while the vast cargo hold was pressurized.

It flew for the first time on 26 November 1969 and

found employment moving Rolls-Royce RB.211 engines and nacelles from the UK to California for Lockheed's L-1011 TriStar programme. Passing though several further owners, it fell foul of regulatory issues in 2006 and was grounded.

Guppy 201

The final and most capable of the Guppies was the Guppy 201, commissioned by Sud-Aviation for its air transport network in support of Europe's multi-national Airbus programme. Two machines were initially constructed, based on KC-97 airframes and structurally similar to the Super Guppy, but with Allison 501 engines in nacelles taken from the Lockheed P-3A Orion maritime aircraft. The Guppy 201 flew for the first time on 24 August 1970 and as Airbus Industrie expanded its operation two more aircraft were commissioned. Built by UTA Industries in France, after Airbus had purchased rights for the design, the final Guppy 201s flew for the first time in 1982 and 1983.

All four machines worked hard supporting Airbus as its product range expanded, continuing in service until replaced by the SATIC A300-600ST Beluga from October 1996. One Guppy 201 remains active, supporting NASA space programmes.

NASA Guppy 201

NASA's Guppy 201 was the fourth aircraft built for Airbus. Now based at Ellington Field, Houston, it directly supports activities at Johnson Space Center.

UTA used components from the Pregnant Guppy to build the machine, after Stratocruiser/C-97 parts became unavailable.

Boeing 727 (1963)

Boeing was still working hard and investing heavily in long-haul jets when it looked to build a short/medium-haul jetliner. The trijet 727 emerged as a result, sweeping all before it as Boeing dominated another emerging market.

Even as Boeing was still working on the Model 720, the domestic version of its 707, it was aware that the aircraft would be unsuitable for smaller U.S. airports, where older equipment including the Constellation and DC-6, and newer machines such as the Convair CV-240 and Lockheed L-188 Electra, were operating. These aircraft were cheap to own and operate, but they were slow. Europe offered a modern jet alternative in the Sud Caravelle, but the aircraft was too small for U.S. needs. Then there was the de Havilland Trident, an aircraft some way off its first flight, but looking likely to snatch the high-capacity short/medium-haul jet market.

De Havilland had adopted a rear-mounted trijet configuration for the Trident and availability of Pratt &

Whitney's powerful, fuel-efficient JT8D turbofan allowed Boeing to use a similar layout, leaving the new aircraft's wing clear of engines and more easily optimized to the demanding performance required. Boeing began work on its Model 727 in February 1956, designing an aircraft that would satisfy multiple requirements, including the need for high-speed cruise to reduce seat-mile costs.

High speeds required a swept wing that was as clean as possible, but the need to fly into smaller airports with short runways, perhaps under hot-and-high conditions, could only be satisfied by a wing delivering maximum lift.

Transportes Aereos Portugueses (TAP) flew 727-100 models as well as the -200 Advanced, the latter including CS-TBW.

Inherited Fuselage
Boeing used the 707's upper fuselage design for the 727, simplifying production.

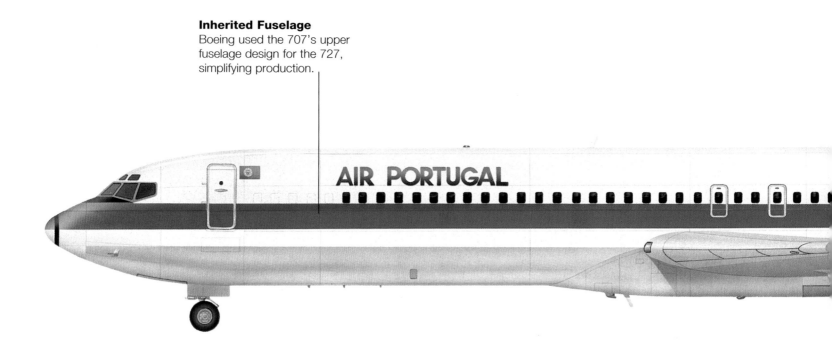

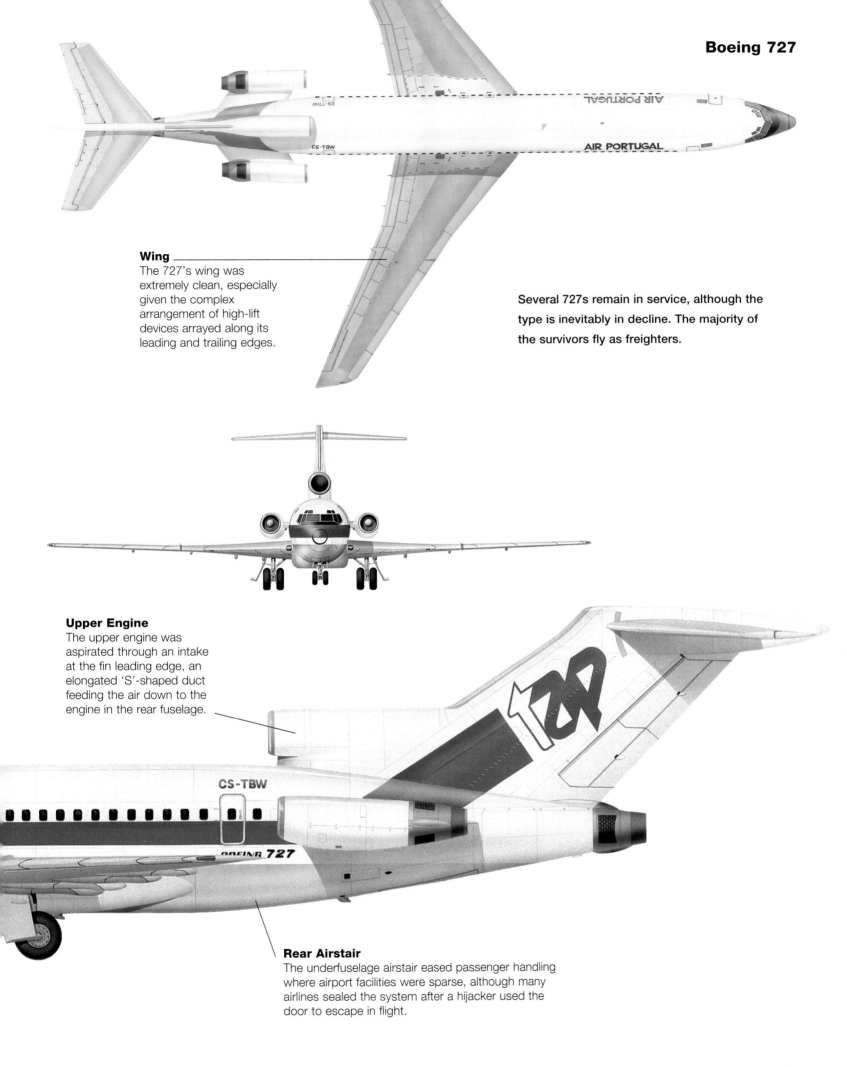

Wing
The 727's wing was extremely clean, especially given the complex arrangement of high-lift devices arrayed along its leading and trailing edges.

Several 727s remain in service, although the type is inevitably in decline. The majority of the survivors fly as freighters.

Upper Engine
The upper engine was aspirated through an intake at the fin leading edge, an elongated 'S'-shaped duct feeding the air down to the engine in the rear fuselage.

CS-TBW

BOEING 727

Rear Airstair
The underfuselage airstair eased passenger handling where airport facilities were sparse, although many airlines sealed the system after a hijacker used the door to escape in flight.

Boeing 727

Boeing's engineers met all these requirements brilliantly, creating an advanced wing with powerful lift-generating flaps on its trailing edge and a mix of slats and leading edge flaps along almost the entire leading edge. Roll control was by ailerons, augmented by a set of eight spoilers on the upper surface of each wing. These also acted as airbrakes and lift dumpers, so that the wing was

Specification (727-200)

Type:	short/medium-range airliner
Dimensions:	wing span 32.92m (108ft), length 46.69m (153ft 2in), height 10.36m (34ft)
Maximum take-off weight:	95,027kg (209,500lb)
Powerplant:	three 64.50kN (14,500lb) thrust Pratt & Whitney JT8D-9A turbofan engines
Maximum cruising speed:	964km/h (599mph)
Range with maximum payload:	4392km (2729 miles)
Service ceiling:	15,240m (50,000ft)
Flight crew:	3
Passengers:	up to 189 in single-class accommodation

American Airlines initially operated its 727-100 aircraft under the title 'Astro-Jet', derived from the 707 Astrojet name used for its Boeing 720 services.

optimized for short take-off performance, short landings and high-speed cruise.

In another masterstroke Boeing used the upper fuselage of the 707, speeding design, standardizing flight decks and saving money on production tooling. The relatively wide cabin also allowed the 727 to seat passengers six abreast in layouts previously only available to long-range transcontinental jets.

Of particular importance to operators using less well-equipped airports, the 727 had to be capable of flying sectors with a minimum of support. Boeing therefore provided integral airstairs at the forward passenger door and a retractable stairway under the tail. An auxiliary power unit (APU) was fitted for engine starting, as well as generating electrical power and delivering cabin air-conditioning prior to engine start. Finally, the 727's undercarriage and wings were made strong enough to support multiple landings at high weights, so that it could be filled with fuel at its departure point, then make multiple stops without refuelling. Such features facilitated austere operations, but also allowed for quick turnarounds, maximizing profits.

Trijet Triumphant

With the promise of orders from Eastern Air Lines and United Airlines, Boeing began building the 727 in April 1960. There must have been considerable relief on 5 December when Eastern finally signed for 40 aircraft and United for 20, with 20 options. The first aircraft took off for its maiden flight from Boeing's Renton, Washington facility at 11.33 on 9 February 1963. After just over two hours it landed at Paine Field to begin the test programme proper.

Orders continued to come in as testing reached a successful conclusion, with Federal Aviation Administration (FAA) approval granted to the 727-100 in December 1963. A 727 world sales tour was already under way, the aircraft impressing at hot-and-high airports and 'meeting' its rival, the Trident, at Karachi. Both All Nippon and Japan Airlines had been impressed by the Trident, but required the higher-capacity variant that would not be available until at least 1966. They had also seen the 727 during its tour and the

Boeing's ability to take off from Osaka's short runway with a full load at 35°C (95°F), compared to the Trident, which was payload restricted, led both to order the U.S. type.

Meanwhile, Eastern had begun services in February 1964 and Lufthansa in April, and Boeing was developing a convertible 727-100C. Easily switched from all-cargo to all-passenger configuration in less than two hours it was ideal for operators moving freight overnight and passengers during the day. With its order book bulging, the 727 became the most widely used commercial jet, but the best was yet to come.

In November 1967 Boeing gained FAA approval for the stretched 727-200, with more power and seating for 189 passengers, compared to the 131 of the -100. Subsequently improved as the 727-200 Advanced, the model allowed Boeing to dominate the market into the 1980s, when airlines began replacing their trijets with the 727's natural successor, the Model 757.

727-200

A 3.05m (10ft) fuselage plug ahead of the wing revolutionized the capability of the already popular 727. Reinforced for heavier weights, the aircraft was powered by the standard JT8D-9, although customers could specify more powerful -11 or -15 engines. The Advanced aircraft was heavier again and

boasted increased range, ensuring that the 727 remained viable until Boeing had a replacement available. A total of 1832 727s was built, the last of them, a 727-200F freighter, going to Federal Express in 1984. All were built at the Renton facility, shown here with -200s on the line.

The Modern Era

With Boeing and Douglas building fine medium and long-haul jets, the competition was on to bring similar standards of service to short-haul and regional sectors. Europe led the way, the Sud-Est Caravelle establishing the viability of short-range jets, while BAC looked set to dominate with the One-Eleven. But Douglas created its DC-9 masterpiece in record time, taking the market with a programme so ambitious it broke the company. Boeing's latecomer to the short-haul sector, the 737 remains in production and set for major upgrade, its huge success only latterly challenged by the Airbus consortium and its A320 family.

By the mid-1960s, jet technology had matured sufficiently for the first widebody airliners to evolve, epitomised by the Boeing 747, challenged for passenger capacity only recently by Airbus, with the A380. The supersonic airliner also came and went, while another new genre of aircraft emerged, the small capacity regional jet.

Facing page: The Boeing 767 epitomises the medium/long-haul widebody, as well as encapsulating the family approach to airliner design. Using the 767-200 airframe as its starting point, Boeing offered the 767 with multiple engine choices, a variety of weight options and in stretched variants for more passengers.

⌖ BAC One-Eleven (1963)

The One-Eleven was an excellent short-haul jet that struggled to find meaningful orders in spite of breaking through into the U.S. market. It faced stiff competition from the Douglas DC-9 and Boeing 737, its British manufacturer unable to match American might.

The UK's Percival company produced a number of successful lightplanes during the interwar period, applying much of the experience gained to produce more than 1000 training and liaison aircraft during World War II. In 1944 it became part of the Hunting Group, continuing in operation as Hunting Percival and producing the Percival Prince, a small piston-engined airliner, among other designs. In 1957 the 'Percival' title was dropped, aircraft design and production continuing under the Hunting title. Hunting had long considered the potential for a

small jet-powered airliner, working through turbojet and turbofan concepts as powerplant technologies evolved. In September 1960 it came under the control of BAC before any of its jet airliner designs had reached fruition, although its H.107 concept for a 48-seat machine was adopted and enlarged to become the 65-seat BAC.111, to be powered by Rolls-Royce Spey turbofans. British United Airways

West Germany's Bavaria Fluggesellschaft bought four Series 400s for use on holiday flights.

Fuselage Length
Only the Series 500 aircraft were stretched, all other production variants featuring the original fuselage length of the Series 200.

Crew
The One-Eleven was among the first airliners designed for two-crew operation.

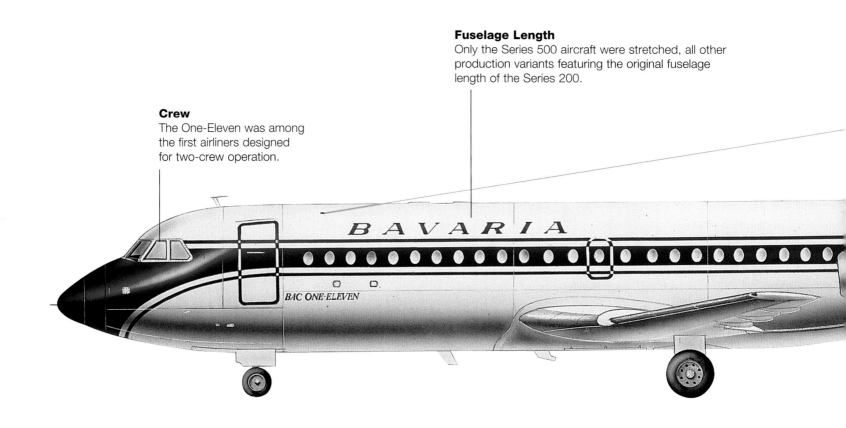

(BUA) ordered the type in May 1961, marking it out as the first British airliner built against a launch order from an independent airline.

BAC stuck to the formula of rear-mounted engines for a clean wing of maximum aerodynamic efficiency around the airfield and when cruising. It also chose a T-tail configuration and an unusually short undercarriage, which allowed easy loading and unloading of baggage from holds that were little more than 1m (3ft 3in) above the ground. An APU allowed a degree of freedom from airport services and the potential for single-point pressure refuelling also shortened turnaround times, as did the integral airstair in the underside of the rear fuselage and a second optional stair at the forward passenger door.

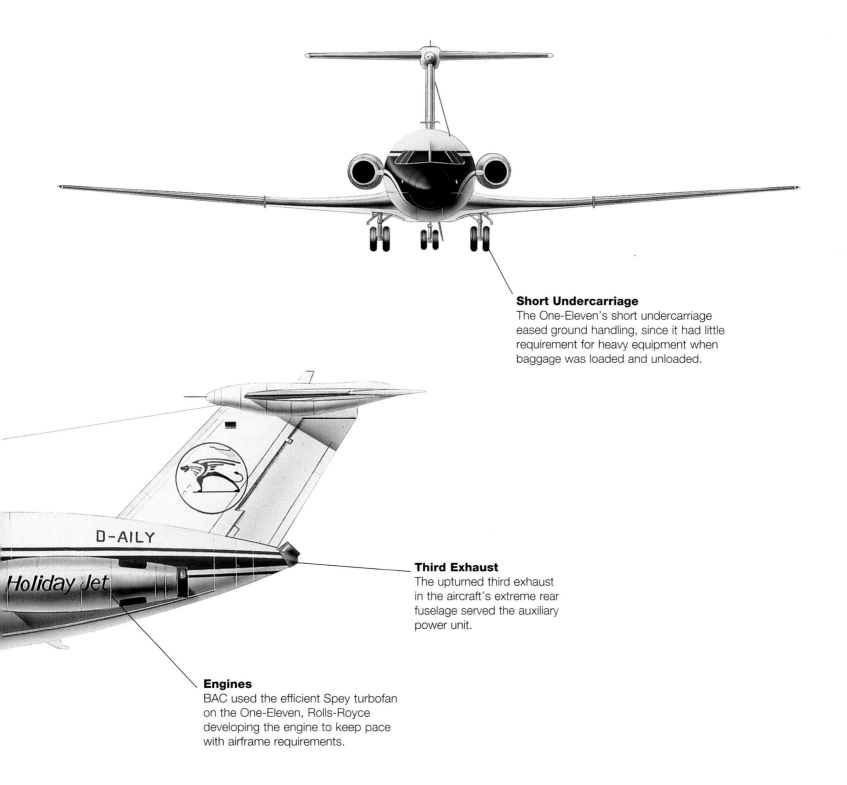

Short Undercarriage
The One-Eleven's short undercarriage eased ground handling, since it had little requirement for heavy equipment when baggage was loaded and unloaded.

Third Exhaust
The upturned third exhaust in the aircraft's extreme rear fuselage served the auxiliary power unit.

Engines
BAC used the efficient Spey turbofan on the One-Eleven, Rolls-Royce developing the engine to keep pace with airframe requirements.

BAC One-Eleven

These excellent qualities were insufficient to tempt BEA, however, which remained firmly committed to the Trident. The new BAC airliner emerged as the One-Eleven, designated Series 200 in its initial form and flying for the first time on 20 August 1963. A deep-stall accident, similar

Specification (One-Eleven Series 500)

Type:	short-haul airliner
Dimensions:	wing span 28.50m (93ft 6in), length 29.67m (97ft 4in), height 7.47m (24ft 6in)
Maximum take-off weight:	47,400kg (104,500lb)
Powerplant:	two 55.60kN (12,550lb) thrust Rolls-Royce Spey Mk 512DW turbofan engines
Maximum cruising speed:	871km/h (541mph)
Maximum range:	3484km (2165 miles)
Maximum cruising altitude:	10670m (35,000ft)
Flight crew:	2
Passengers:	up to 119 in single-class accommodation

Romania's Romaero established a production line that delivered nine Series 516RC aircraft. These brought One-Eleven production to 245 aircraft.

to that which claimed the penultimate Series 1 Trident, ended its carer on 22 October, but BAC handled the crisis well and sales were unaffected. The One-Eleven Series 200 entered BUA service on 9 April 1965, further customers bringing production to 56 airframes.

Developing the One-Eleven

Nine Series 300 aircraft followed, with more power and a greater fuel load, while the Series 400 was essentially similar, but suited to the U.S. regulations governing two-crew operation through an enforced weight restriction and with slightly modified control actuation. BAC had a heavyweight rival in the form of Douglas and its DC-9, especially in the U.S. market, but nevertheless managed to sell 30 out of 69 Series 400s built to American Airlines, also selling One-Elevens to Braniff, Mohawk and Aloha.

When BEA announced that it needed a replacement for the Vickers Viscount, BAC offered the One-Eleven Series 500, with a wider wing span and yet more power. The type flew for the first time on 17 February 1968 and BEA was sufficiently impressed to buy 18 out of the run of 89 produced. The Series 500 spawned the Series 475, which used the former's wings and powerplant, allied to the short fuselage of the Series 400 to produce an aircraft optimized for hot-and-high operation. In fact, the Series 475 was far more than a hot-and-high One-Eleven, because it was also protected against damage caused by debris striking the airframe, suiting it to semi-prepared strips of the type used by Faucett, a Peruvian carrier that took all nine of the aircraft.

Five further One-Eleven iterations failed to progress into production. After BOAC and BEA merged to form British Airways (BA), the airline called for a new short-haul jet. BAC initially offered the Series 600 with a developed Spey producing 81kN (18,000lb), but

ultimately put a less ambitious type forward, but BA seemed to have adopted BOAC's Boeing policy and opted for the 737-200.

The Series 600 had used a revised high-lift wing flown on the Series 670 prototype, which had been developed as a replacement for the Japanese NAMC YS-11 twin turboprop, but failed to find customers. British Airways subsequently turned down a second 81kN (18,000lb) Spey-engined One-Eleven, the Series 700, while the same designation was applied to an equally unsuccessful stretch. Another stretch was the Series 800, with longer wings and powered by CFM56 engines, which morphed into the wider X-Eleven of 1976. British Aerospace abandoned the latter after its formation by combining Hawker Siddeley and BAC in 1977, when the decision was made to join the Airbus Industrie consortium.

British Airways Service

British Airways never bought new One-Elevens, but took on BEA's fleet when the airline merged with BOAC. The new carrier subsequently added second-hand examples, raising its fleet to more than 30 machines at its peak during the late 1980s, the majority of them Series 500s. British Airways retired its last One-Eleven in 1993.

Douglas DC-9, MD-80/90 and Boeing 717 (1965)

Douglas beat Boeing to the short-haul jet market and for a while its DC-9 was the world's best-selling jetliner. But the company overstretched itself and it was left to McDonnell Douglas to develop the even more successful MD-80.

Even as the Boeing 707 and Douglas DC-8 were becoming established in service, the industry became aware of the stark contrast between the latest long-haul airliners and the motley collection of largely piston-driven types covering shorter routes. Turbojet power was widely considered to lack the economy for such services, so that Lockheed, with its L-188 Electra, and Vickers, with the Viscount, developed turboprop solutions.

In France, however, Sud-Est had taken the bold step of producing a short-haul jet and its successor, Sud-Aviation, was making headway with the Caravelle in the U.S. market. For its part, Douglas was also convinced that jet power was the only viable option, scheming a 'small DC-8',

which retained four engines in the form of Pratt & Whitney JT10s and carried the designation DC-9. When United and Eastern ordered Boeing 727s in 1960, Douglas abandoned the DC-9 concept in favour of a jet serving the market for a smaller aircraft than the 727, in a segment where Boeing had no competing type.

There followed a period during which Douglas and General Electric courted Sud-Aviation over the development

Air Cal operated its MD-80 fleet in competition with that of PSA, the airlines particularly vying for traffic on the San Francisco–Los Angeles route.

Cockpit
Customers could specify an EFIS cockpit for their MD-80 series aircraft. This early EFIS equipment employed heavy CRT displays, but represented a leap in capability over conventional instruments.

Fuselage
The DC-9 had been designed for around 80 passengers, but successive stretches allowed the MD-82 to carry 155.

In Service
Many hundreds of aircraft from the DC-9/MD-80/MD-90/717 series remain in service and freighter conversions are likely to out-serve the passenger variants.

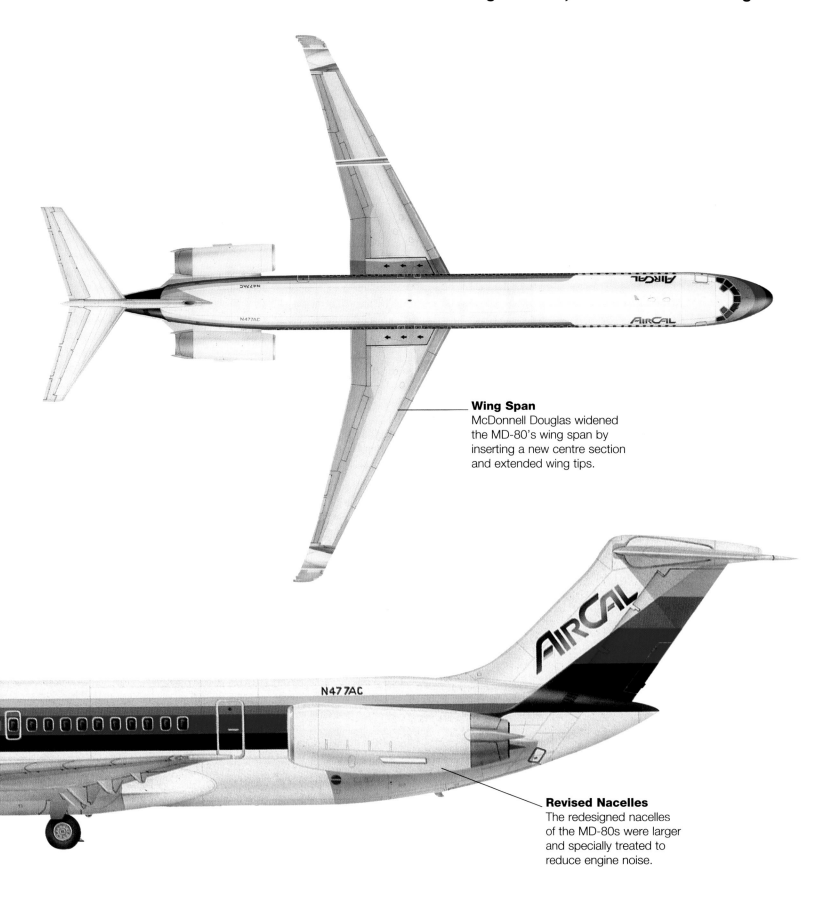

Wing Span
McDonnell Douglas widened the MD-80's wing span by inserting a new centre section and extended wing tips.

Revised Nacelles
The redesigned nacelles of the MD-80s were larger and specially treated to reduce engine noise.

of an improved Caravelle, but the type was becoming dated – it had first flown in 1955 – and would in any case offer capacity close to that of the 727. When BAC announced its One-Eleven, an airliner in exactly the category Douglas had been considering, the U.S. manufacturer withdrew from the Caravelle programme to concentrate on a new design, presented to the airlines from 1962 as the D-2086.

Superficially similar to the Caravelle and One-Eleven, the Douglas was engineered with the power and high-lift wings required for operations from the shorter runways of the USA's still largely underdeveloped regional airports. Douglas benefitted from Pratt & Whitney's development work on the JT8D for the Boeing 727, choosing to power what was now the DC-9 with a pair of JT8Ds. Somewhat overpowered for the aircraft's needs, the Pratts, combined with the

Hawaiian Airlines took delivery of this DC-9-51 in July 1978. McDonnell Douglas built 96 DC-9-50s between 1974 and 1981.

DC-9's inherent suitability for fuselage stretches, conferred tremendous development potential.

Delta Launch

In April 1963 Delta Airlines committed to buy 15 DC-9s, with a similar number on option, sufficient for Douglas to formally launch the programme. With the One-Eleven close to first flight and already winning U.S. orders, Douglas was obliged to move fast with the DC-9, flying the first machine on 25 February 1965 and achieving certification for the DC-9-10 initial production version in November. It produced a series of primary DC-9 variants with a bewildering array of powerplant, weight and other options, alongside versions developed against specific customer requests. The first of several stretches lengthened the fuselage by 4.57m (15ft), adding 25 passengers to the 80 carried by the DC-9-10 and creating the DC-9-30. By now Boeing had reacted to the short-haul requirement, with the 737, but the DC-9-30, which offered similar capacity, was ready for service from early 1967, before the 737's April first flight.

The DC-9-20 and -40 were both matched closely to SAS specifications and built in small numbers, but serve to illustrate the serious problems that Douglas was beginning to encounter. Its willingness to embark on such limited projects was combining with the huge demand for DC-9s to cause severe financial problems. Many DC-9s had been sold at favourable prices to encourage sales, but demand had been so great that Douglas had never managed to bed the type fully into production and its workers were flat out and struggling to learn their jobs. The demands of the Vietnam War on aircraft and spares production were also

Specification (MD-82)

Type:	short/medium-haul airliner
Dimensions:	wing span 32.87m (107ft 10in), length 45.06m (147ft 10in), height 9.04m (29ft 8in)
Maximum take-off weight:	66,680kg (147,000lb)
Powerplant:	two 88.94kN (20,000lb) thrust Pratt & Whitney JT8D-217A turbofan engines
Maximum cruising speed:	850km/h (528mph)
Range:	3000km (1800 miles)
Flight crew:	2
Passengers:	up to 172 in single-class accommodation

taking an expensive toll, so that the unit cost of the DC-9 was considerably higher than expected and every single aircraft was being delivered at a loss.

New Management

McDonnell saved Douglas from bankruptcy, taking over in April 1967 and creating McDonnell Douglas. The new management brought production under control and as well as producing DC-9-30 cargo variants, introduced the DC-9-50, with more power and a 4.34m (14ft 3in) stretch compared to the -30. Seating 139 passengers, the -50 was an excellent aircraft, but its high-powered

Germany's Aero Lloyd operated this DC-9-32 from 1982. It passed to Midwest Express in 1994.

JT8Ds were loud in a world increasingly concerned about aircraft noise. Swissair was the first airline to call for a quieter DC-9, after people living around its Swiss airports complained about the noise increase of its new DC-9-50s compared to the -30s it had previously operated. The U.S. government was also planning strict noise regulations and McDonnell Douglas embarked on a radical redesign to produce the DC-9-80, also known as the Super 80 and designated MD-80 by the time it entered service.

MD-80 and MD-90

Stretching the DC-9-50 fuselage by another 4.34m (14ft 3in), McDonnell Douglas produced the baseline for the MD-80 series. The wing was modified with increased span thanks to a new centre section and while the JT8D was retained, it was as the -209, in acoustically treated nacelles. Digital avionics found their way onto the flight deck for the first time, while an EFIS was available to order.

The first of the series, an MD-81, completed its maiden flight on 18 October 1979 and launch customer Swissair took its first example on 12 September 1980. Subsequent models included the hot-and-high MD-82 and the more powerful, longer-ranged MD-83. The MD-87 was 5m (16ft 5in) shorter for a maximum of 130 passengers, while the JT8D-219 engined MD-88 flew for the first time on 15 August 1987 and introduced an EFIS as standard. The MD-80 series remained in production until 1999, adding 1191 orders to the 976 received for the original DC-9 variants.

In 1989, McDonnell Douglas had launched a re-engined MD-80 designated MD-90, although subsequent variants dispensed with the hyphen, the standard model becoming the MD90-30. Stretched yet again by a modest 1.45m (4ft 9in), the aircraft seated 172 passengers and was powered by IAE V2525-D5 turbofans. First flown on 22 February 1993, the MD-90 was delivered from September 1997, by which time McDonnell Douglas had been subsumed into Boeing. Customers included Japan Air System (illustrated).

The new owner discontinued MD-90 production in 2000, but ran with the MD-95, which McDonnell Douglas had announced in 1994 as a 130-seat regional variant powered by BMW Rolls-Royce BR710 turbofans. Boeing somewhat bizarrely redesignated the type 717, repeating a 1950s' designation, and took 155 orders, delivering the aircraft between 1999 and 2006.

Ilyushin Il-62 'Classic' (1967)

Working to the unusual requirements of the Soviet system, Ilyushin produced the USSR's first long-haul jet transport. The Il-62 proved capable and reliable in service, but never matched the efficiency of Western equivalents.

The Soviet Union was largely self-sufficient in commercial aircraft from its inception, with the notable exceptions of the Lisunov Li-2 'Cab', based on the Douglas DC-3, and Czech LET L-410 Turbolet, a small twin-engined turboprop. Its domestic requirements were very different to those of the free world, since emphasis was placed on creating simple, rugged and easily maintained machines that could be operated from austere airfields, often in harsh weather conditions. Aeroflot, the state airline, was concerned with maintaining vital services rather than turning a profit, so that achieving efficiency and passenger comfort were no better than secondary aims.

Aeroflot's international services, especially those to Western destinations, were considered rather more

important, however, since they provided the opportunity for the Soviets to demonstrate their aviation prowess to the wider world. In 1957 the Tupolev Tu-114 'Cleat' flew for the first time and soon became the mainstay of Aeroflot's long-haul services. An impressive and unusual turboprop, with swept wings and massively powerful engines, it offered accommodation and range performance comparable to those of the 707-320B, although the Tu-114 was considerably slower in the cruise.

Soviet officials had realized at the time of the Tu-114's maiden flight that a long-haul jetliner was required and in 1958 Ilyushin was handed a specification demanding an aircraft capable of carrying 150 passengers over 8000km (4971 miles) at 900km/h (559mph). In common with

Thanks to its more efficient engines and greater fuel capacity, the Il-62M offered a considerable range increase compared to the Il-62.

Flight Crew
While Western airlines were steadily reducing flight crew, the Il-62 entered service with a crew of five.

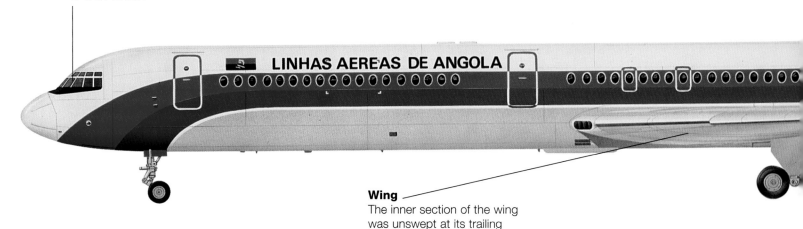

Wing
The inner section of the wing was unswept at its trailing edge and carried large flaps. The wing mounted an array of high-lift devices, spoilers and ailerons.

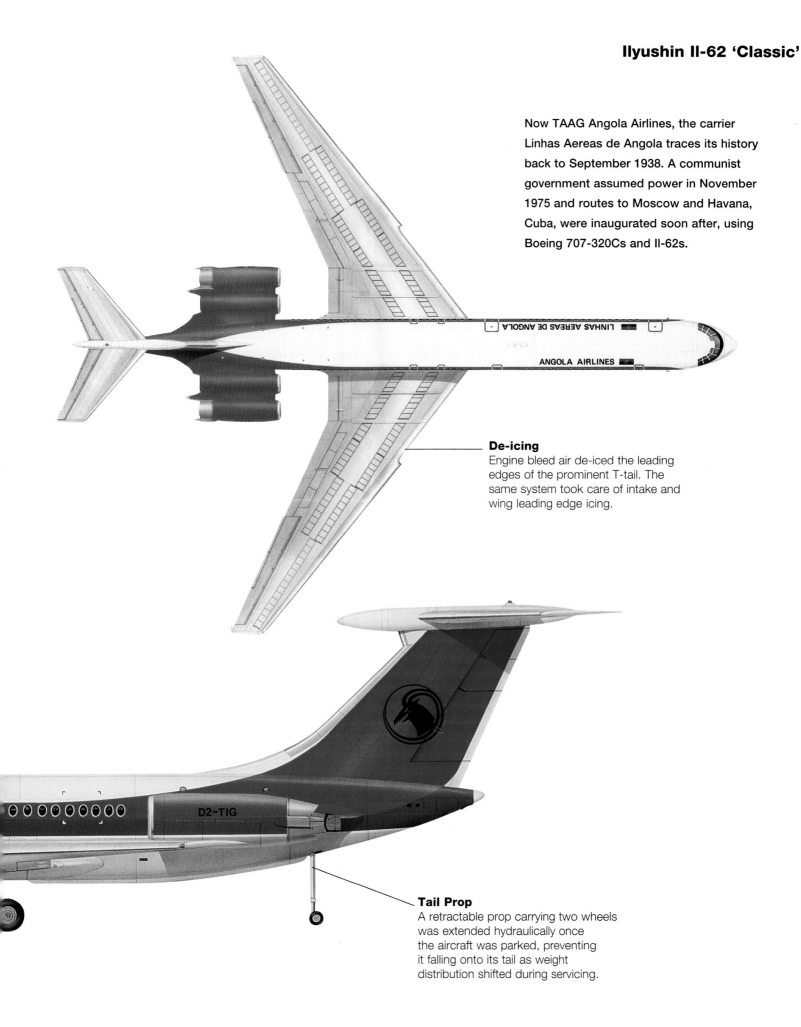

Now TAAG Angola Airlines, the carrier Linhas Aereas de Angola traces its history back to September 1938. A communist government assumed power in November 1975 and routes to Moscow and Havana, Cuba, were inaugurated soon after, using Boeing 707-320Cs and Il-62s.

De-icing
Engine bleed air de-iced the leading edges of the prominent T-tail. The same system took care of intake and wing leading edge icing.

Tail Prop
A retractable prop carrying two wheels was extended hydraulically once the aircraft was parked, preventing it falling onto its tail as weight distribution shifted during servicing.

Ilyushin Il-62 'Classic'

designers in the UK and U.S., the Ilyushin team realized the benefits of the rear-engine arrangement pioneered by the Sud-Est Caravelle and decided upon two pairs of podded engines for their Il-62 design. Given its similar requirements and the choice of podded engine pairs, the Soviet airliner immediately took on a resemblance to the Vickers VC10, leading Western commentators to suggest that it was a straight copy – it was not.

A new turbofan, the Kuznetsov NK-8 was commissioned as powerplant, but unavailable for the first prototype, which took its maiden flight on 3 January 1961, fitted with four Lyul'ka AL-7 turbojets. These less powerful engines were good for proving that the aircraft would fly, but otherwise limited performance severely. A second prototype and three pre-production aircraft followed, all initially powered by the AL-7, although

The VC10's engine nacelles were mounted in a 'spectacle' arrangement, but a short joining section separated those of the Il-62.

NK-8-4 engines were gradually retrofitted on the latter three machines.

The airframe was considerably revised during testing, the pre-production aircraft losing the prominent forward-fuselage fairings of the prototypes, while the wing required considerable re-working. The drooped outer leading edge was increased in span and chord, fences added and the wing tips revised. Given the unavailability of engines and extensive wing modifications required, development became protracted and Aeroflot was only able to begin service trials with the Il-62 on 10 March 1967.

Specification (Il-62M)

Type:	'Classic' long-haul airliner
Dimensions:	wing span 43.20m (141ft 9in), length 53.12m (174ft 3½in), height 12.35m (40ft 6in)
Maximum take-off weight:	165,000kg (363,757lb)
Powerplant:	four 107.70kN (24,200lb) thrust Soloviev D-30KU turbofan engines
Maximum cruising speed:	900km/h (560mph)
Range with maximum payload:	7800km (4846 miles)
Service ceiling:	12,800m (42,000ft)
Flight crew:	5
Passengers:	up to 186 in single-class accommodation

Classic Service

Reliable information on Soviet technologies was difficult to gather during the Cold War, and to ease the identification of new aircraft types the Air Standardisation Coordination Committee, originally formed by Canada, the UK and the U.S., but later including Australia and New Zealand, allocated codenames to new Soviet aircraft as they were identified. Transport aircraft designations began with the letter 'C' and the Il-62 was known as 'Classic'. Also adopted by the NATO countries, these designations are popularly but erroneously also known as 'NATO codenames'.

Aeroflot began full 'Classic' services on 15 September 1967, finally bringing the Soviet Union into the era of pure jet long-range transport. Production was now primarily for the national carrier, but Il-62s were also exported to states under Soviet influence and allied nations, including China (for CAAC) and Cuba (Cubana).

With the Il-62 performing well, Ilyushin looked to improve the design with more modern Soloviev D-30KU turbofans and other changes, including a fin fuel tank, upgraded avionics and provision for baggage and freight to be loaded in containers. The latter reduced turnaround times since the aircraft's holds had previously been compatible only with bulk cargo.

The combination of more efficient engines and fin tank extended the range of the new Il-62M variant by 1100km (684 miles) over that of the Il-62 and allowed the type to remain the cornerstone of Aeroflot's long-haul operation from its service entry in 1974 into the 1990s. It replaced Il-62s with other operators, as well as winning new customers, including TAAG Angola and Linhas Aereas de Moçambique.

From 1978 a further upgraded version became available as the Il-62MK, its structure restressed for higher take-off weights and accommodation revised for as many as 195 passengers, with wider aisles allowing access for passenger service carts and overhead baggage bins. By 1990, 245 Il-62s of all variants had been built with 25 in work at the dissolution of the Soviet Union.

Il-62 Survivors

Il-62s served airlines around the world, but never in huge numbers. Late in 2014 the aircraft remained in regular passenger service with a handful of operators, having outlived the contemporary British and U.S. types, although in many cases Il-62 users were left with little choice but to adopt the less economical Soviet airliner.

North Korea's Air Koryo had five Il-62Ms in service, having lost a sixth to an accident in 1983. Kazakhstan's Air Trust had a single Il-62M and Russia's KAPO-Gorbunova had a single Il-62M airliner and three converted Il-62MF freighters, all apparently active, with another aircraft stored and available for purchase.

Boeing 737 (1967)

Boeing continues to achieve phenomenal success with the smallest member of its jetliner family. The 737 remains the best-selling jet airliner of all time and its latest variants offer unthinkable performance compared to the original model of 1967.

Boeing announced its Model 737 to a barely lukewarm reception from the airlines in 1964, yet it expects to deliver the first example of the latest iteration, the 737 MAX, late in 2017, confident in the future success of what has become the world's best-selling jetliner. This peculiar turn of events began with the fleet renewal plans of the major U.S. carriers – American, Delta, Eastern and United – which called for a short-haul jet to replace old piston and turboprop equipment.

Boeing's focus had been on developing the 707 and bringing the 727 to service, so that the new requirement caught it somewhat off guard, while BAC and Douglas, with the One-Eleven and DC-9, respectively, were poised to take orders. And they did, American signing for One-Elevens,

while Delta ordered DC-9s. Boeing had yet to launch an airliner programme against anything other than a U.S. order, but the 737 impressed neither Eastern nor United and instead it took a Lufthansa order for 21 aircraft.

Still Boeing yearned for a domestic buyer and after Eastern ordered DC-9s, it offered to cover United's immediate short-haul needs with 727s, leased on favourable terms until the 737 became available. United committed to 40, with 30 options, and Boeing began work in earnest.

Below is an example of a 737-200 Advanced, leased to British airline Amberair in 1988. More than 1100 examples of the popular Model 200 were built between 1967 and 1988.

Nose Section
Boeing took the 727 nose section and cockpit, mating them to a shortened 727 fuselage to create the 737. The 737's lineage can therefore be traced directly back to Boeing first jetliner, since these were originally 'borrowed' from the 707.

Short Undercarriage
As with the BAC One-Eleven, the 737's short undercarriage eased ground handling. Later it caused design headaches when modern engines with large-diameter fans were introduced.

Success Defined

While airframers in Europe, the U.S. and the U.S.SR were exploiting the benefits of rear-mounted engines, Boeing discounted this set-up for its 737 on the basis of its inherent weight penalty compared to placing the engines underwing. Thus it installed the jet's Pratt &Whitney JT8Ds in sleek nacelles, mounted directly to the wing underside, negating the need for a conventional pylon and allowing an unusually short undercarriage to be used, saving weight and facilitating ground handling.

The fuselage was a shorter version of that used on the 727, while the trijet also supplied the 737's cockpit and nose sections, so that the forward fuselage profile of even the very latest 737s is almost identical to that of the earliest 707. On 9 April 1967 the first prototype,

Engine Position
When Boeing re-engined the 737 with CFM56 turbofans it was forced to abandon the type's original underwing engine nacelle design, shown here on this 737-200.

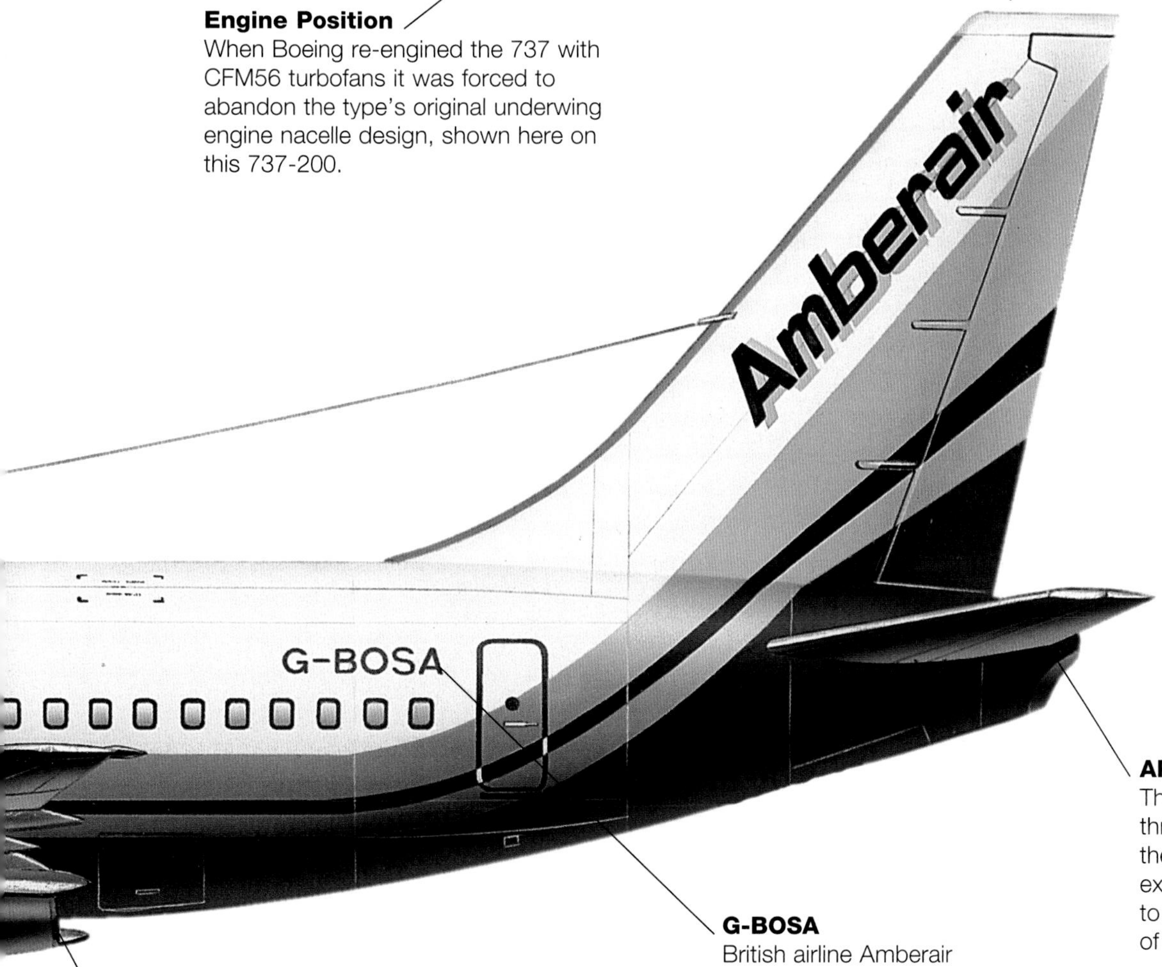

APU Exhaust
The 737's APU exhausts through a prominent outlet in the tip of the rear fuselage. This exhaust outlet has been revised to an installation similar to that of the 787 on the 737 MAX.

G-BOSA
British airline Amberair leased G-BOSA, a 737-200 Advanced, in 1988.

Thrust Reversers
The JT8D engines were originally housed in short nacelles with their thrust reversers opening horizontally below the wing. These decreased braking efficiency and a redesign, with vertically opening reversers at the end of much longer nacelles, was required.

Boeing 737

built to 737-100 standard for 103 passengers, took off on its maiden flight. The engine installation immediately gave trouble, creating excess drag and braking problems, since reverse thrust tended to 'lift' the aircraft, taking weight off the mainwheels and reducing brake effectiveness.

Months of redesigning solved the problems, but the market found the -100 too small and with just 30 sold, Boeing was forced to produce the stretched 737-200, with more fuel and, in its initial form as delivered to United, 115 passenger seats. But still Boeing struggled to sell its 'baby', introducing the 737-200C convertible and 737-200QC 'quick-change' convertible, as well as a 'gravel kit' for rough-field operations to maximize the aircraft's appeal. Eventually the orders trickled in sufficiently for the airline community to view the 737 as a realistic proposition and from the 281st aircraft, Boeing began delivering the 737-200 Advanced.

Seating 130 passengers and modified for operations into smaller airports, the Advanced at last put the 737 onto a firm footing and Boeing continued to improve the model through features including carbon composite construction, which on the later production aircraft shaved as much as 454kg (1000lb) off structural weight.

Lufthansa took this 737-300 in 1986. The airline has been a staunch supporter of Boeing products throughout its post-war history.

Specification (737-800)

Type:	short/medium-haul airliner
Dimensions:	wing span 35.80m (117ft 5in), length 39.50m (129ft 6in), height 12.50m (41ft 2in)
Maximum take-off weight:	79,015kg (174,200lb)
Powerplant:	two 107.60kN (24,200lb) thrust CFM International CFM56-7B24 turbofan engines
Maximum cruising speed:	Mach 0.785
Maximum range:	5765km (3582 miles)
Service ceiling:	12,500m (41,000ft)
Flight crew:	2
Passengers:	up to 189 in single-class accommodation

The Advanced was good enough to compete effectively with the MD-80 series developed out of the DC-9 by McDonnell Douglas, but in 1981 Airbus Industrie announced its intention to create a modern rival and Boeing looked to work it already had in hand to keep the 737 at the top of its game.

Big Fan

The alliance of General Electric and SNECMA in CFM International had produced the big-fan CFM56, the first high-bypass turbofan suitable for smaller aircraft and already in use on the DC-8-70 series. The combination of a large-diameter fan with the 737's short undercarriage challenged Boeing's ingenuity and even with the engine hung on a pylon ahead of the wing there was insufficient ground clearance. The solution was found in moving the engine accessories to the side, encasing the entire assembly in an unusual nacelle of 'flattened oval' section. A revised cabin interior and electronic flight instrumentation system (EFIS) cockpit were also major features of the new design, which first flew in 737-300 form, for 149 passengers, on 24 February 1984. USAir took the first delivery on 28 November and Boeing further exploited the power available form the CFM56 in the stretched 737-400, seating up to 170 passengers and creating an aircraft capable of replacing much of the older equipment in the charter and IT markets. It also returned the 737 to its -200 roots, with the short-body 737-500, whose long range allowed it to carry 108 passengers over 5552km (3450 miles).

Together, the 737 models from -100 to -500 are today regarded as the 'Classic' aircraft, because as Airbus continued to insert technology into the A320 series, so Boeing launched the Next Generation (NG) 737 in 1993. The final Classic 737s, two -400s, were delivered to CSA Czech Airways on 28 February 2000, the first of the NGs, a 737-700 having gone to Southwest Airlines in December 1997.

NG and Max

Boeing proposed three NG variants, the 737-300X, -400X and -500X. The -400X would be longer than the Classic -400 and to emphasize this and the fact that the NG had a new wing, more powerful CFM56 engines with full-authority digital engine control (FADEC), revised cabin features and improved performance, the designations were revised as 737-700, -800 (illustrated) and -600, respectively.

Subsequently Boeing realized that the airframe could be further stretched for 189 passengers as the 737-900 and extending that aircraft's range with the 737-900ER for service from April 2007, produced an unexpected but opportune replacement for the 757.

The introduction of an all-new Sky Interior with cues from the 787 Dreamliner revitalized the NG and the 1000th Sky-equipped aircraft, a -800, went to Norwegian in February 2014. Nevertheless, on 30 August 2011 Boeing had announced the NG's successor, the 737 MAX. To be available in 737-7, -8 and -9 variants, the MAX adds the new technology CFM International LEAP-1B to improved NG airframes for a quantum leap in efficiency. Once again the aircraft's short undercarriage has caused problems, Boeing increasing the length of its nose gear by 20cm (8in) to provide ground clearance for the engine's even larger fan. MAX deliveries are expected from late 2017.

Fokker F28 Fellowship and 70/100 (1967)

With the F28 Fokker took the pioneering attitude of its F27 thinking and applied it to regional jet transport. The short-field F28 spawned the F100 and F70, which became the famous planemaker's final products.

Fokker had worked hard to convince airlines that turboprop rather than piston power was the way ahead for regional operations, but when BEA called for a high-speed jet-powered regional aircraft, the Dutch manufacturer became concerned that the turboprop too would soon be outmoded. It therefore announced a new jet project in 1961. Known as the F28 Fellowship, it was extremely similar in appearance to the BAC One-Eleven, but with a maximum passenger capacity of 65 compared to the One-Eleven's minimum of 89. The Fellowship's wing was optimized for operations from

short runways and it would be powered by the Rolls-Royce RB.183 turbofan.

A surprisingly international venture, the F28 was produced through agreements with West Germany's MBB, which produced the rear fuselage, engine nacelles and pylons, and VFW, which built the forward fuselage and tail; and Shorts in Northern Ireland for the wings and undercarriage doors. Fairchild-Hiller considered its own FH-228 development for the North American market, but subsequently settled on selling the standard F28 into the region.

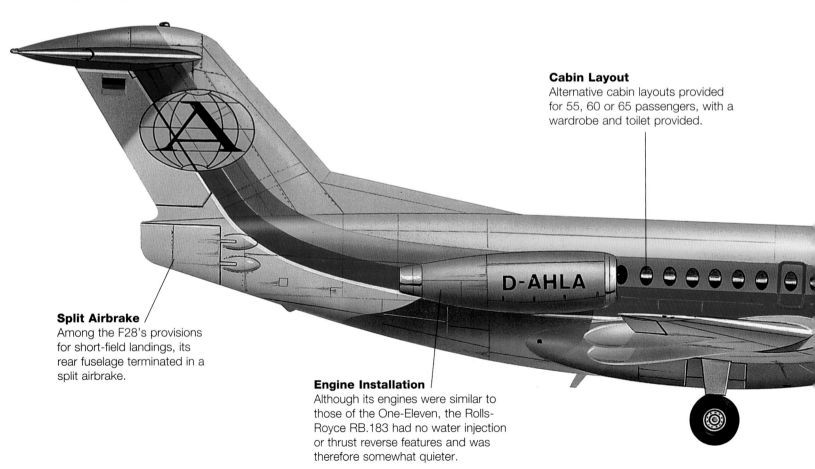

Cabin Layout
Alternative cabin layouts provided for 55, 60 or 65 passengers, with a wardrobe and toilet provided.

Split Airbrake
Among the F28's provisions for short-field landings, its rear fuselage terminated in a split airbrake.

Engine Installation
Although its engines were similar to those of the One-Eleven, the Rolls-Royce RB.183 had no water injection or thrust reverse features and was therefore somewhat quieter.

There were two F28 prototypes, flown on 9 May and 3 August 1967, with first delivery to West German carrier LTU on 24 February 1969. By now Fokker had signed up several customers, but between them their orders totalled just 22 aircraft and the manufacturer was obliged to begin an aggressive marketing campaign. By its nature, however, the F28 appealed in small numbers to more specialist operators, thanks to its relatively small capacity and field performance, and although Fokker's marketers were bringing in new orders, they were seldom for more than two or three aircraft each.

Extended Fellowship

The original model had become known as the F28 Mk 1000 or F28-1000, and Fokker set about increasing the type's popularity and versatility with a series of

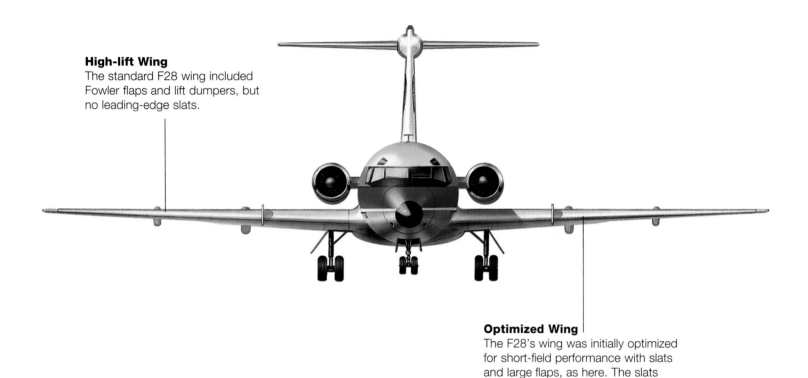

High-lift Wing
The standard F28 wing included Fowler flaps and lift dumpers, but no leading-edge slats.

Optimized Wing
The F28's wing was initially optimized for short-field performance with slats and large flaps, as here. The slats were omitted on some later variants.

A short-lived West German airline, Aviaction took three F28-1000 jets in 1971. Its operations were unsuccessful and Fokker repossessed them in 1973.

developments. First came the F28-2000 in 1970, stretched for 79 passengers, while the Mk 1000C was a short-fuselage combi with a large freight door. Adding an even higher-lift wing of extended span to the short

Air Mauritanie operated this F28-6000 in the early 1980s. The long-fuselage Mk 6000 had a slatted wing.

fuselage produced the Mk 5000, while the same wing combined with the long fuselage generated the Mk 6000.

These aircraft had re-podded RB.183 Mk 555-1H engines that generated less noise and allowed increased weights. The same motors featured on the Mk 3000 and Mk 4000, variants of the Mk 5000 and Mk 6000, respectively, with the slats of the high-lift wing deleted. Still sales were slow, but a continuous trickle of orders kept the F28 production line active until 1986, by which time 241 aircraft had been sold.

Final Fokkers

In November 1983 Fokker took another bold step in regional aircraft design, announcing its intention to develop a new-generation regional jet when the airlines, ironically, were yet to be tempted away from the economics of the turboprop. The company had considered Super F28 and 150-seat F29 designs, and discussed the possibility for joint development of an MDF 100 with McDonnell Douglas, but the aircraft launched

Specification (Fokker 100, Tay 650 engines)

Type:	short-haul airliner
Dimensions:	wing span 28.08m (92ft 1½in), length 35.53m (116ft 6¾in), height 8.50m (27ft 10½in)
Maximum take-off weight:	44,450kg (98,000lb)
Powerplant:	two 67.19kN (15,000lb) thrust Rolls-Royce Tay 650 turbofan engines
Maximum operating speed:	837km/h (520mph)
Maximum range:	2956km (1836 miles)
Service ceiling:	10,670m (35,000ft)
Flight crew:	2
Passengers:	up to 107 in single-class accommodation

in 1983 was a 100-seat development of the F28, designated Fokker 100, or F100.

It was launched alongside the F50, a factor that later stretched Fokker's capacity and caused delays. The F100 was thoroughly modern, with a new wing, power from 61.60kN (13,850lb) thrust Rolls-Royce Tay 620 turbofans and an EFIS cockpit. The cockpit specification was modified late in the design process and weights increased, prior to a first flight on 30 November 1986.

Fokker again entered into production agreements for various airframe components. Daimler Benz Airbus built the centre fuselage and tail, Shorts the wings and Dowty the nose gear, while Northrop Grumman and Menasco in the U.S. took care of the engine nacelles and thrust reversers, and main undercarriage, respectively. The engine nacelles, control surfaces, cabin floor and several fairings were all of weight-saving composite construction.

Launch customer Swissair placed the F100 into service on 3 April 1988, while an alternative variant with 67.19kN (15,000lb) Tay 650s flew for the first time on 8 July. In 1989 American Airlines placed Fokker's largest ever order, for 75 of these more powerful aircraft, while USAir took the first delivery on 1 July 1989.

Although it examined an enlarged F100, Fokker next developed the 70-seat F70. Similar in length to the short-fuselage F28 and powered by Tay 620 engines, the aircraft suffered a difficult gestation while Fokker was taken over by DASA. The confused situation led to the F70 flying for the first time on 2 April 1993, ahead of programme launch at the Paris Air Show in June – where it secured 15 orders and five options. Further small orders came in and the type entered service, with Sempati Air of Indonesia, on 9 March 1995.

But Fokker was struggling under its new ownership, with well-thought-out rivals appearing on the market while the Dutch company turned out beautifully built but expensive products. By January 1996, DASA had become Daimler-Benz and this new entity withdrew funding that month. Fokker declared bankruptcy on 15 March and delivered its last aircraft, an F70 for KLM cityhopper, on 18 April 1997.

Private Fokkers

The Force Aerienne Populaire de Benin was among a handful of operators to fly VIP or corporate F28/100/70 aircraft. It took this F28-4000 in 1982, but retained it in service only until 1984. The very first F70 delivery was made to a corporate customer, Ford Motor Company, which took a 48-seat corporate shuttle on 25 October 1994.

Tupolev Tu-144 'Charger'
(1968)

The Soviet Union was first into the air with a supersonic transport, the Tu-144 offering scintillating performance, but its service career was cut short after two fatal accidents. Only 13 aircraft flew and services were cancelled on 1 June 1978.

A 1963 study noted that on average, every Aeroflot service saved its passengers 24.9 hours in travel time compared to alternative methods of surface transport. For people in important positions, such as doctors or senior military personnel, this time saving was vital to increase productivity. There were obvious benefits in facilitating even faster air travel and calculations suggested that a fleet of 75 supersonic transports (SSTs) would increase this time saving to more than 36 hours per passenger. Given its vast territory, supersonic transport had obvious benefits for the USSR.

The problems of noise disturbance caused by the unavoidable 'booms' that an aircraft moving at supersonic speed creates, which became such an issue for the Anglo-French Concorde programme, were dismissed by the authorities. Andrei Tupolev, whose design bureau was commissioned to produce the SST, simply claimed that the noise was similar to 'thunder'.

An SST programme was initiated in July 1963 and while Tupolev was made responsible for developing the airframe of what became the Tu-144, the type's engine was entrusted to Kuznetsov, which modified the NK-8, already

CCCP-77144 was the fourth production Aeroflot Tu-144 'Charger' and ought to have been registered CCCP-77104, but was given an out-of-sequence registration to reflect its designation. It appeared at the 1975 Paris Air Show.

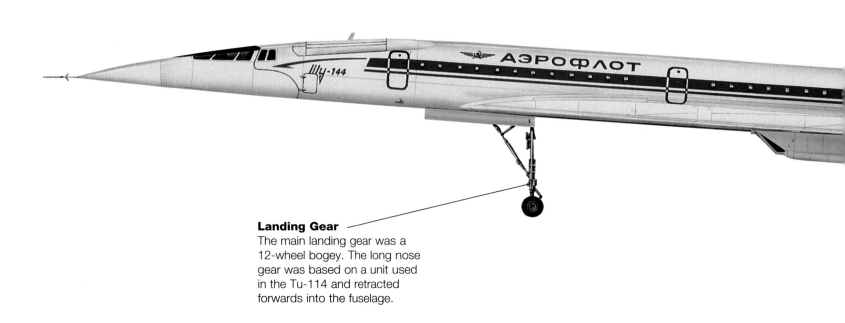

Landing Gear
The main landing gear was a 12-wheel bogey. The long nose gear was based on a unit used in the Tu-114 and retracted forwards into the fuselage.

proven on the Il-62, to satisfy the trying requirements of supersonic cruise. An afterburner, or reheat, commonly used to increase the power of military engines at the expense of much increased fuel consumption, was added, along with a variable exhaust nozzle. An intake system capable of delivering subsonic airflow to the engine

regardless of flight regime was also designed, in materials capable of withstanding the enormous kinetic heating generated at supersonic speed.

In November 1962, Britain and France had formally agreed the development programme that would lead to Concorde; although the Tu-144 was in many ways a more

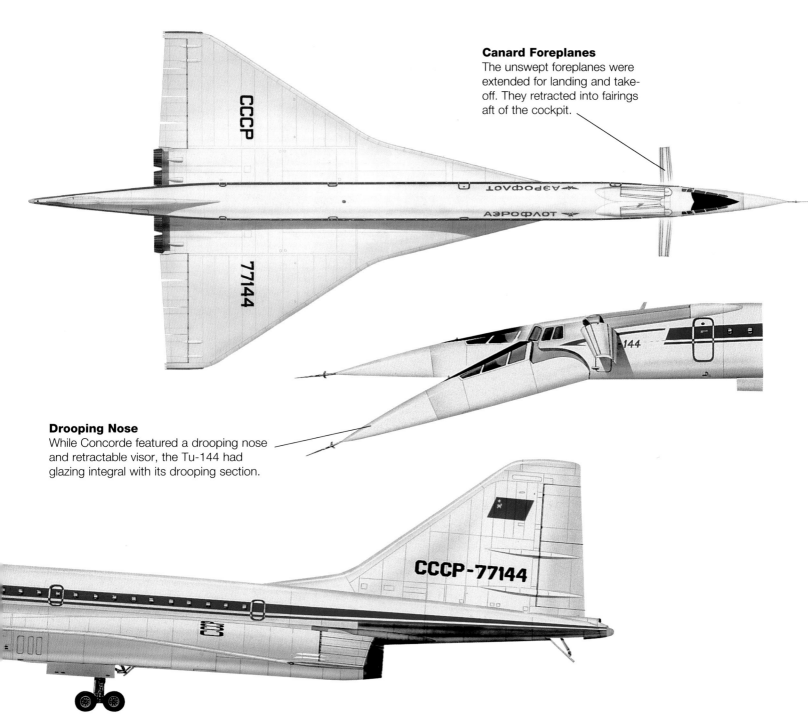

Canard Foreplanes
The unswept foreplanes were extended for landing and take-off. They retracted into fairings aft of the cockpit.

Drooping Nose
While Concorde featured a drooping nose and retractable visor, the Tu-144 had glazing integral with its drooping section.

With powerful engines and advanced aerodynamics, the 'Charger' showed great promise, but was a challenging aircraft to operate. It was slightly faster than Concorde, but its career ended prematurely.

Tupolev Tu-144 'Charger'

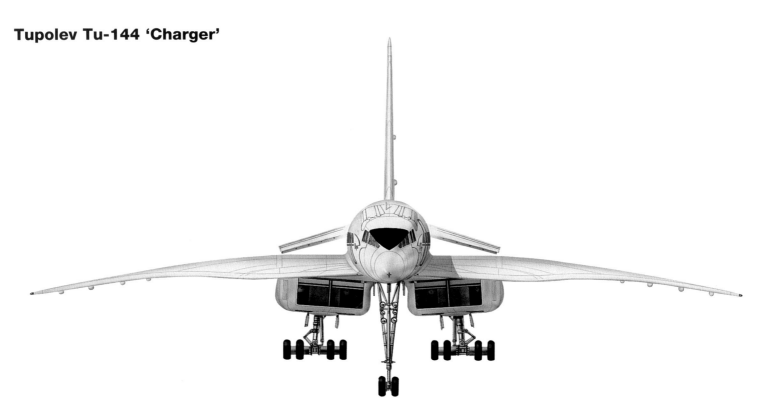

ambitious programme, the Soviets were quick to exploit aspects of Concorde research. French authorities arrested an Aeroflot official in Paris carrying Concorde drawings, while a French airport worker was approached to provide samples of Concorde tyre rubber from the runway at Le Bourget. Developing tyres capable of withstanding the high landing speeds inherent in SST operations was particularly challenging, and complicated for the Soviets when the French produced a dummy rubber compound and inserted it into the Tu-144 programme.

Specification (Tu-144 'Charger')

Type:	long-haul supersonic airliner
Dimensions:	wing span 28.80m (94ft 6in), length 65.70m (215ft 6in), height 12.85m (42ft 4in)
Maximum take-off weight:	180,000kg (396,830lb)
Powerplant:	four 127.29kN (28,660lb) thrust Kuznetsov NK-144 afterburning turbofan engines
Maximum cruising speed:	2500km/h (1553mph)
Maximum range:	6500km (4030 miles)
Maximum cruising altitude:	18,000m (59,000ft)
Flight crew:	3
Passengers:	up to 140 in single-class accommodation

The Tu-144 prototype resembled Concorde, but was quite different in detail, while the production aircraft were far closer to the Western aircraft in design.

Tu-144 Defined

In overall configuration the Tu-144 resembled Concorde, but it was designed for higher cruising speeds. The engines were grouped in a central fairing, similar to the powerplant installation on the North American XB-70 Valkyrie. Antonov designed the Tu-144's wing, the airliner's tailless layout having been proven on the Mikoyan-Gurevich A-144 'Analog', a MiG-21 fitted with a sub-scale Tu-144 style wing.

Dramatically swept at 76°, the wing's giant inboard section connected with an outboard section swept at 57°. Fuel was carried in the wings and lower fuselage, Tupolev later adopting a fuel-pumping system for transonic trimming, similar to that in Concorde. And just like Concorde, the Tu-144's nose was made to droop, improving pilot visibility at the high angles of attack naturally assumed by delta-winged aircraft on landing and take-off.

First Flight

The Tu-144 flew for the first time on 31 December 1968, its four-man test crew all sitting on ejection seats. Flight test continued into 1970 and a high speed of Mach 2.4 (the ratio of the aircraft's speed compared to the local speed of sound) was achieved, although the prototype had yet to be fitted with an airliner cabin. It was revealed to the public at Sheremetyevo on 21 May 1970, but when the first production Tu-144 emerged two years later, it was to a radically altered design. The wing planform and control surfaces had been dramatically modified, the fuselage was 6.30m (20ft 8in) longer, the engines separated into two discrete nacelles similar to those of Concorde and a pair of dramatic canard foreplanes added to the upper forward fuselage for improved low-speed handling.

The aircraft's weight had increased by 50 tonnes, much of it through increased fuel capacity so that production machines could achieve the design range of 6500km (4039 miles). A revised machine flew for the first time in 1973, before a second was lost at that year's Paris Air Show. Aeroflot began operational trials in 1974 and on 26 December 1975 cargo flights between Moscow and Alma Ata began. The 3260km (2026-mile) stage was often completed in less than two hours from pushback to shutdown.

Passenger flights began over the same route on 1 November 1977, but following the fatal crash of an aircraft involved in engine testing, they were cancelled after just 102 schedules. The accident had been the result of a fuel system failure that was remedied, but passengers were never again carried. A Tu-144D variant with improved engines for afterburnerless cruise was flown, but subsequently abandoned.

Paris Crash

Registered CCCP-77102, the second production-standard Tu-144 appeared at the 1973 Paris Air Show. At the end of its display routine on 3 June the aircraft pitched steeply upwards before stalling. It broke up as the pilot attempted to recover, the debris falling on houses and killing eight people on the ground and all of the crew.

No conclusive cause for the accident has been identified, but some sources suggest that a French Dassault Mirage IIIR reconnaissance-fighter may have distracted the pilot as it attempted to gather images of the Tu-144's canards. Other suggestions put the crash down to pilot error or equipment failure.

Tupolev Tu-154 'Careless'
(1968)

Designed to the exacting requirements of the Soviet civil air fleet, the Tu-154 built on Tupolev's earlier jet airliners to produce an aircraft of exceptional performance. Once the cornerstone of Aeroflot's short/medium-haul fleet, the Tu-154 finally fell foul of noise regulations and competition from more economical Western types.

Tupolev had built the USSR's first jet airliner by designing a new fuselage for the Tu-16 bomber, the short/medium range Tu-104 'Camel' entering full service on 15 September 1956. The huge Tu-114 'Cleat' long-range turboprop followed it into the air on 15 November 1957 and the Tu-124 'Cookpot', a short-haul aircraft based on the Tu-104, first flew on 24 March 1960.

Around the time of the Tu-124's service entry in 1962, the authorities commissioned Tupolev to design a new, more efficient short-haul aircraft and the manufacturer decided upon the popular rear-engine configuration for the new twin. Designated Tu-134 and given the ASCC reporting name 'Crusty', the aircraft began passenger service in September 1967, by which time its configuration had already informed the design of a larger, medium-haul trijet, the Tu-154 'Careless'.

The authorities of the Soviet civil air fleet required a jet to replace the Tu-104 and Ilyushin Il-18 'Coot' and Antonov An-10 'Cat' turboprops then serving Aeroflot's domestic network. Tupolev was given a testing specification for the Tu-154, calling for a reduced-payload maximum range of 6000km (3725 miles) flying off a

Balkan Bulgarian Airlines flew the Tu-154M from 1985, just five years before the first Western aircraft, Boeing 737s, joined its fleet.

Cabin Doors
The Tu-154B introduced an extended cabin with a second entry door, just ahead of the wing leading edge.

Anhedral Wing
Tupolev's airliner designs were notable for their anhedralled (downward-angled) wings.

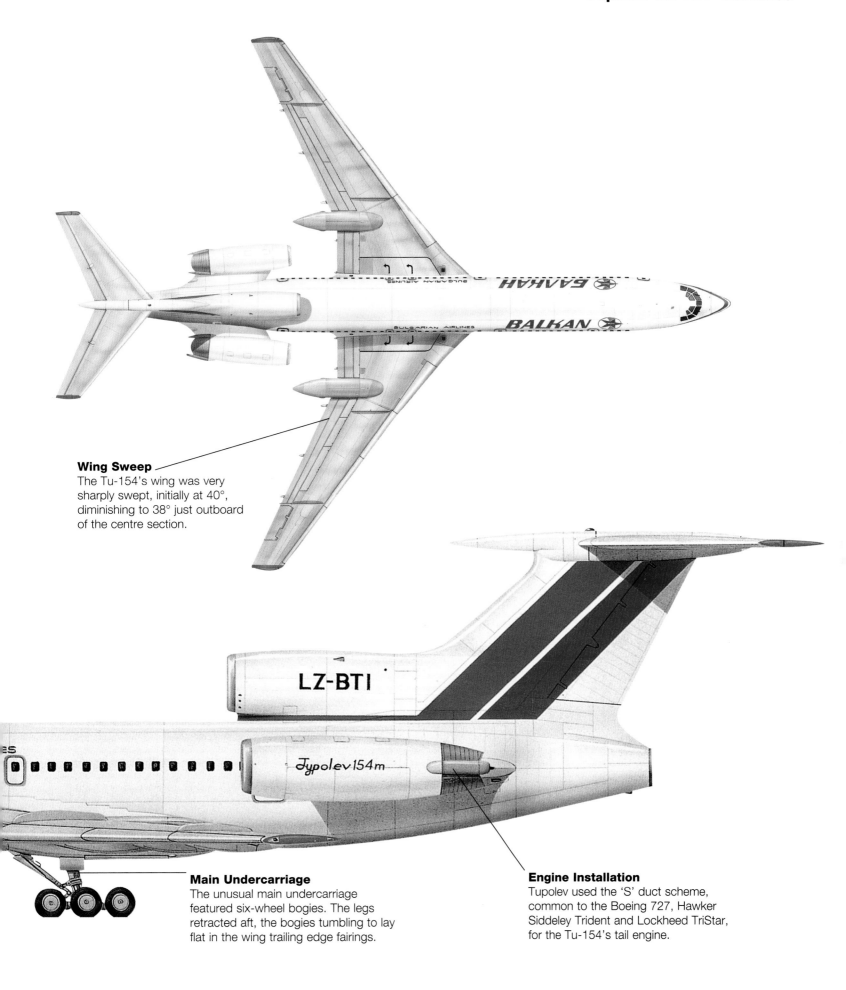

Wing Sweep
The Tu-154's wing was very
sharply swept, initially at 40°,
diminishing to 38° just outboard
of the centre section.

Main Undercarriage
The unusual main undercarriage
featured six-wheel bogies. The legs
retracted aft, the bogies tumbling to lay
flat in the wing trailing edge fairings.

Engine Installation
Tupolev used the 'S' duct scheme,
common to the Boeing 727, Hawker
Siddeley Trident and Lockheed TriStar,
for the Tu-154's tail engine.

Tupolev Tu-154 'Careless'

2000m (6500ft) semi-prepared runway. This trying field performance was achieved through the installation of three powerful Kuznetsov NK-8-2 turbofans and wings equipped with extensive high-lift devices, including slats and triple-slotted flaps. In layout the aircraft was very similar to the Boeing 727-200, albeit smaller and lighter, but considerably more powerful.

Six-wheel main undercarriage bogies were fitted in order to spread the aircraft's weight evenly over the gravel or compacted earth runways that it might be expected to operate from. These retracted aft, the wheels resting in fairings extending behind the wing.

Specification (Tu-154M 'Careless')

Type:	short/medium-haul airliner
Dimensions:	wing span 37.55m (123ft 2½in), length 47.90m (157ft 1¾in), height 11.40m (37ft 4¾in)
Maximum take-off weight:	100,000kg (220,460lb)
Powerplant:	three 104kN (23,380lb) thrust Soloviev D-30KU-154-II turbofan engines
Maximum cruising speed:	950km/h (590mph)
Range with maximum payload:	3900km (2425 miles)
Maximum cruising altitude:	11,900m (39,000ft)
Flight crew:	3
Passengers:	up to 180 in single-class accommodation

The Tu-154's unusual anhedral wing and the oval shape of its centre intake gave the aircraft a distinctive appearance.

'Careless' in Service

The Tu-154 flew for the first time on 4 October 1968 and scheduled passenger service began on 9 February 1972. The aircraft appeared on international routes from 1 August, when it visited Prague for the first time, and the majority of the original production machines was provisioned for 128 passengers.

By 1971, Tupolev had designed an improved Tu-154A. Available for regular service from 1975, it featured more powerful NK-8-2U engines and a centre section fuel tank, among other improvements. In a peculiar arrangement, the fuel in this tank could only be distributed into the aircraft's primary fuel system on the ground and was therefore simply a means of carrying supplies for refuelling at airfields away from home. Passenger capacity was increased to 168.

The Tu-154 had been equipped for auto-landing in poor visibility from the outset, but in the Tu-154B introduced from 1977, the instrumented landing system (ILS) avionics associated with this capability were switched from Soviet provenance to the French Thomson-CSF/SFIM system. The improved 'B' was also heavier, with additional cabin doors and provision for 180 passengers. It remained in production only until 1980, when the Tu-154B-2 replaced it. Now the centre section fuel was useable in-flight, a new radar was fitted and the main undercarriage bogies made to rotate laterally for crosswind landings.

Tupolev offered a Tu-154S freighter from 1982 and two years later began building the ultimate 'Careless', the Tu-154M. Originally designated Tu-164 and produced by modifying a B-2, the revised machine was powered by more efficient Soloviev D-30KU-154-II engines, fed by inlets of greater area to satisfy their increased air requirements. New nacelles were developed for the side engines and the APU moved from its former position in the tail to a location in the centre fuselage.

The high-lift devices and spoilers on the wing were considerably improved and the tailplane redesigned. In the cabin, non-flammable furnishings were installed, along with enclosed overhead luggage bins. The Tu-154M flew for the first time in 1982 and the initial pair of production aircraft reached Aeroflot on 27 December

1984. A Tu-154M-100 variant with Western avionics was produced late on in the Tu-154 programme, but very few of the 1000 or so aircraft built were to this advanced standard.

By early 2015, Tu-154 numbers were diminishing rapidly. The aircraft cannot be made compliant with Stage 3 noise regulations and is therefore banned from operating into many countries, including those of the EU. In the region of 40 Tu-154s were thought to remain active, representing a huge decline, since the type remained the mainstay of Aeroflot's domestic services as recently as the mid-2000s.

'Careless' Operators

Aeroflot was by far and away the major Tu-154 operator, taking the majority of production, but several aircraft, especially Tu-154Ms, were exported to Soviet client states and those under Soviet influence. After the break up of the Soviet Union in the early 1990s, the country's air transport system was opened to competition and new airlines proliferated as entrepreneurs worked to challenge Aeroflot.

In many case these airlines – there were at least 100 by the

end of 1993 – purchased cheap second-hand equipment from the Aeroflot regional branches, typically founding domestic services on a handful of Tu-154Ms. The subsequent availability of more efficient Airbus A320 and Boeing 737 airliners meant that the few survivors of these early operators re-equipped relatively quickly, while Europe's strict noise regulations also curtailed operations, so that the choices of destination outside the CIS became limited.

Boeing 747 (1969)

Boeing's continuous drive and industrial daring led to the next commercially valid major step in commercial aviation after the introduction of jet power – the widebody. It pioneered the market with the 747, which remains in production more than four decades after its first flight.

The first of the long-haul passenger jets had barely entered service when Boeing began to consider an even larger airliner. Air travel had quickly become so popular that airports and airspace were becoming congested and the introduction of larger aircraft, rather than of more, smaller aircraft, was a possible solution.

Douglas found the DC-8 inherently stretchable, but the 707 was less suitable for such extensive structural alteration and Boeing instead decided to use work that both it and Pratt & Whitney had performed on a military programme as the basis for an airliner wider and larger than anything that had come before. In 1964 the U.S. Air Force had issued its CX-HLS requirement for a logistics transport so large that the engine makers were obliged to develop new technologies to power it.

Boeing, Douglas and Lockheed submitted airframe proposals, with Lockheed successful, while General Electric and Pratt & Whitney made engine submissions, of which the former was announced winner. Reluctant to abandon their investment, Boeing and Pratt began work on a new generation of widebody transport, designed for as many as 10 passenger seats across. This giant aircraft relied on the massive thrust generated by Pratt & Whitney's high-bypass JT9D turbofan.

Boeing had taken several ideas to the airlines before arriving at a design essentially traditional in configuration but on a very grand scale. Potential customers had disliked Boeing's double-fuselage and double-deck proposals, but Pan Am had been a staunch supporter of Boeing's efforts from the outset, and as soon as Boeing

Japan's All Nippon Airlines (ANA) took 747 airliners and freighters, including the 747SR. The SR was developed as a high-capacity, high-frequency aircraft for Japan's domestic market, while Nippon Cargo Airlines operated the 747F.

Main Undercarriage
The heavy 747 requires multiple-wheel undercarriage units to spread its weight more evenly over airport surfaces.

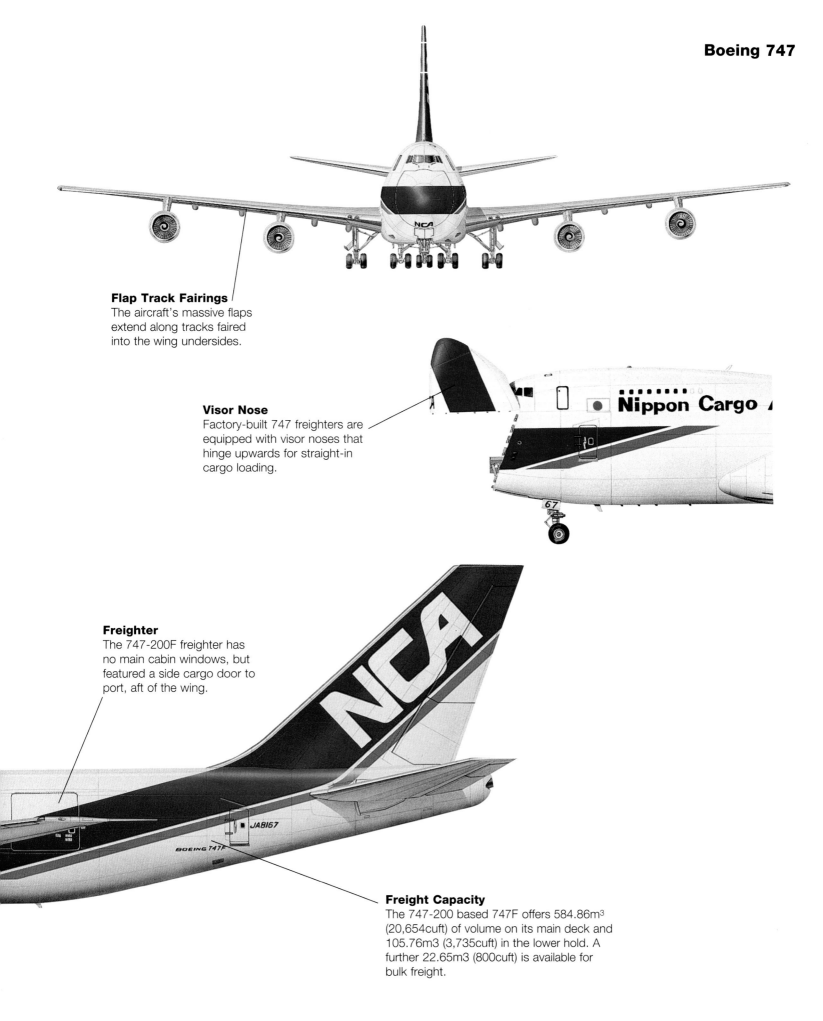

Flap Track Fairings
The aircraft's massive flaps extend along tracks faired into the wing undersides.

Visor Nose
Factory-built 747 freighters are equipped with visor noses that hinge upwards for straight-in cargo loading.

Freighter
The 747-200F freighter has no main cabin windows, but featured a side cargo door to port, aft of the wing.

Freight Capacity
The 747-200 based 747F offers 584.86m³ (20,654cuft) of volume on its main deck and 105.76m3 (3,735cuft) in the lower hold. A further 22.65m3 (800cuft) is available for bulk freight.

Boeing 747

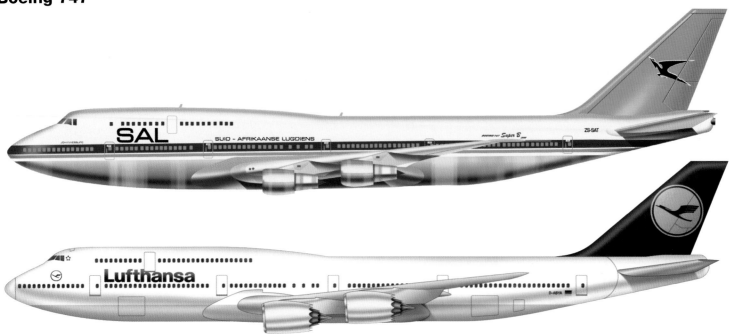

produced plans for a 10-abreast airliner, it signed up. On 13 April 1966 the airline ordered 25 of what became the Boeing 747, in a $525 million commitment that was then the largest commercial order ever.

Building the Jumbo

The popular nickname 'Jumbo Jet' appeared early on in the 747 programme as the aircraft was revealed with its huge fuselage topped by an upper deck

Specification (747-400 with RB.211 engines)

Type:	long-haul widebody airliner
Dimensions:	wing span 64.44m (211ft 5in), length 70.67m (231ft 10¼in), height 19.41m (63ft 8in)
Maximum take-off weight:	396,891kg (875,000lb)
Powerplant:	four 258kN (58,000lb) thrust Rolls-Royce RB.211-524G turbofan engines
Maximum speed:	984km/h (612mph)
Range at highest take-off weight:	13,214km (8211 miles)
Initial cruising altitude:	9998m (32,800ft)
Flight crew:	2
Passengers:	up to 421 in typical three-class accommodation

A stretched upper deck was the primary difference between the 747-300, here shown in South African Airways service, and 747-200. Lufthansa introduced the 747-8 into service during 2012.

containing additional passenger seats and the cockpit, an advanced, high-lift wing sharply swept at 37° for cruise efficiency and four-jet powerplant. In a project of extremes, the JT9D was, at the time, the most powerful jet engine in existence and mounting it on the 747 presented a major engineering challenge that stretched Boeing and Pratt to the extreme. The project also left Boeing exposed financially, since it was obliged to make huge investments in infrastructure to build the monster, and although orders were coming in, load factors were not rising as quickly as anticipated and the aircraft soon found itself operating under the high fuel prices of the 1973 crisis.

Pan Am had involved itself in the 747's development, and was naturally the first to place it into service. On 22 January 1969 it flew from New York to London, although engine overheating – the engines had caused numerous problems that flight testing on a B-52 had failed to illuminate – had caused a last-minute delay. TWA began 747 services between New York and Los Angeles on 25 February and soon the type was operating long-haul routes with multiple operators and spanning the globe. But it was now that the slow rate of increase in passenger numbers became apparent and the 747 might have seemed a huge mistake. Convinced that it was not, Boeing continued the aircraft's development.

Jumbo Variations

More powerful engines were sure to evolve and so they did, allowing Boeing to offer heavier 747s for longer ranges. It announced its intention to build the first such development in June 1968, the 747-200B entering service as a passenger carrier with KLM in February 1971, while -200C combi and -200F freighter variants were also built. The -200 series also offered airlines a choice of powerplant, between the JT9D, General Electric CF6 and Rolls-Royce RB.211, establishing a precedent that airlines subsequently came to expect.

Next Boeing enlarged the 747's passenger capacity by extending its upper deck, the resulting 747-300 flying for the first time on 5 October 1982. Customers could choose between the -200 and -300 variants, but the next 747 iteration, the high-tech 747-400, replaced all previous variants in production. First flown on 29 April 1988, the -400 employed an EFIS for its two-crew cockpit, replaced the JT9D engine option with Pratt & Whitney's PW4056, featured a longer-span wing with winglets and provided

for extra range through a tailplane fuel tank, as well as aerodynamic refinements.

Northwest Airlines placed the -400 into service in February 1989 and Boeing went on to deliver it in several variants, easily outselling the earlier machines. Boeing completed the series with the 747-400ER Extended Range airliner for Qantas and 747-400ERF freighter. The company had dominated the long-haul widebody market for three decades, but the increasing threat from Airbus, especially with the announcement of what became the A380, caused Boeing to rethink the 747.

It decided to stretch the fuselage for the first time, adding a longer-span wing with raked tips, more fuel and General Electric GEnx-2B67 engines, modified from those of the 787 and exploiting work done on the Dreamliner's 'electric architecture'. This 747-8I (Intercontinental), or just 747-8, continues to sell slowly, while the 747-8F freighter has found favour for its excellent economics, especially since Airbus elected not to proceed with a freighter A380.

Special Variants

The 747's unusual passenger capacity and weight-lifting capabilities have suited it to small numbers of orders for military forces. The U.S. Air Force operates a pair of VC-25A aircraft, illustrated here, modified with special accommodation and extensive communications systems, for presidential transport. It also has four E-4B aircraft in the National Airborne Operations Center role. The VC-25 and E-4 are based on the 747-200, while the now cancelled AL-1A laser-armed anti-ballistic missile aircraft was based on the 747-400F. Elsewhere, the Japan Air Self-Defense Force operates a pair of 747-400s as government

transports, while Iran took a 747-100 variant equipped as an inflight-refuelling tanker.

Several companies offer commercial freighter conversions, but perhaps the most radical airline development was the 747SP (Special Performance), designed to offer long ranges off shorter runways. Boeing built 45 SPs, identified by their 14.87m (48ft 8in) fuselage shrink, taller fins and enlarged tailplane span, the aircraft offered extreme performance, but by the time they were becoming established in service, Boeing had developed the -200B to cover similar ranges.

Aerospatiale/BAC Concorde (1969)

Concorde presented perhaps the most recognizable shape ever to fly. It reigned as the world's only viable supersonic transport for almost three decades before a tragic accident cut short its career. Regarded among the greatest technological achievements ever, its performance is unlikely to be repeated for many years to come.

Few aircraft are as instantly recognizable or have gained such publicity – positive and negative, depending on national sensitivities – as Concorde. Described by NASA engineers as more complex than the Apollo programme, Concorde achieved sustained supersonic passenger services, operating over the Atlantic from 1976 until 2003.

Aerospace manufacturers in Britain and France had studied supersonic transport technology during the late 1950s, realizing that the massive resources needed to bring such a machine into service were beyond any

G-BOAB was the eighth production Concorde, entering BA service after its first flight in 1976.

one nation, let alone a single company. British work had culminated in the BAC 223, while Sud-Aviation had created the Super Caravelle. Both were paper projects and their design teams had independently arrived at very similar configurations, albeit that the French wing was rather more advanced.

In November 1962 the nations formalized their SST plans, agreeing to combine the BAC design with the ogival wing of the Super Caravelle. Bristol Siddeley was chosen to adapt the afterburning Olympus turbojet it had produced for the abortive BAC TSR.2 strike aircraft into an SST engine, in cooperation with SNECMA, although Rolls-Royce absorbed Bristol Siddeley in 1966. The

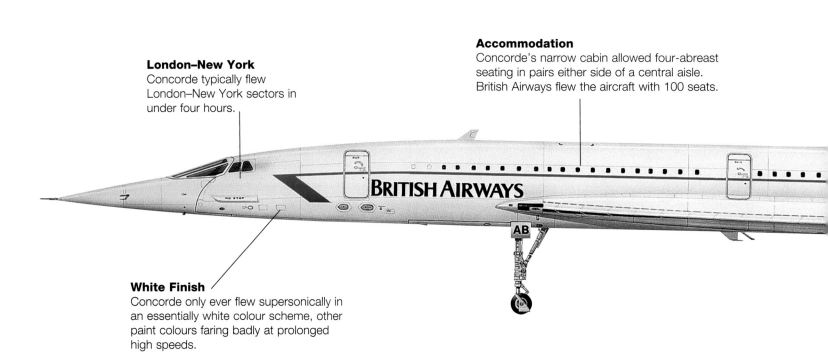

London–New York
Concorde typically flew London–New York sectors in under four hours.

Accommodation
Concorde's narrow cabin allowed four-abreast seating in pairs either side of a central aisle. British Airways flew the aircraft with 100 seats.

White Finish
Concorde only ever flew supersonically in an essentially white colour scheme, other paint colours faring badly at prolonged high speeds.

aircraft would cruise around Mach 2.2, since slower speeds were felt to bring too little improvement in journey times to tempt passengers onto the jet, while achieving higher speeds would stretch the technological possibilities too far.

The product of this joint working would be named Concorde and exercise the political and industrial capacities and goodwill of the two nations to the

extreme. There were challenges at every stage, from powerplant, through intake and nacelle design, to materials and aerodynamics. The UK flew three dedicated test beds – the BAC 221 assessed high-speed delta handling, the Handley Page HP.115 did the same at low speeds and an Avro Vulcan bomber was used for engine testing. The BAC aircraft was modified from a Fairey Delta 2, an airframe that had

Nose Undercarriage
The nose undercarriage leg was set 11.58m (38ft) aft of the cockpit, making for tricky taxiing characteristics.

Drop Nose
The pilot would lower the nose to improve visibility of the runway and taxiways.

Transonic Trimming
In the transonic regime an aircraft's centre of pressure moves aft, forcing the aircraft to rotate nose-down around its centre of gravity. Concorde employed special trimming tanks around which fuel was pumped to trim out this nose-down attitude that would otherwise have been countered with drag-inducing upward elevon deflection.

G-BOAB

Aerospatiale/BAC Concorde

Specification

Type:	long-haul supersonic airliner
Dimensions:	wing span 25.60m (83ft 10in), length 61.66m (202ft 4in), height 12.20m (40ft)
Maximum take-off weight:	185,070kg (408,000lb)
Powerplant:	four 169.20kN (38,050lb) thrust Rolls-Royce/SNECMA Olympus 593 Mk 610 afterburning turbojet engines
Maximum speed at cruising altitude:	Mach 2.04
Maximum range	6481km (4030 miles)
Service ceiling:	18,290m (60,000ft)
Flight crew:	3
Passengers:	up to 131 in single-class accommodation, but 100 in British Airways aircraft

introduced the drooping nose concept to improve pilot visibility on landing and take-off. All three aircraft were very successful, although the Vulcan suffered a fiery fate after an Olympus 593 test engine exploded during full-power ground runs.

Given the UK's 60/40 lead in powerplant development, Sud-Aviation took the 60/40 lead on airframe design.

There remained fundamental differences, however, including the question of design range, the French preferring a short-haul aircraft to the British requirement for transatlantic range. The latter won out and by early 1969 the two prototypes, one built in France, the other in Great Britain, were being prepared for flight.

Sud-Aviation was airborne first, flying aircraft 001 on 2 March, BAC taking 002 aloft on 9 April. Concordes 01 and 02 followed, acting as further prototypes, although labelled as pre-production machines. The former, a British machine, flew on 17 December 1971 and the latter, a French aircraft, on 10 January 1973, by which time Sud-Aviation had merged with Nord-Aviation and SEREB to form Aerospatiale.

Testing Times

A lengthy flight test programme befitting the aircraft's complexity followed, the Anglo-French team encountering many challenges, as did their Soviet counterparts on the Tu-144. Tupolev was developing its aircraft to a state requirement, however, while Concorde could expect orders from its national flag carriers, Air France and BOAC, but had to attract major orders from other airlines if its huge development costs were to be met and a profit turned.

Interest in Concorde grew as testing reached its conclusion and major airlines, including Pan Am and TWA, expressed interest. But the U.S. aerospace

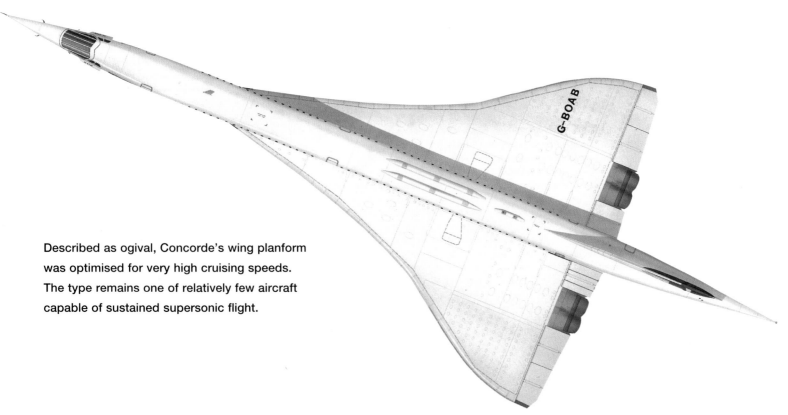

Described as ogival, Concorde's wing planform was optimised for very high cruising speeds. The type remains one of relatively few aircraft capable of sustained supersonic flight.

British Airways

British Airways, the UK flag carrier, used its Concordes to great effect, maintaining regular schedules, especially on the prestigious route to New York. Many individuals became frequent fliers, including senior business leaders, the rich and famous valuing the time saved across the Atlantic as well as the cachet of Concorde flying. This aircraft, G-BOAB, was retired at London Heathrow in 2000.

industry was not at all keen on U.S. airlines buying Concorde, since it had no viable projects of its own to offer as alternatives. When opposition to the potential nuisance from sonic booms grew, especially around the airports into which Concorde would fly, the U.S. manufacturers, according to some sources, actively fuelled the issue.

Now Concorde was restricted to supersonic flight over water, essentially limiting it to transatlantic and transpacific flights, and high-speed cruising over land, although even without environmental concerns, the oil crisis of 1973 had driven oil prices sky high – airliners with afterburners no longer made economic sense.

All potential operators but Air France and BOAC withdrew their interest and even then Concorde orders were pitifully small, the national carriers each taking

seven. In all just 20 aircraft were built, only 16 of them to production standards, and dividing the programme's massive costs over the 14 airframes delivered meant that Concorde would never cover its costs.

BOAC had merged with BEA to become British Airways by the time Concorde's operators began simultaneous services on 24 May 1976. Both carriers worked hard to offer premium services with their small fleets, as well as supersonic experience flights, charters and other 'specials', eventually turning over handsome operating profits, although they never scratched the surface of the aircraft's development costs. But then Air France lost a Concorde shortly after take-off from Paris in 2000. It never again flew a scheduled Concorde service and although BA performed extensive modification work to prevent a similar accident happening again, it retired its fleet in 2003.

McDonnell Douglas DC-10 and MD-11 (1970)

McDonnell Douglas entered the widebody market with the DC-10, a fine aircraft that became blighted by a series of accidents. The DC-10's successor, the MD-11 failed to deliver on performance promises, but both types have become valued as freighter conversions.

Like Boeing, Douglas had been unsuccessful in the CX-HLS programme and was keen to recoup at least some of its investment. Having proposed a 650-seat transport to the military, the company scaled back its ambition for the commercial market, identifying, as had Lockheed, space for a widebodied transport smaller than the 747. An aircraft of around 250 seats would be ideal for the U.S. domestic market, but obliged the Douglas product to go head-to-head with Lockheed's TriStar.

Meanwhile, a severe financial crisis had forced Douglas to seek a partner and on 28 April 1967 it merged with McDonnell, it falling to the new McDonnell Douglas company to launch the DC-10 in February 1968, with 50 orders already signed. The aircraft would be a trijet with a tail-mounted engine that employed a straight nacelle, with air intake, engine and exhaust in line. It was a configuration that made re-engining potentially more practical than in trijets with 'S' ducts and rear-fuselage

Now known as FedEx, the global parcel company is a major operator of DC-10 and MD-11 freighters, with around 61 MD-10-10/30 and 64 MD-11s in its global fleet late in 2014.

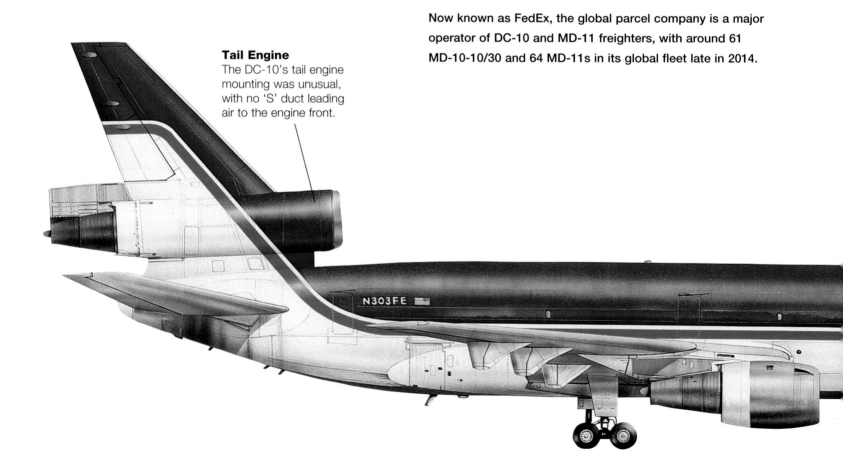

Tail Engine
The DC-10's tail engine mounting was unusual, with no 'S' duct leading air to the engine front.

N303FE

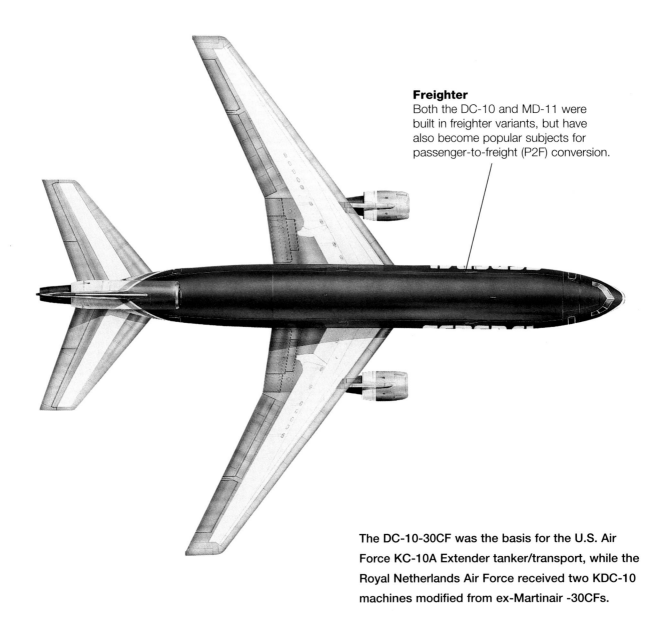

Freighter
Both the DC-10 and MD-11 were built in freighter variants, but have also become popular subjects for passenger-to-freight (P2F) conversion.

The DC-10-30CF was the basis for the U.S. Air Force KC-10A Extender tanker/transport, while the Royal Netherlands Air Force received two KDC-10 machines modified from ex-Martinair -30CFs.

Federal Express
Built in 1973, this aircraft remained in operation with FedEx in 2015.

FedEx Cockpit
FedEx has modernized its DC-10 fleet to produce the MD-10, equipped with an EFIS cockpit similar to that of the MD-11.

McDonnell Douglas DC-10 and MD-11

British Caledonian operated a variety of DC-10-10 and DC-10-30 aircraft, the latter including this machine.

mounted engines, as on the Boeing 727 and TriStar. The first of the initial DC-10 Series 10, or DC-10-10, aircraft completed its maiden flight on 29 August 1970, on the power of three General Electric CF6 engines. In the event, of the 446 aircraft subsequently built for civilian service, only 42 were built with an alternative engine, the Pratt & Whitney JT9D-20 powering DC-10-40s for

Specification (MD-11)

Type:	long-haul airliner
Dimensions:	wing span 51.66m (169ft 6in), length 61.21m (200ft 10in), height 17.60m (57ft 9in)
Maximum take-off weight:	273,300kg (602,500lb)
Powerplant:	three 268.24kN (60,300lb) thrust Pratt & Whitney PW4460 turbofan engines
Maximum cruising speed:	932km/h (579mph)
Design range:	13,358km (8300 miles)
Service ceiling:	9935m (32,600ft)
Flight crew:	2
Passengers:	up to 410 in single-class accommodation

Northwest Orient and the JT9D-59A equipping those of Japan Airlines.

American Airlines and United Airlines received the first DC-10-10s in a joint delivery ceremony on 29 July 1971. The model could accommodate up to 380 passengers ten-abreast, but was typically furnished for between 250 and 300. It remained in production until 1982 and 122 were built, the majority for major U.S. airlines.

Next McDonnell Douglas produced the DC-10-20, the Pratt-engined variant requested by Northwest Orient for engine commonality with its 747 fleet. Brought to market as the DC-10-40, it flew for the first time on 28 February 1972 and although it satisfied Northwest when it entered service on 13 December, the JT9D-20 was less powerful than the CF6D and not until the more powerful JT9D-59A became available did the -40 win another order, from JAL, for delivery between 1976 and 1981.

Long-haul Success

McDonnell Douglas achieved its greatest DC-10 success with the long-haul DC-10-30, with more power and a maximum take-off weight as much as 40 per cent greater than that of the original model, at 263,088kg (580,000lb).

An additional main undercarriage leg, introduced on the Series 20, was added under the wing centre section to better distribute the aircraft's greater weight and the variant took off for its maiden flight on 21 June 1972.

Swissair began transatlantic services with the -30 on 15 December 1972 and became the model's largest original operator, although it only took 13, illustrating the DC-10's trend for multiple small sales to lots of airlines – McDonnell Douglas never achieved the large-scale orders that Boeing managed. The last of 266 DC-10-30s and the last commercial DC-10 built went to Nigeria Airways in 1989.

A series of engine problems had caused disruption for the first few months of DC-10 operations, but then the first in a series of major accidents struck. A Turkish Airlines DC-10-10 suffered a cargo door failure and crashed near Paris in May 1974, with all 346 souls aboard lost. In June 1979 an American Airlines DC-10-10 lost its port engine on take-off at Chicago O'Hare, the

entire unit detaching and the aircraft coming down shortly after. Then, in November, an Air New Zealand DC-10-30 flew into Mount Erubus, Ross Island, Antarctica, during a sightseeing flight.

Only the Turkish accident could be blamed on flaws in the aircraft and then only indirectly, but the DC-10's reputation was irreparably damaged and its fate effectively sealed when a United Airlines DC-10-10 crashed at Sioux City, Iowa, in July 1989 after catastrophic engine failure.

Other, minor DC-10 variants included the DC-10-10CF convertible, hot-and-high DC-10-15 for Mexican Airlines and Mexicana, DC-10-30CF convertible and -30AF or -30F freighter, and extended-range DC-10-30ER. McDonnell Douglas examined a twin-engined 'shrink' as a rival to the Airbus A300, as well as a DC-10-60 stretch. The former was shelved, while the latter worked through MD-100 and MD-XX designations, before emerging as the MD-11.

MD-11

McDonnell Douglas elected to move away from the traditional DC (Douglas Commercial) designation system for its ultimate DC-10 iteration, preferring a new 'MD' designator. The aircraft represented the culmination of work that began with the -30 based DC-10-60 series, an aircraft considered outdated by airlines facing increasing fuel costs.

By 1982, McDonnell Douglas had replaced the design with the MD-100, equipped with the latest technologies for two-crew operations, and with advanced aerodynamics and new engines for improved economy. Unlike the -61 and -63 stretches, the MD-100 was of regular DC-10 length and again failed to garner interest.

Now McDonnell Douglas proposed the MD-XX, a stretch with CF6-80C2 or Pratt & Whitney PW4000 engines, launched formally as the MD-11 series on 30 December 1986 against a

number of commitments, many of which failed to mature, so that by late 1987 McDonnell Douglas was faced with only 30 firm orders.

The MD-11 flew for the first time on 10 January 1990 and the type entered service with Finnair on 20 December. Several small orders followed, but the MD-11 was not performing well and although the airframe and engine manufacturers worked hard to improve its range performance, it never reached brochure figures. The final two of 200 MD-11s built were MD-11F freighters delivered to Lufthansa Cargo in January 2001.

Lockheed L-1011 TriStar
(1970)

Lockheed produced an exceptional airliner with the trijet TriStar, but financial difficulties delayed the type's development and by the time a long-range variant was available, the majority of potential customers were already flying the rival DC-10-30.

By the mid-1960s, American Airlines had identified the potential for a 250-seat aircraft to serve its domestic routes and Lockheed began developing a widebody machine on this basis in 1966. By 1 April 1968 the company had accumulated 144 orders for its L-1011, from airlines including Eastern and TWA but ironically not American, which had signed for DC-10s.

Lockheed had schemed the L-1011 as a twin, but added a tail engine when the design became somewhat larger,

choosing the name TriStar to suit. It built a new facility for TriStar construction and flew the first prototype on 16 November 1970. The aircraft included Rolls-Royce RB.211 engines and the latest in technology, remaining at the forefront of development throughout its production run, but at this early stage Lockheed found itself in serious trouble.

The TriStar was Lockheed's final airliner design, the company subsequently concentrating on military aircraft.

BA TriStars
BEA had ordered nine TriStar 1 aircraft and these were delivered to British Airways in October 1974. Eight TriStar 200s and six 500s followed and BA performed several conversions to TriStar 50 and 100 standards.

Accommodation
BA typically flew its TriStar 500 with seats for 18 first class and 217 economy passengers.

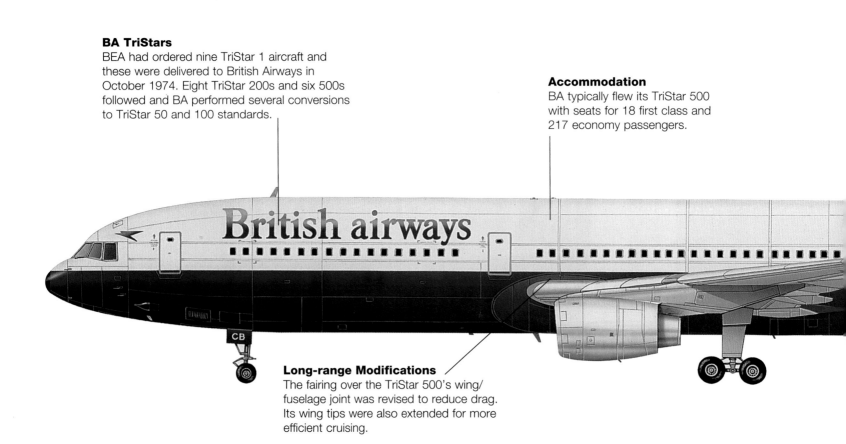

Long-range Modifications
The fairing over the TriStar 500's wing/fuselage joint was revised to reduce drag. Its wing tips were also extended for more efficient cruising.

Noise Reduction
A fillet inserted at the leading edge of the third engine's intake reduced cabin noise in the rear of the aircraft.

Entering service in May 1979, British Airways TriStar 500s served its long, thin routes to the Arabian Gulf, the Caribbean and U.S. East Coast. They served only briefly – BA was delighted to ease cash flow problems by selling them to the Royal Air Force in 1982.

Lockheed L-1011 TriStar

It had overrun development costs on the C-5 Galaxy airlifter significantly and these expenses, combined with the huge investment in the TriStar, had brought the company to its knees. The U.S. government moved to subsidize the airliner programme, but production slowed dramatically as employees were laid off. On 4 February 1971 the situation worsened dramatically. Rolls-Royce was also in deep financial trouble and the TriStar's design, with the tail engine mounted in the rear fuselage and fed with air by an 'S' duct, precluded the easy substitution of an alternative engine type.

Specification (TriStar 500)

Type:	long-haul airliner
Dimensions:	wing span 50.09m (164ft 4in), length 50.05m (164ft 2½in), height 16.87m (55ft 4in)
Maximum take-off weight:	228,610kg (504,000lb)
Powerplant:	three 222.35kN (50,000lb) thrust Rolls-Royce RB.211-524B turbofan engines
Maximum cruising speed:	973km/h (605mph)
Range with maximum passenger load:	9697km (6025 miles)
Maximum operating ceiling:	13,135m (43,000ft)
Flight crew:	3
Passengers:	up to 333 in single-class accommodation

Aircraft N1011 was the prototype TriStar. It remained with the programme throughout, taking on various test bed and proving roles.

The British government saved Rolls-Royce and the L-1011 programme continued, but it had incurred delays and lost orders so that while McDonnell Douglas sold 446 DC-10s, Lockheed delivered only 250 TriStars. Eastern took the first TriStar 1 on 5 April 1972, beginning scheduled services on 9 May, and sales of this domestic variant eventually outstripped those of the DC-10-10 equivalent.

Search for Range

With the TriStar in service, the airlines began their inevitable call for increased range. Lockheed responded with a bewildering array of modifications and production variants, some of the latter also produced by conversion of older airframes. The TriStar line delivered Series 1 aircraft in three Groups, each to a different empty weight as structural weight came down. These aircraft could be brought to a common maximum take-off weight by the TriStar 50 conversion, while the TriStar 100 modification added extra fuel tanks to TriStar 1 Group 3 aircraft for additional range. The TriStar 100 was also built as new.

The TriStar 150 delivered additional range through modification of Group 1 and 2 jets, while a number of TriStar 100s received more powerful RB.211-524B or B4 engines for improved hot-and-high performance, bringing them to TriStar 200 standard; 24 TriStar 200s were also built as such. Only six TriStar 250 aircraft were produced, all by modification from Group 3 standard with more fuel than the earlier conversions and more power. They were all for Delta.

Finally, the TriStar 500 was a production-only variant, with a shortened fuselage, greater fuel capacity and active control ailerons. The aircraft was the longest-ranged of the TriStars, easily transatlantic and ideal for so-called 'long, thin routes' requiring long range but generating insufficient passengers for larger aircraft.

The Series 500 typified the high technology incorporated into the TriStar programme, introducing Lockheed's active control system (ACS). This automatically reacted to aerodynamic loads caused by manoeuvring or turbulence, for example, deflecting the ailerons to counter their effects. Passenger comfort was improved and the wing off-loaded, so that longer tips could be fitted without any requirement for structural reinforcement. These tips increased aspect ratio and

reduced cruise drag for greater fuel economy. The TriStar had matured into an effective long-haul airliner, but the trevails of 1970–71 when Lockheed and then Rolls-Royce had cheated bankruptcy, had delayed development of the longer-ranged variants. By the time Lockheed began serious development work, the DC-10-30 was already flying; the definitive TriStar 500 entered flight test in 1978, but the DC-10-30 had entered transatlantic service in December 1972.

Only 50 TriStar 500s were completed, the last flying for the first time on 3 October 1983. Latterly with the Las Vegas Sands Corporation having served the Saudi Arabian Royal Flight, this aircraft is now in storage, while its sister ship may remain active. Only one other TriStar is known to be airworthy, Orbital using an aircraft modified as the 'Stargazer' to launch its Pegasus rocket. The most prolific recent TriStar operator, the Royal Air Force, flew a mix of aircraft in passenger transport and tanker/transport roles, retiring the type in March 2014.

Whisperjets

Among the TriStar's many qualities was its relatively low noise signature – it was noticeably quieter than the Boeing 747 and McDonnell Douglas DC-10, and Lockheed made the most of the fact in its marketing. Eastern Airlines also used the type's aural qualities as a selling point, labelling its L-1011s 'Whisperjet'. This aircraft, N301EA, was the second TriStar off the production line, first flown on 15

February 1971 and reaching Eastern in March 1973 after a period of flight testing. A Group 1 TriStar 1, it finished its career with AeroPeru and was broken up in March 1998. The Group 1 aircraft were build numbers 2 to 12 (operating empty weight 114,624kg/252,700lb), Group 2 were 13 to 51 (112,220kg/247,403lb) and Group 3 from 52 to the end of TriStar 1 production (108,864kg/240,000lb).

Airbus Industrie A300 and A310 (1972)

With the pioneering A300, Airbus Industrie proved its sceptics – especially those across the Atlantic – wrong and mounted a credible challenge to U.S. domination in the heavy airline market. The A310 development further strengthened the Europeans' credibility with its unprecedented performance.

After the Comet debacle and the apparent inability of British manufacturers to see beyond the niche requirements of their home airlines, the success of joint European working in overcoming the technical challenges of Concorde offered a glimmer of hope that a European entity might one day challenge U.S. dominance in the big jet market.

Europe's aircraft makers had reached very similar conclusions to their colleagues across the Atlantic, noting the need for a short- to medium-haul widebody with seating for between 200 and 250 passengers. Very similar observations had led Douglas to create the DC-10 and Lockheed the TriStar, and now a European team of the UK's Hawker Siddeley and the French companies Breguet and Nord began working on a new design.

Designated HBN 100, it was largely conventional in configuration and planned for a pair of Rolls-Royce turbofans. On 10 April 1969 the British withdrew, however,

West German IT airline Hapag-Lloyd took its first of four A310-200s in January 1988. It also received four A310-300s, having previously flown the A300B4-200.

Flight Deck
For its time the A310's flight deck was revolutionary, with six 16cm × 16cm CRT screens delivering all the primary diagnostic, flight and navigation data.

Engines
Airbus used U.S. engine technology on the A310, initially offering a choice of General Electric CF6 or Pratt & Whitney JT9D powerplants and later replacing the latter option with the PW4152.

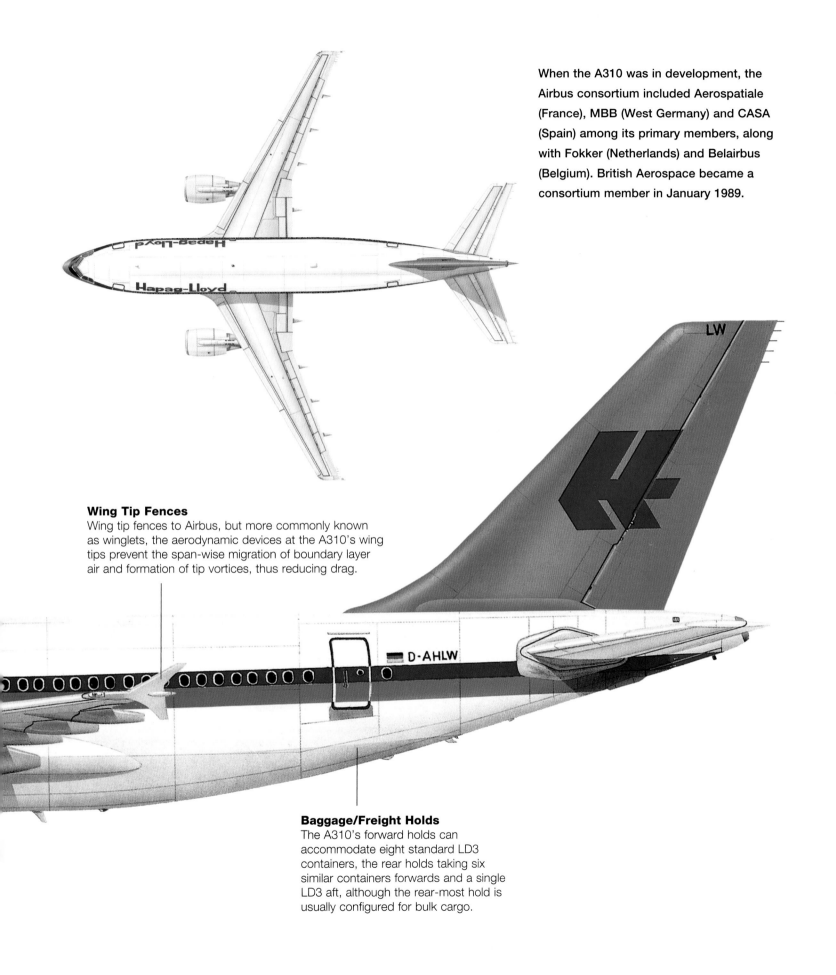

When the A310 was in development, the Airbus consortium included Aerospatiale (France), MBB (West Germany) and CASA (Spain) among its primary members, along with Fokker (Netherlands) and Belairbus (Belgium). British Aerospace became a consortium member in January 1989.

Wing Tip Fences
Wing tip fences to Airbus, but more commonly known as winglets, the aerodynamic devices at the A310's wing tips prevent the span-wise migration of boundary layer air and formation of tip vortices, thus reducing drag.

Baggage/Freight Holds
The A310's forward holds can accommodate eight standard LD3 containers, the rear holds taking six similar containers forwards and a single LD3 aft, although the rear-most hold is usually configured for bulk cargo.

Rolls-Royce opting to concentrate on the RB211 for the TriStar, although Hawker Siddeley eventually returned as a subcontractor, having the lost a potentially leading role. The title European Airbus had already been used for the programme, the design and manufacturing organization formally taking the title Airbus Industrie in December 1970.

With Rolls-Royce out of the equation, Airbus chose the General Electric CF6-50, essentially similar to the engine selected for the DC-10, to power what it temporarily designated the A250, but subsequently identified as the A300B, the number indicating the aircraft's maximum passenger load. It was designed for typical stage lengths of 2200km (1367 miles), but to return a profit over ranges as short as 650km (404 miles).

Although France's Sud-Aviation now took design lead, Hawker Siddeley took responsibility for the aircraft's extremely advanced wing, which employed a less complex set of high-lift devices than contemporary U.S. wings and used a superbly efficient aerofoil section.

Building the Airbus

Four development aircraft were planned, without a prototype. There was a possibility that the fourth of these A300B1 aircraft would be completed with RB211 engines, completing a circle intended to tempt BEA into an order, but in the event they all flew on General Electric power. There were differences between them, however, since Air France was keen to see an additional 24 passenger seats fitted and the second pair were completed to A300B2 standard, lengthened by 2.65m (8ft 8½in) through plugs inserted fore and aft of the wing.

Although it wore Air France colours, this A300B2, the fourth built, remained with Airbus Industrie until 1977, when it was delivered to Air Inter.

Air France subsequently placed the first A300 order, for just six A300B2 jets, but with options on a further ten. Now Airbus offered the A300B4, in hopes of increasing the model's appeal. Featuring a new centre wing tank and revised fuel system, its range was increased to 3700km (2300 miles) and it quickly won support – from Iberia, which placed its first order on 14 January 1972 and took a total of six aircraft. Lufthansa had been slow to commit to Airbus and had been keen to see a

Specification (A310-300, PW4156A engines, highest weight)

Type:	medium-haul airliner
Dimensions:	wing span 43.89m (144ft), length 46.66m (153ft 1in), height 15.80m (51ft 10in)
Maximum take-off weight:	164,000kg (361,550lb)
Powerplant:	two 249kN (56,000lb) thrust Pratt & Whitney PW4156A turbofan engines
Long-range cruising speed:	Mach 0.8
Maximum range:	9630km (5984 miles)
Flight crew:	2
Passengers:	up to 280 in single-class accommodation

reduced-capacity A300, but eventually signed for three A300B2s and four options on 7 May 1973.

The first A300B1 had been rolled out at Toulouse alongside the second production Concorde on 28 September 1972, flying for the first time on 28 October. An intensive period of test and demonstration flights followed before Air France placed the first A300B2 into service between Paris and London on 23 May 1974. As the type slowly became established, so Airbus revised its designation system, regular weight models taking a -100 suffix, those with higher weights -200. When SAS ordered a Pratt & Whitney JT9D-powered version, it was delivered as the A300B2-300.

Convertible and freighter versions of the B4 subsequently appeared as the A300C4-200 and A300F4-200, respectively, but far more B2 and B4 freighters were produced by conversion than on the production line. Most dramatically, Airbus worked on the stretched A300B4-600, subsequently redesignated

A300-600, with a new EFIS cockpit, revised wing with drag-reducing wing tip fences and other changes, and accommodation for 361 single-class passengers. The -600 flew for the first time on 8 July 1983, followed by the A300C4-600 in April 1984. The -600 had replaced the A300B4 series in production by early 1985 and revolutionized the type's sales prospects, especially when Airbus introduced the extended-range A300-600R, which first flew on 9 December 1987 against an American Airlines order.

The all-freight A300-600F similarly turned around the A300's fortunes as a freighter, becoming a firm favourite of FedEx, with which it entered service on 27 April 1994 after a maiden flight on 2 December 1993. Meanwhile, Airbus was also working on a smaller capacity A300B10, but this gained a new wing as well as a shortened fuselage and became the A310. The last aircraft off the A300/A310 production line was a -600F for FedEx, delivered in July 2007.

A310

The A300B10 morphed into the production A310, essentially a shortened A300 featuring a new, even more aerodynamically efficient wing designed by British Aerospace, which joined the programme late and therefore absorbed input from West Germany's MBB and VFW-Fokker, and France's Aerospatiale, which had already begun wing design work. Configured from the outset with an EFIS cockpit for two-crew operations, the A310 also featured revised tail and engine pylon assemblies. Optimized for smaller passenger loads over longer ranges

than the A300, the A310 was recognized as the most efficient airliner of its era, thanks largely to its exceptional wing. Aircraft were assembled on the A300 line, such was the commonality between the types, and the A310 first flew on 3 April 1982. A range of variants offering engine choices, increased weights and longer ranges followed, the ultimate A310-300 including a tailplane fuel tank (a similar installation was used on the A300-600R), for a full-payload range of 8300km (5157 miles).

De Havilland Canada DHC-7 Dash 7 (1975)

De Havilland Canada employed its extensive experience in building rugged STOL aircraft to develop a uniquely capable turboprop airliner. The Dash 7 not only satisfied a niche capability, but helped create a new genre of operation.

In the post-war period de Havilland Canada (DHC) busied itself with a series of aircraft of exceptional short take-off and landing (STOL) performance. Aimed in the first instance at the civilian market, the first of these rugged machines were the single-engined DHC-1 Beaver and DHC-3 Otter. The latter inspired the DHC-6 Twin Otter twin-engined turboprop, marking DHC's entry into the airliner market proper, albeit with an aircraft of only 19-seat capacity.

De Havilland Canada realized that many of the airlines operating the DHC-6 also required a larger aircraft, either to fly alongside the Twin Otter, or to replace it as their

operations grew. But they served smaller airports, or fields where access for traditional aircraft was difficult and the large turboprops then available – the Fokker F27, for example – were unsuited to such operations. DHC therefore set about creating a large turboprop suitable for these niche airlines.

It took the basic configuration of the Pratt & Whitney Canada (P&WC) PT6A-20 powered Twin Otter and enlarged it into an aircraft capable of accommodating 50 passengers on the power of four more powerful PT6A-50 engines. Designated DHC-7, the aircraft was named Dash 7 and optimized for flights of around one-hour duration,

High Wing
The DHC-7's high wing kept its propellers and engine intakes clear of possible foreign object damage and kept its fuselage close to the ground for independence from airport services.

Engines
Each of the Dash 7's PT6A-50 turboprops turns a four-bladed Hamilton Standard 24 PF propeller.

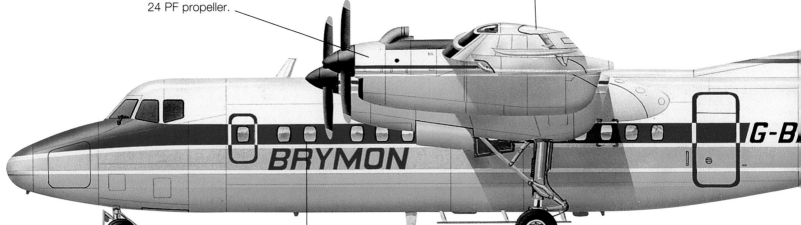

Passenger Accommodation
Standard seating is for 50 passengers, but 56 can be accommodated in a high-density layout.

having taken off in just 689m (2260ft) and landing in no more than 594m (1950ft). It was also exceptionally quiet, a quality that combined with its STOL capabilities to open up an entirely new airport genre.

The Dash 7's high-aspect ratio wing ensured excellent cruising capabilities, while the wash of its propellers augmented airflow over the wing and its large flaps, providing even greater lift. Raising the wing spoilers, setting the propellers to ground fine pitch and applying the wheel brakes brought the Dash 7 rapidly to a stop on landing, the change in propeller pitch alone reducing wing lift by around 90 per cent.

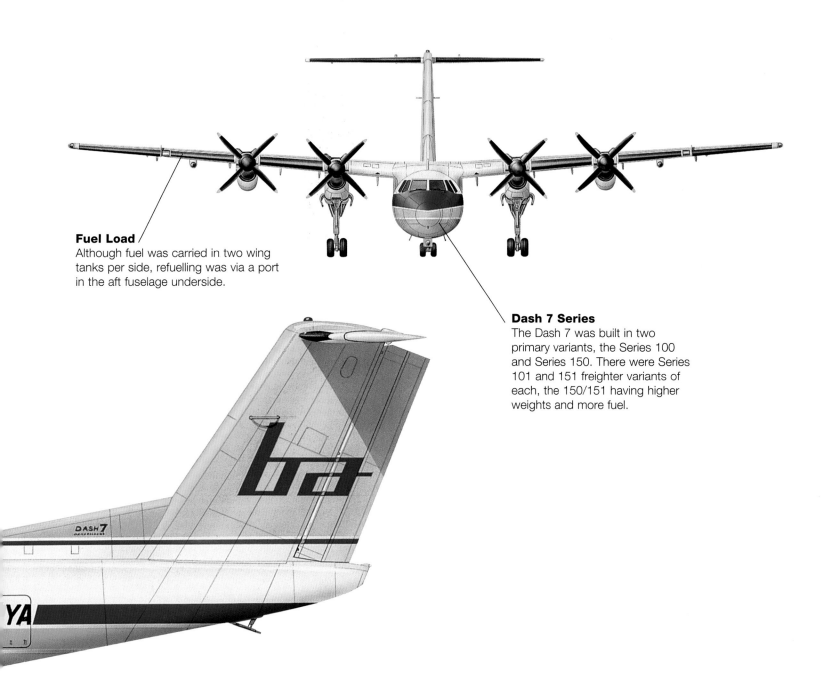

Fuel Load
Although fuel was carried in two wing tanks per side, refuelling was via a port in the aft fuselage underside.

Dash 7 Series
The Dash 7 was built in two primary variants, the Series 100 and Series 150. There were Series 101 and 151 freighter variants of each, the 150/151 having higher weights and more fuel.

Brymon Airways was a primary operator of the DHC-7 in the UK. It was instrumental in creating London City Airport, based on the Dash 7's ability to fly off the airfield's short runway.

De Havilland Canada DHC-7 Dash 7

Into Service

De Havilland Canada flew the new propliner for the first time on 27 March 1975, having begun work on the design during 1972. Type approval was granted by the Canadian Department of Transport on 19 April 1977

Specification (DHC-7 Dash 7 Series 100)

Type:	short-haul STOL airliner
Dimensions:	wing span 28.35m (93ft), length 24.59m (80ft 8in), height 7.98m (26ft 2in)
Maximum take-off weight:	19,958kg (44,000lb)
Powerplant:	two 1120shp Pratt & Whitney Canada PT6A-50 turboprop engines
Maximum cruising speed:	431km/h (268mph)
Range with 2948kg (6500lb) payload:	2180km (1355 miles)
Maximum cruising altitude:	7000m (23,000ft)
Flight crew:	2
Passengers:	up to 56 in single-class accommodation

This Dash 7 was the hundredth built and the fourth for Indonesian carrier Pelita Air Services.

and at the end of the year, Denver, Colorado-based Rocky Mountain Airways placed the Dash 7 into service. Another of the type's early operators illustrates the significance of the aircraft's capabilities, since before it took the DHC-7, Greenlandair had relied on the Sikorsky S-61 helicopter for many of its services.

The Dash 7's STOL performance was always its primary selling point in a very niche market, and DHC played it to the full. It promoted a Separate Access Landing System where the aircraft would use short sections of runway to perform STOL operations, using its unique capabilities to operate into and fly from sections of runway unavailable to other types. Ransome Airlines employed the system in New York and at Washington National, and Golden West Airways at San Francisco, while Maersk Air used it in Copenhagen. But where the Dash 7 was a real game-changer was at the world's downtown city airports.

Once the preserve of helicopters, smaller business aircraft and general aviation types, these facilities could now be opened up to airliner services with the Dash 7. The aircraft's low noise signature quickly allayed fears over noise pollution – in tests at Meigs Field Airport,

Chicago, its engines could barely be heard over the city's regular road traffic. Its STOL performance allowed the steep approaches and departures typically required for city airports and it needed the minimum of runway space from which to operate.

The Dash 7 therefore became the aircraft that allowed the city airports in Montreal and Toronto to expand and, perhaps more significantly, it was part of the deal that prompted the British government to approve the development of London City Airport in the heart of the capital's Docklands area. Dash 7 operator Brymon

Airways teamed with developer John Mowlem to promote the airport based on the DHC-7's capability to service it safely and with a minimum of noise disruption, and today inner city airports are widely accepted.

Of the 114 production Dash 7s that had been built by the time the line closed in 1988, a few dozen remained in service with civilian and military operators into 2015. Those airlines with Dash 7s still in their fleets tend to serve destinations with airports just as challenging as those for which the aircraft was originally designed and for which no obvious replacement has been forthcoming.

Dash 7 Legacy

The Dash 7's history is inextricably linked with that of Toronto, the DHC-7 production line having been established at nearby Downsview. Later the aircraft was instrumental in establishing full airline operations at the city's Billy Bishop Airport, located just offshore in the

waters of Lake Ontario. The Dash 8, from de Havilland Canada's successor, Bombardier, subsequently became the cornerstone of Billy Bishop's operation and there is every possibility that the Bombardier CSeries will continue the tradition.

Boeing 767 (1981)

Boeing trailed Airbus in the medium-haul, widebody twinjet market, after the success of the European A300 took the U.S. manufacturers by surprise. Its 767 contender was nonetheless an excellent aircraft that continues in production for commercial and military customers.

Boeing was initially content to leave the medium-haul widebody market to Lockheed and McDonnell Douglas. In keeping with contemporary U.S. thinking, it was also quick to dismiss Airbus Industrie as any threat to its position, but the European airframer shocked the world, first by developing its A300 and then by its quick success.

When Airbus developed longer-ranged A300 variants, the type became a natural replacement for older TriStar and DC-10 equipment, as well as the 707 Intercontinentals that remained in service. Boeing was obliged to respond with a medium-haul, widebody twin of

its own, while neither Lockheed nor McDonnell Douglas were able to compete. In fact Boeing had already been working through possible twin-jet configurations under the title 7X7.

A wide range of radical solutions had been dismissed by the time the company finally announced its 767 in July 1978. Boeing's launch coincided with that of the Airbus Industrie A310, demonstrating how far ahead of the game the Europeans were. At first glance the 767 looked

Air Seychelles took delivery of S7-AAS in 1989, naming it *Aldabra* – later it became *Isle of Aldabra*.

Passenger Load
The 767-200 typically flies with around 224 passengers in three classes, although 290 can be squeezed into an all-economy configuration.

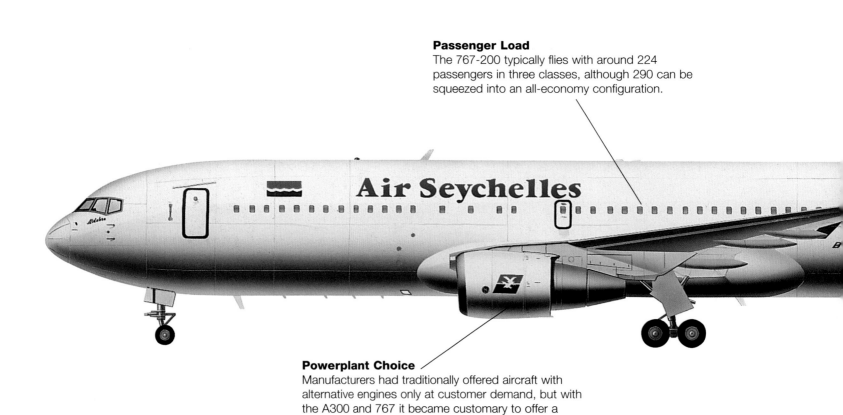

Powerplant Choice
Manufacturers had traditionally offered aircraft with alternative engines only at customer demand, but with the A300 and 767 it became customary to offer a choice from the outset.

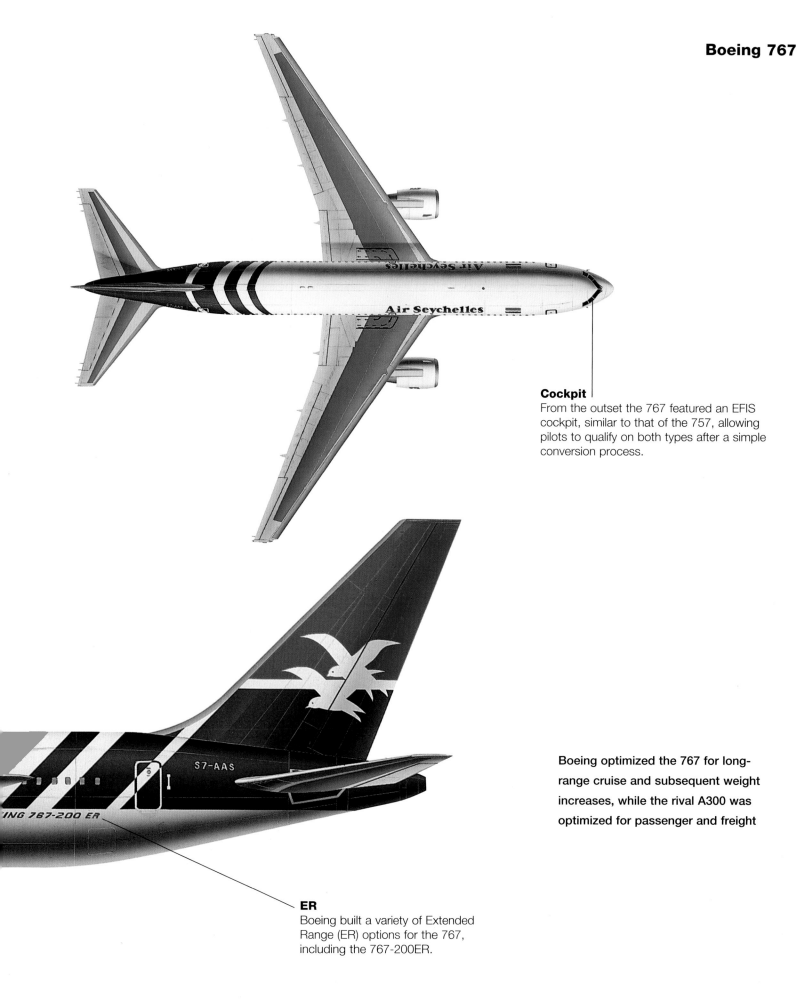

Cockpit
From the outset the 767 featured an EFIS cockpit, similar to that of the 757, allowing pilots to qualify on both types after a simple conversion process.

Boeing optimized the 767 for long-range cruise and subsequent weight increases, while the rival A300 was optimized for passenger and freight

ER
Boeing built a variety of Extended Range (ER) options for the 767, including the 767-200ER.

Boeing 767

very much like the A300 and critics suggested that Boeing was following its rival's high-tech lead, but closer inspection revealed that the U.S. jet was rather different in ambition.

The 767 was narrower than the A300, creating less drag, but also more cramped conditions for passengers in the eight-abreast seating that was standard on the Airbus. It was also impossible to load standard freight containers. On the other hand, the 767's wing was considerably larger than the A300's, lending itself not only to long-range cruise at high altitude, but also laying the foundations for subsequent fuselage stretches and increases in take-off weight.

Specification (767-200, JT9D-7R4D engines)

Type:	medium-haul airliner
Dimensions:	wing span 47.57m (156ft 1in), length 48.51m (159ft 2in), height 15.85m (52ft)
Maximum take-off weight:	136,080kg (300,000lb)
Powerplant:	two 213.51kN (48,000lb) thrust Pratt & Whitney JT9D-7R4D turbofan engines
Maximum speed:	914km/h (568mph)
Design range:	5852km (3636 miles)
Altitude at maximum take-off weight:	11,950m (39,200ft)
Flight crew:	2
Passengers:	up to 290 in single-class accommodation

All Nippon Airways took this 767-300 in July 1987. It remained with the airline until 2012, when it was withdrawn into storage.

Selling the 767

Small numbers of European jet airliners had entered service with U.S. carriers since the Caravelle, but the A300 had won favour on a new level. Boeing could still rely on parts of the traditional domestic market for orders, but in some cases its most ardent supporters were already flying the A300, having been offered no alternative when the Airbus salesmen came calling. Eastern Airlines and Pan Am were among Boeing regulars already flying the Airbus, but sufficient opportunities remained for significant sales, beginning with a 30-aircraft order from United, which allowed formal 767 launch on 14 July 1978.

A powerplant choice between the Genral Electric CF6 and Pratt & Whitney JT9D was offered from the outset, the Pratt-engined variant flying first, on 26 September 1981. The GE-powered 767 completed its maiden flight on 30 July 1982 and United took first delivery, of a JT9D aircraft, on 19 August. The early 767-200s soon proved their efficency and on this basis Boeing began exploiting the model's growth potential, producing the 767-200ER (Extended Range), with a variety of gross weights on offer, the highest of which took range out to 12,611km (7836 miles), compared to 6000km (3730 miles) for the baseline aircraft. Like the A310, the 767-200ER was optimized for long, thin routes, but with considerably more range.

An obvious next step was to increase capacity and this Boeing achieved with a 6.42m (21ft 1in) stretch through plugs fore and aft of the wing. The resulting 767-300 flew for the first time on 30 January 1986 and entered service with launch customer JAL on 25 September. The -300 was initially offered with the CF6 and JT9D, but Pratt subsequently replaced its engine with the PW4000, while a Rolls-Royce option was added with the RB211-524H. The 767-300ER inevitably followed, offering a range of maximum take-off weights and flying for the first time on 9 November 1986.

Boeing had cleverly extracted range and capacity from the 767 design, but Airbus was already working on its A300/310 successor, in an interesting pair of related aircraft, the A330 twin and A340 quad. The U.S. manufacturer responded with a further stretch to create the 767-400ER, but the market was never enthusiastic about

the variant and although the 767 remained in production as an airliner into 2015, it was as the -300ER.

Freighters and Tankers

The 767 had other talents that Boeing was keen to explore. As the 767-300F it made an excellent freighter, launched against a 60-aircraft order from UPS in January 1993 and first delivered in October 1995. The 767 was also chosen as the platform to satisfy a Japanese requirement for an airborne warning and control system (AWACS) aircraft after the 707 airframe used as the basis of the E-3 Sentry had completed production. The Japanese subsequently took KC-767 tankers, and Boeing separately developed the KC-46A tanker/transport for the U.S. Air Force, expecting to deliver the first production aircraft early in 2016.

767-400ER

Stretching the 767-300 and increasing fuel capacity compared to the -300ER, Boeing created the medium/long-haul 767-400ER, first flown on 9 October 1999. The model introduced the distinctive fuel-saving raked wing tips subsequently used on some 777 models, and was optimized as a replacement for longer-ranged DC-10 and TriStar

survivors, as well as the A300-600, A310 and MD-11, in which market it went head-to-head with the A330.

Boeing invested heavily in the -400ER, but even a world tour was insufficient to energize the market and only 38 aircraft were ordered, 21 for Delta, 16 for Continental and one for a private customer.

BAe 146 and Avro RJ (1981)

The Hawker Siddeley HS.146 eventually emerged as the impressive BAe 146 after a long and trying gestation that at one time threatened to scupper the UK's national aircraft industry. Reinvented as the Avro RJ, the series became the best-selling British jetliner.

Many years of concept definition preceded Hawker Siddeley's 1973 announcement of a new jet-powered transport seating up to 93 passengers and suitable for STOL operations from austere or semi-prepared airfields. The aircraft was also designed for a low noise signature – important for urban short-field operations in an era when aircraft noise was being recognized as an important issue.

Designated HS.146, the machine was, somewhat surprisingly, powered by four Lycoming ALF502 turbofans, whose low fuel consumption and noise provided the exacting performance required – no two engines at the time could have achieved the design goals. The high-set wing was tapered, but barely swept.

It carried huge trailing edge flaps for maximum lift, but thanks to the modest sweepback, no slats were required on the leading edge, simplifying design and saving weight.

The high wing configuration kept the fuselage close to the ground, ideal for easy servicing at poorly-equipped airports, especially if integral airstairs were fitted. Also in keeping with the aircraft's STOL capabilities, its rugged undercarriage featured widely spaced main gears for

The 146 found considerable favour as a feederliner for U.S. hub airports. Presidential Airways flew this 146-200 in Continental Express livery.

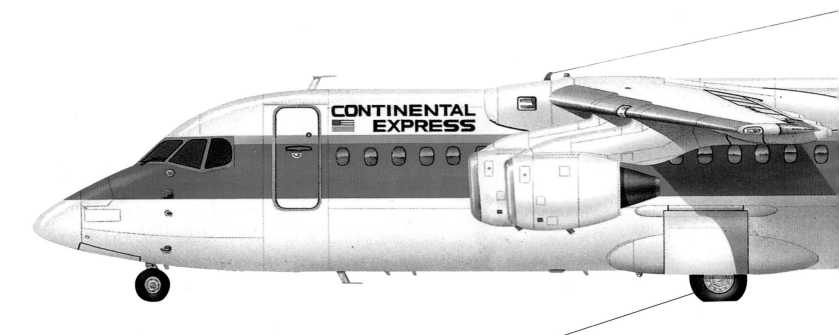

Main Undercarriage
Mounted on the sides of the centre fuselage, the retracted main undercarriage requires blister fairings to fully cover it. Wheel track is greater than that of the Lockheed C-130 Hercules military airlifter.

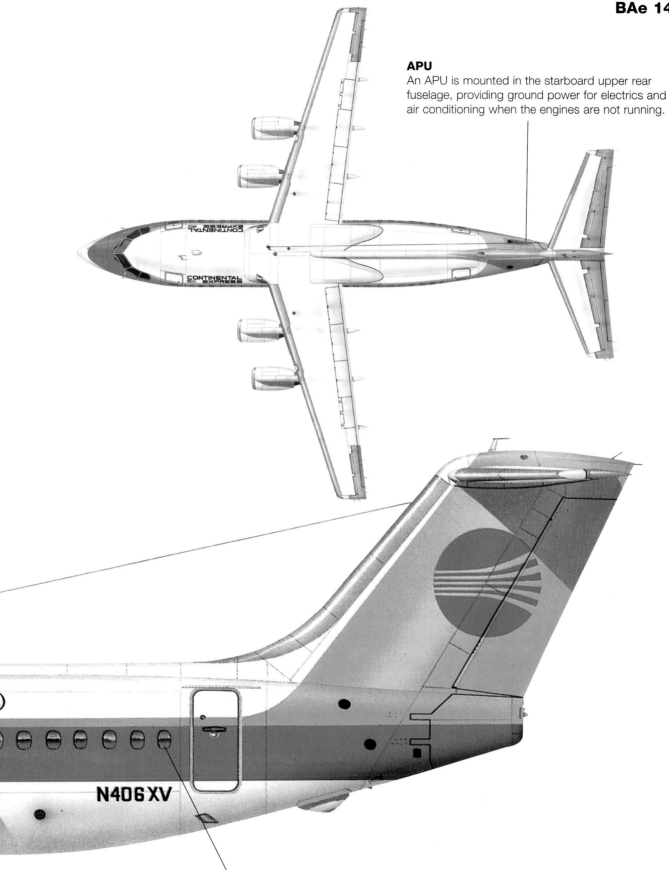

APU
An APU is mounted in the starboard upper rear fuselage, providing ground power for electrics and air conditioning when the engines are not running.

Cabin Comfort
Passenger comfort had been a priority for Hawker Siddeley, which aimed to offer Boeing 747-standards of accommodation. It therefore designed the 146 with a wide cabin and actually used 747 seats in its early mock-ups.

The British Royal Air Force's 32 (The Royal) Squadron operates the 146 on utility, VIP and Royal transport duties.

optimum stability. Steep approach angles were expected as a regular operational challenge and a split airbrake at the extreme rear fuselage delivered impressive speed control; combined with wing spoilers and powerful wheel brakes, it made thrust reverse provision unnecessary, further saving on weight and complexity. Finally, the tailplane was set high on a broad fin, well clear of the jet efflux. The fin ensured directional stability in the event of an outer engine failure at low speed.

On, Off and On Again

Launched with £92 million in government funding, the HS.146 quickly ran into trouble. It looked likely to make a financial loss, causing investors concern over Hawker Siddeley's wellbeing and, crucially, the prospects

Specification (146-200)

Type:	regional airliner with STOL capability
Dimensions:	wing span 26.21m (86ft), length 28.60m (93ft 10in), height 8.59m (28ft 2in)
Maximum take-off weight:	42,184kg (93,000lb)
Powerplant:	four 31kN (6970lb) thrust Lycoming ALF502R-5 turbofan engines
High-speed cruising speed:	669km/h (416mph)
Range with maximum payload:	2094km (1301 miles)
Flight crew:	2
Passengers:	up to 112 in single-class accommodation

Large numbers of 146 and RJ aircraft remain in service, many of the former as freighters. The RJ continues on important regional services, especially in Europe, with airlines including Malmö Aviation.

of the nationalized British Aerospace (BAe) that the government was working to create from the merger of Hawker Siddeley and BAC. The situation was remedied in October 1974 when the HS.146 was cancelled, although employees at Hawker Siddeley's Hatfield works, where much of the development work had been done, were so vehement in their protests at the decision that a trickle of funding was maintained.

Thus, when BAe came to review the HS.146 shortly after its creation in 1977, it discovered a useful aircraft with considerable market potential and the programme was formally relaunched after receiving government backing on 10 July 1978. Now little time was lost and the BAe 146-100 prototype became airborne for the first time on 3 September 1981. The type entered service with Dan-Air on 27 May 1983, serving Innsbruck from the UK, the Austrian airport having never before enjoyed a jet service.

The 146 was the ideal platform for the 1980s' rise in city airports, typically with short runways, demanding approach and take-off profiles and strict noise restrictions. The 146-100 satisfied all these requirements with ease and also allowed operators already established at such airports to expand from their turboprop – typically Dash 7 – equipment, onto jets.

146 Series

With the 146-100 excelling in service, it became clear that some operators would gladly compromise a little on the aircraft's STOL performance in order to gain more passenger seats. The stretched 146-200 therefore flew for the first time on 1 August 1982, quickly supplanting the -100 in production. Seating around 100 passengers, the -200 first went to Air Wisconsin, the 146's wide cabin allowing six-abreast seating.

When the model began entering widespread service with Pacific Southwest Airlines (PSA), however, its accommodation was found a little too tight for the typically larger-built Californian passenger, obliging PSA to reduce

capacity to fewer than 90. BAe therefore stretched the fuselage again, producing the 146-300, which could seat 103 passengers five abreast in its 30.99m (101ft 8in) long fuselage.

All three 146 variants were certificated for operations into London City Airport, where the -100 had proven the viability of jets. They also formed the basis for the 146-QT Quiet Trader freighter and 146-QC Convertible, before the 146 was phased out of production in favour of the modernized Avro RJ.

Avro RJ

During the early 1990s BAe consolidated 146 production at its Woodford facility near Manchester, UK, reviving the old Avro title for the organization. Woodford had already built 146s alongside Hatfield, flying its first in 1988, but now it was to manufacture an upgraded variant under the designation Avro RJ. The four-model RJ series was subsequently produced with EFIS cockpits and more powerful AlliedSignal (which had taken over Lycoming) and subsequently Honeywell LF507 engines. The RJ70 was equivalent to the 146-100, RJ85 to the -200 and RJ100 to the -300, while

the RJ115 was essentially an RJ100 equipped for higher weights.

The first RJ, an RJ85, completed the type's first flight on 23 March 1992 and the first production aircraft, an RJ100, went to Crossair on 2 April 1994. Offering 146 capability with modern systems, the RJs sold well, but BAE Systems (BAe had merged with Marconi Electronic Systems to form BAE Systems on 30 November 1999) cancelled a further upgraded variant, designated RJX, after only three aircraft had been built.

Boeing 757 (1982)

Airbus had once again forced Boeing's hand when the U.S. manufacturer announced the 757 as a replacement for ageing 727s and challenger to the A321. The new twinjet offered operators exceptionally efficient service and demonstrated unexpectedly long range.

Boeing studied replacement options for the 727 short/medium-range trijet through the early 1970s, the availability of the Airbus A300 adding impetus to a project that by 1976 was designated 7N7. Various ideas based on re-engining and stretching the 727 had been abandoned, so that the 7N7 featured a pair of high-bypass turbofans under its wings, which were all new, and a T-tail configuration.

As it became clear that the larger iterations of 7N7 were likely to be most popular, so the new Rolls-Royce RB211-535 engine emerged as lead powerplant. In 1979

the T-tail idea was dropped in favour of fuselage-mounted tailplanes and the nose and cockpit section from the 767 was adopted, albeit mated to a narrowbody fuselage very similar to that of the 707/727/737.

British Airways and Eastern had placed simultaneous launch orders on 31 August 1978, the British airline having been particularly enthusiastic in its encouragement

Royal Air Maroc, Morocco's flag carrier, took its first pair of 757-200 jets in 1986. It has been faithful to Boeing products since 1970, when it began operating the 727.

Production
Several subcontractors contributed to the 757, most importantly Northrop Grumman, which supplied the rear fuselage. LTV built the fin in conventional alloys, while Shorts was responsible for the inboard flaps and CASA the outers.

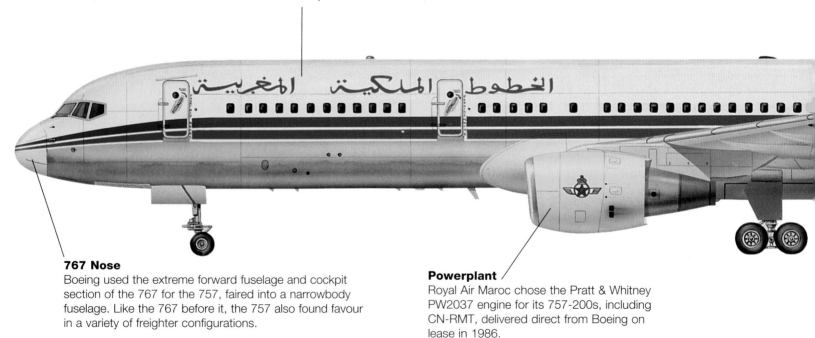

767 Nose
Boeing used the extreme forward fuselage and cockpit section of the 767 for the 757, faired into a narrowbody fuselage. Like the 767 before it, the 757 also found favour in a variety of freighter configurations.

Powerplant
Royal Air Maroc chose the Pratt & Whitney PW2037 engine for its 757-200s, including CN-RMT, delivered direct from Boeing on lease in 1986.

Carbon Composites
Weight-saving composites were used for the elevator and rudder skins, as well as aileron, flap, slat and spoiler components.

Fuel Capacity
In basic form the 757-200 held 42,597 litres (11,253 U.S. gal) of fuel.

Boeing 757

of Rolls-Royce's involvement. In fact the two UK companies worked together in attempting to persuade the national aerospace industry to build 757 wings rather than supporting Airbus Industrie. The attempt failed and although Rolls-Royce never offered an engine for the A300/310, British Airways subsequently purchased aircraft from the Airbus A320 series.

757 Defined

An order drought followed the initial signings, continuing until April 1980, when orders for just three aircraft each

Nepal Airlines has operated nine different 757-200s, including 9M-ACA, delivered in September 1988.

came from Aloha and Transbrasil. Both airlines specified a new variant of the proven CF6, to be developed by GE in cooperation with Sweden's Volvo Flygmotor and labelled CF6-32. Delta followed with a more significant order – for 60 aircraft – in November, eventually announcing its engine choice as the Pratt & Whitney PW2037, promoted by the manufacturer as the world's most efficient turbofan.

American was next to order, again specifying the PW2037 and, Aloha and Transbrasil were soon forced to switch to the P&W unit after General Electric withdrew the CF6-32. The first 757 was Rolls-Royce powered, however, the RB211-535C proving spectacularly competent from the type's maiden flight on 13 January 1982. Boeing had combined the latest technologies and design philosophy in the 757 to produce an extremely efficient 727 replacement and A300 challenger, but had not pushed the boundaries in the way it had with the 727 and 747, for example. Like the 767, the 757 featured an EFIS cockpit with comprehensive mechanical backup and although it introduced some new navigation equipment and employed graphite-composite construction, it was essentially conventional throughout. The type entered service with Eastern on 1 January 1983, debuting in Europe with British Airways on 9 February.

Perhaps the most surprising 757 feature was the Rolls-Royce engine, which proved more reliable than any

Specification (757-200, RB211-535E4 engine)

Type:	short/medium-haul airliner
Dimensions:	wing span 38.05m (124ft 10in), length 47.32m (155ft 3in), height 13.56m (44ft 6in)
Maximum take-off weight:	113,395kg (250,000lb)
Powerplant:	two 178.37kN (40,100lb) thrust Rolls-Royce RB211-535E4 turbofan engines
Maximum cruising speed:	Mach 0.8
Maximum range:	7070km (4400 miles)
Cruising altitude:	11,795m (38,700ft)
Flight crew:	2
Passengers:	up to 231 in single-class accommodation

commercial engine that had gone before. Engine removals due to failure were almost non-existent and the RB211's efficiency enabled considerable expansion beyond the 757's predicted 3700km (2300-mile) range to 7080km (4400 miles). Several airlines later exploited this range for long-haul operations over thin routes, even on transatlantic services, on which the aircraft became even more efficient when retrofitted with winglets.

Stretched at Last

Boeing had considered offering various lengths and other variations of 757, but by the time the aircraft entered service it had settled on building only the 757-200, offered with a choice of Pratt & Whitney and Rolls-Royce engines. As such the jet sold extremely well, especially to U.S. domestic carriers, which appreciated its ability to operate their longer and shorter sectors with equal efficiency. But there had always been some potential

customers, especially in Europe, which suggested the aircraft's capacity was insufficient to make the most of its long range. These airlines wanted an aircraft of equal performance but with more seats, to reduce seat/mile costs on longer services and increase revenue.

When Airbus began satisfying such customers with longer-ranged A321 options, Boeing announced the 757-300, revealed in 1996 with a 7.10m (23ft 4in) stretch and single-class accommodation for up to 289 passengers. The aircraft was especially suited to IT and charter work, Condor, Germany's specialist in the market, emerging as launch customer with a 2 September 1996 order for 12 757-300s. The 'stretch' flew for the first time on 2 August 1998 and Condor took the first customer aircraft on 10 March 1999, but sales were disappointing and production ceased after 55 aircraft had been delivered. By the time production of all 757 variants finished on 28 November 2005, 1049 aircraft had been delivered.

757 Service

America West Airlines was typical of the many U.S. domestic operators that made extensive use of the 757. It took four -200s from new, for delivery between December 1987 and November 1989, as well as taking several others on lease. American was among the major U.S. customers, taking 126 757-200s; other major operators included Delta (116) and United (148, including nine -300s). In Europe British Airways was a primary customer, taking its fiftieth

and last 757-200 on 11 June 1999. The 757 also found favour with IT and charter operators all over the world.

Boeing now offers the 737-900 and -900ER as 757 replacements. They hold as many as 220 passengers in single-class accommodation, but their range falls short and several operators continue to canvass Boeing for a genuine 757 replacement.

Saab 340 and 2000 (1983)

Saab worked with Fairchild to produce the exceptional SF340 turboprop, then struck out alone to develop the improved 340B and high-performance 2000. Denied contemporary sales by the first regional jets, today the Saab 2000 remains a popular aircraft.

Keen to enter the regional turboprop market, Sweden's Saab concluded that it needed a foreign partner to share the financial burden of developing and marketing such a machine. In particular, it had hoped for a U.S. partner and in June 1979 signed a preliminary deal with Fairchild Republic, under which Saab engineers began working alongside their U.S. colleagues at Fairchild's Long Island, New York, facility.

The Swedes had already created the Saab 1084 design for a high-wing civil and military aircraft, and this was refined into a low-wing proposal for the commercial market only. Seating between 35 and 37 passengers, it would exploit the latest in airframe, digital avionics and propulsion technologies to achieve the most favourable operating economics possible.

Considerable use was made of weight-saving composites, although much of the primary structure remained metal. Nevertheless, further weight was saved by extensive use of bonding instead of riveting. The advanced wing offered very low drag and mounted a pair of General Electric CT7 turboprops of 1700shp each, driving four-bladed composite propellers. The result of this ambitious input from the Fairchild and Saab designers was, ironically,

Bar Harbor operated its Saabs in Continental Express colours, feeding passengers into the mainline carrier's hubs.

Passenger Seating
The 340 typical accommodates 37 passengers in 12 rows of three, with the 37th seat at the front of the cabin to starboard and facing aft.

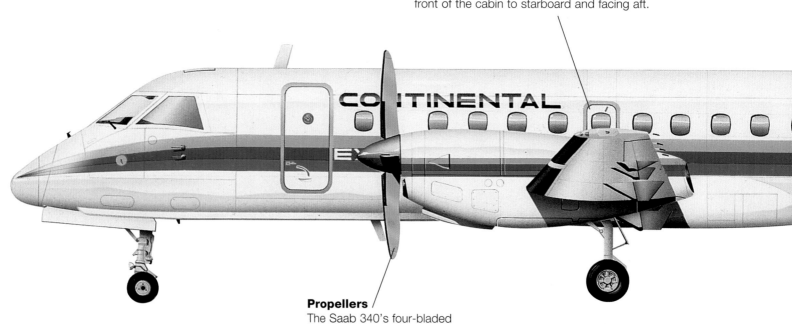

Propellers
The Saab 340's four-bladed Dowty propellers featured composite blades and elegant spinners.

Delivered in 1986, this Saab 340A was built after Fairchild had become a subcontractor to Saab. The companies had embarked on the programme as partners.

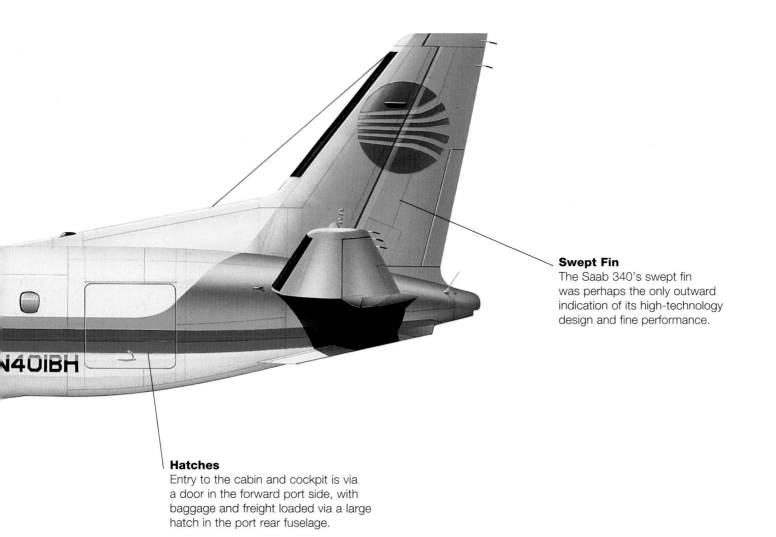

Swept Fin
The Saab 340's swept fin was perhaps the only outward indication of its high-technology design and fine performance.

Hatches
Entry to the cabin and cockpit is via a door in the forward port side, with baggage and freight loaded via a large hatch in the port rear fuselage.

SE-ISA was the second Saab-Fairchild SF340. It was later rebuilt as the 340B prototype.

Specification (Saab 340B)

Type:	turboprop regional airliner
Dimensions:	wing span 21.44m (70ft 4in), length 19.73m (64ft 8¾in), height 6.86m (22ft 6in)
Maximum take-off weight:	12,927kg (28,500lb)
Powerplant:	two 1750shp General Electric CT7-9B turboprop engines
Maximum cruising speed:	522km/h (325mph)
Range at long-range cruising speed:	1807km (1123 miles)
Standard service ceiling:	7620m (25,000ft)
Flight crew:	2
Passengers:	up to 37 in single-class accommodation

an aircraft of entirely conventional appearance, designated as the Saab-Fairchild 340A.

Production Responsibility

The two companies divided production between themselves, although Saab undertook final assembly in Sweden and certification was initially to Swedish standards. Fairchild designed the empennage, engine nacelles and wings, Saab the remainder of the airframe. A public announcement on 25 January 1980 revealed the new airliner to the world and Saab began construction of a new factory specifically to manufacture it. Five prototypes were built, the first completing its initial flight on 25 January 1983.

Switzerland's Crossair had ordered the SF340 in November 1980 and debuted the aircraft in service on 14 June 1984. It quickly proved capable and popular, allowing Saab to break into the lucrative U.S. feederliner market; Cincinnati's Comair was second into service with the SF340A in October 1984. But all was not well at Fairchild, which withdrew as a programme partner in 1985, remaining involved only as a subcontractor. Saab took full control from 1 November and then assumed responsibility for empennage and wing production, expanding its Swedish facility to do so from 1987. Fairchild closed for business in 1988 and from the 110th example the aircraft became the Saab 340A.

Hot-and-High

The 160th aircraft was produced to a new standard, designated 340B and optimized for hot-and-high operations, with greater power from CT7-9B engines and a wider tailplane. The prototype had flown for the first time in April 1989 and deliveries commenced in September.

Meanwhile, Saab had been working on a re-engined, stretched variation launched late in 1988 as the Saab 2000. While it remained under development, elements of the new aircraft's technology were used to improve the 340B, producing the 340B Plus, first delivered to American Eagle/Wings West in April 1994.

Among its new features the aircraft boasted a Saab 2000 interior, active noise suppression and longer wing tips. It could be specified with modifications for rough-field operation, including structural reinforcement and the application of resistant coatings to the undersides. Typically seating between 35 and 37 passengers three

abreast, the Saab 340 in all its variants had become a stalwart of U.S. feederliner and commuterliner routes, the American Eagle and Northwest Airlink operators flying in excess of 250 examples between them. A little more than 450 Saab 340s were manufactured, however, and around 200 of these remained in service into 2015, some as cargo aircraft, but many remaining as primary passenger-carrying equipment.

Ironically, Saab found continued demand for the 340 and 2000 after it had closed the production line in 1999 and continues to manage healthy demand for used aircraft in the second-hand and leasing markets. Indeed, such is the aircraft's popularity that in May 2013 a cabin upgrade was agreed between Saab and seat-manufacturer Acro. Using the latest in technologies to increase passenger appeal, the lightweight seats are also sculpted to provide additional legroom, so that even at 71cm (28in) pitch (the industry minimum) passengers experience the impression of 76cm (30in) pitch. Performance limitations mean that no additional seats are installed in the 340, but there is potential for Saab 2000 capacity to be expanded from a typical 50–53 seat configuration to 56, with no reduction in comfort.

Saab 2000

During the 1990s the Saab 340 became outdated as airlines looked for larger aircraft that could operate at near-jet speeds over short routes, but at a fraction of jet costs. Saab therefore redesigned the 340 as the 50-seat 2000, launched in December 1988 with an order for 25, plus 25 options, from Crossair.

Stretched by 7.55m (24ft 10in) compared to the 340, the 2000 could seat up to 58 single-class passengers and featured an EFIS cockpit. Power came from a pair of 4152shp Allison GMA 2100 turboprops driving six-bladed propellers and Saab worked hard to reduce cabin noise, including development of an active noise-reduction system.

The prototype first flew on 26 March 1992, but stability issues delayed service entry until 30 September 1994, when Crossair received its first aircraft. Later the airline painted one of its 2000s in a special scheme to promote the musical The Phantom of the Opera. In service the Saab 2000 excelled, but came to market just as Bombardier and Embraer were beginning to make jet services over short routes at near-turboprop economics possible. Saab was unable to maintain production in the face of such competition, and curtailed the 2000 at the 63rd aircraft in 1999.

De Havilland Canada DHC-8 Dash 8 and Bombardier Q Series (1983)

De Havilland Canada satisfied demand for a turboprop regional airliner of intermediate capacity with its DHC-8, moving its focus away from outright STOL performance. Today the aircraft remains a market leader as the radically-developed Bombardier Q400 NextGen.

While customers appreciated the Dash 7's STOL performance, there were many sectors on which it was not required, while there were also airlines keen to purchase a turboprop offering capacity between the 19 or 20 seats of the Twin Otter and 50 of the Dash 7. For these potential customers the soon-to-fly Fokker 50 was too large, while the F27 was being phased out of production. Embraer was entering the market with its EMB-120 Brasilia, beginning a rivalry that continues between the Brazilian company's

E-Jet and Bombardier's CSeries, while the ATR 42 was in development, establishing another challenger for de Havilland Canada and, ultimately, Bombardier, today's Q400 and the ATR remaining competitors. It was into this arena that de Havilland Canada launched the Dash 8.

The manufacturer chose to disclose its Dash-X work at the 1979 Paris Air Show, taking an order for two aircraft from NorOntair, a DHC-6 operator based in Ontario, in April 1980. Four prototypes of what had now become the Dash 8 were

Typical of de Havilland Canada's loyal home customers, City Express operated Dash 8-100s out of Toronto Island Airport – later named Billy Bishop Airport – during the late 1980s and early 1990s.

Fuel
The Dash 8 was designed with integral tanks in its wings, outboard of the engines, holding 3160 litres (835 U.S. gal) of fuel.

Passenger Door
The forward passenger door features an integral airstair, while the aircraft's high wing brings doors and hatches close to ground level for easy ground handling.

Passengers
The DHC-8-100 typical accommodates 36 passengers in nine rows of 2+2 seating with a central aisle. Remarkably, the latest Q400 NextGen variant seats up to 86 passengers.

built, the first flying on 20 June 1983 and initial delivery, to NorOntair, followed on 23 October 1984.

Originally designed for 36 passengers, the Dash 8 in its final form was not entirely devoid of STOL capability, but at 1000m (3280ft), its field length was considerably longer than that of the DHC-7. Relinquishing the extreme STOL capabilities of the earlier aircraft left the Dash 8 less compromised in other areas of performance, so that it was able to cruise at considerably higher speeds. This quality was especially important for operators flying short routes in the U.S. market, where near-jet speeds were required, but jet economics made little sense.

Baggage
A large door in the port side of the rear fuselage provides access to the 8.5m³ (300cuft) baggage/cargo hold.

The aircraft retained the high-wing/T-tail configuration of its predecessors, the former mounting two Pratt & Whitney Canada PW120 turboprops, each considerably more powerful – at 1800shp – than the 1120shp engines of the Dash 7. Consideration was given to mounting the Dash 8's main undercarriage in blisters on the lower centre fuselage,

The Dash 8/Q Series has won considerable popularity with regional airlines operating feeder services for the mainline carriers. This Dash 8-100 wears Canadian Regional colours.

but in the end DHC opted for long undercarriage units retracting into the undersides of the engine nacelles. The compromise this represented in terms of additional weight and complexity was thought worth it for the additional stability it gave during crosswind operations.

Specification (Q400 NextGen optional increased gross weight version)

Type:	turboprop regional airliner
Dimensions:	wing span 28.40m (93ft 3in), length 32.80m (107ft 9in), height 8.40m (27ft 5in)
Maximum take-off weight:	29,574kg (65,200lb)
Powerplant:	two 5071shp Pratt & Whitney Canada PW150A turboprop engines
Maximum cruising speed:	667km/h (414mph)
Range with 74 passengers:	2063km (1282 miles)
Maximum operating altitude:	8230m (27,000ft)
Flight crew:	2
Passengers:	up to 86 in single-class accommodation

Dash 8 Developed

With the original variant designated Dash 8 Series 100, DHC-8-100 or Dash 8-100 progressing, DHC's attention turned to the Series 200. Schemed for 2200shp PW122 engines, the design subsequently remained dormant until the early 1990s, while DHC instead moved ahead with the Series 300 stretch, which it announced during 1985.

A pair of fuselage plugs fore and aft of the wing extended the fuselage by 3.43m (11ft 3in), producing a cabin for 50 passengers. Power came from the 2380shp PW123 and, among other changes, wing span was enlarged and maximum weight increased. The model flew for the first time on 15 May 1987 and deliveries began in February 1989.

Boeing had bought DHC in January 1986 and under its ownership the company announced the even longer Series 400 in June 1987. Some 6.83m (22ft 5in) longer than the

Series 300, the latest model was designed for 78 passengers.

Revamping the DHC-8-100's interior and upgrading with PW120A engines produced the Series 100A in 1990, simultaneous with Boeing declaring its intent to divest DHC – the company became part of Bombardier in January 1992. The new owner soon introduced the PW121-powered Series 100B with improved field performance, while adding PW123C engines to the Series 100A improved payload and performance to resurrect the Series 200 designation, in the Dash 8-200A. The subsequent Dash 8-200B employed PW123D engines capable of delivering full power under hot-and-high conditions. There were also Series 300A/B and C variants, applying similar changes to the longer aircraft.

Q Series

With the Dash 8 remaining popular but facing stiff competition, especially from ATR, Bombardier undertook an improvement programme across the range, introducing a noise and vibration suppression (NVS) system and new interiors. The NVS reduced cabin noise by 12dB and by way of recognition Bombardier redesignated the Dash 8 as the Q (for quiet) Series, continuing production of the Q100, Q200, Q300 and Q400 variants.

Production of the three smaller models was subsequently phased out, Bombardier concentrating on the Q400. It has since upgraded the basic aircraft once again and the considerably revised Q400 NextGen continues to win sales worldwide and remains the focus of constant development.

Q400 NextGen

Powered by 5071shp PW150A turboprops driving six-bladed Dowty composite propellers, the NextGen is in many ways a new aircraft. It offers very high cruising speeds, delivering negligible differences in flight time over shorter sectors compared to regional jets. Alternatively, many operators are reaping the benefits of improved fuel economy by cruising just a little more slowly, losing just a few minutes to the jets, but remaining faster than the rival turboprop from ATR over the same distances.

In 2014, Bombardier confirmed its intent to offer Wi-Fi connectivity as a Q400 feature, as well as launching 50- and 68-seat Combi variants, while offering dual-class and 86-seat high-capacity options for the all-passenger variant.

ATR 42 and 72 (1984)

Aerospatiale and Aeritalia joined forces to create a new turboprop regional airliner for the 1980s. The ATR 42 and 72 have proved themselves flexible and economical in service and the latest Series 600 variants continue to sell well.

In 1981 France's Aerospatiale joined with Italy's Aeritalia to form Avions de Transport Regional (ATR) for the design and development of a high-tech turboprop regional airliner to satisfy emerging demand for such a machine. Since that time, consolidation in the European aerospace industry has modified the organization of the original partners, so that ATR is now the result of cooperation between the Airbus Group and Alenia Aermacchi.

Aerospatiale had earlier taken over Nord, which brought with it experience gained on the Nord 262 turboprop airliner and through the international programme that produced the Transall military airlifter.

Aeritalia's turboprop transport knowledge came only from the G222 military transport that it had inherited from Fiat. ATR nevertheless set about designing a 30–50-seat aircraft, applying exceptional technology where it might benefit the machine's economics, but otherwise keeping the design relatively simple.

With serious competitor aircraft also in development from BAe (ATP), de Havilland Canada (Dash 8), Fokker

Delivered to Air Mauritius in 1986, 3B-NAH served the airline's regional routes for almost ten years, before going on to Air Madagascar.

Cabin Configuration
A typical ATR 42 cabin might feature 11 rows of double seats arranged either side of a central aisle, with an additional two aft to port and two rearward-facing seats forward to starboard.

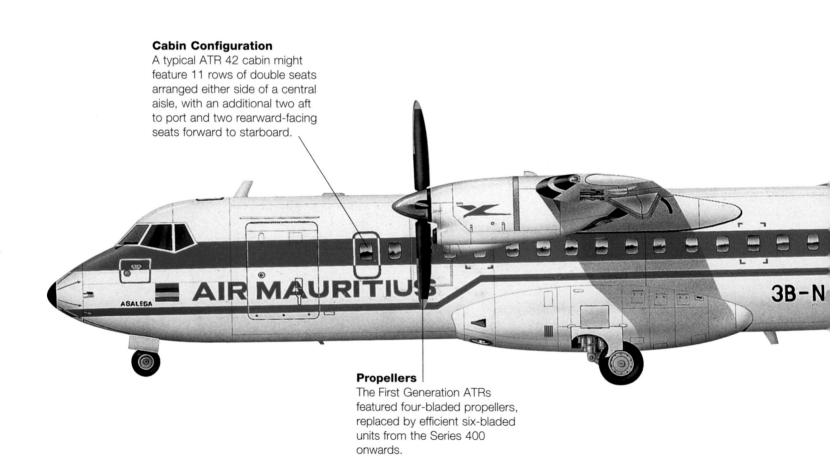

Propellers
The First Generation ATRs featured four-bladed propellers, replaced by efficient six-bladed units from the Series 400 onwards.

(50) and Saab-Fairchild (SF340), the ATR partners
realized that to succeed theirs' must be an exceptional
aircraft. Seating between 42 and 50 passengers, the
ATR 42 was designated as the initial production model
and launched in October 1981. Power was provided by
a pair of Pratt & Whitney Canada PW120 turboprops
and the airframe appeared largely conventional, with

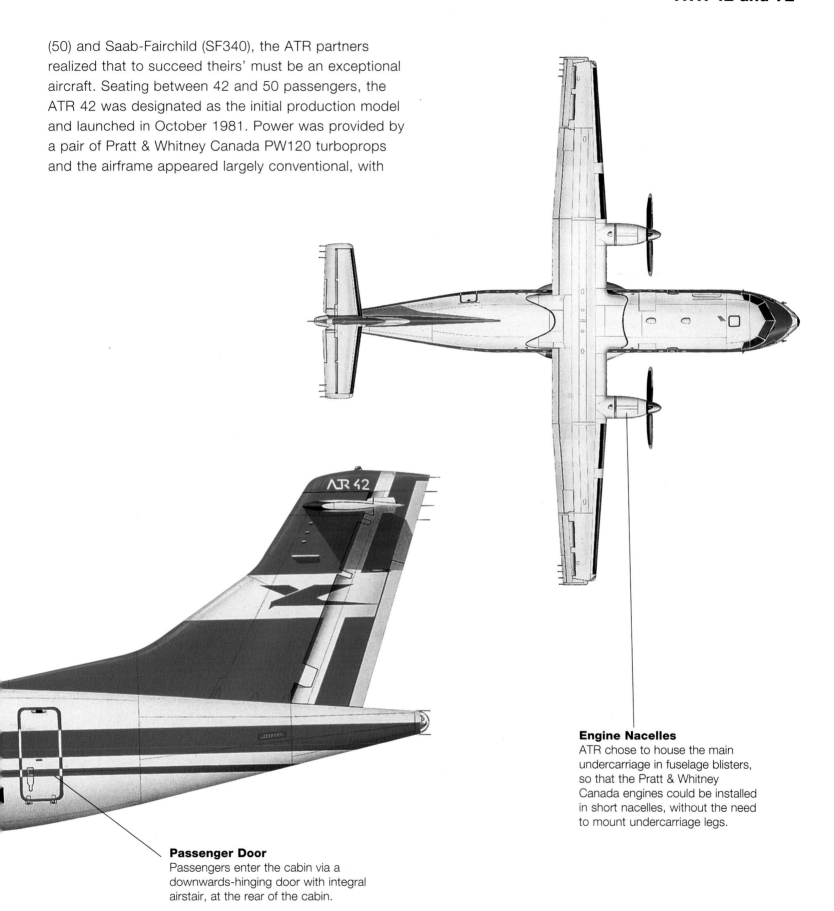

Engine Nacelles
ATR chose to house the main
undercarriage in fuselage blisters,
so that the Pratt & Whitney
Canada engines could be installed
in short nacelles, without the need
to mount undercarriage legs.

Passenger Door
Passengers enter the cabin via a
downwards-hinging door with integral
airstair, at the rear of the cabin.

ATR 42 and 72

From the forward elevation the ATR's bulbous main undercarriage fairings are obvious. The four-bladed propellers are also evident.

a straight high-aspect ratio wing, T-tail and main undercarriage units retracting into fairings on the fuselage sides.

Extensive use of weight-saving composites was made in the aircraft's structure and considerable attention paid to passenger comfort. Propellers generally bring with them a level of vibration and noise lacking in jets, making cabins noticeably noisier and reducing the passenger appeal of turboprop airliners. To combat these effects, ATR introduced noise-reducing systems into the cabin.

Specification (ATR 42-500)

Type:	short-haul turboprop airliner
Dimensions:	wing span 24.57m (80ft 7in), length 22.67m (74ft 5in), height 7.59m (24ft 11in)
Maximum take-off weight:	18,600kg (41,005lb)
Powerplant:	two 2400shp Pratt & Whitney Canada PW127E or M turboprop engines
Maximum cruising speed:	556km/h (345mph)
Range with maximum passenger load:	1327km (824 miles)
Flight crew:	2
Passengers:	up to 50 in single-class accommodation

Split Production

Aerospatiale was responsible for the wing, flaps, engine nacelles, cockpit and cabin, Aeritalia for the fuselage and empennage; final assembly was in the French company's facility at Toulouse. Two ATR 42 prototypes were built, the first making the type's maiden flight on 16 August 1984, followed by the initial production machine on 30 April 1985.

A series of variants emerged, in what ATR now calls the First Generation. Initial production was of the ATR 42-300, with PW120 engines, and 42-320 with PW121s for improved hot-and-high performance. ATR had announced its intention to build the ATR 72 stretch in 1985, flying the first prototype on 27 October 1988. As well as its 4.50m (14ft 9in) longer fuselage, the new aircraft had a wider wing span and more fuel. The First Generation ATR 72 was built as the standard ATR 72-200 with 2400shp PW124B engines and the hot-and-high -210, with PW127s and other changes, including improved noise reduction treatments. An even more powerful variant, with PW127F engines, was designated ATR 72-210A.

The ATR 42-400/500 and ATR 72-500 replaced the early aircraft in production from 1996. Flying for the first time on 12 July 1995, the PW121A engines of the two ATR 42-400s built drove six-bladed propellers, paving the way for the -500, which became the primary -300 replacement and employed the same PW127 turboprop as the ATR 72-210. The equivalent ATR 72-500 also used the PW127 and both types benefitted from a redesigned cabin interior as well as what ATR describes as: 'An efficient and technologically advanced acoustic treatment of the structure, with the installation of dynamic vibration absorbers and skin damping.'

Special Variants

Several specialized ATR variants have been offered for civilian and military applications although the latter market has largely fallen to the rival CN235 and longer C-295, now Airbus Military & Space products and derived from the original Airtech CN235, which found few airline customers in competition with the ATRs and Dash 8. For commercial operators, ATR has produced designs for the ATR 42 Cargo QC and ATR 72 Cargo QC, with quick-change convertible interiors, and ATR 42L with side cargo door, but the passenger variants have dominated production. As Bombardier developed the Q400 into the Q400 NextGen, so ATR produced a new generation of ATR 42 and 72. Entering service from 2011, the -600 series machines feature PW127M engines, a new cabin interior and completely revised avionics. Meanwhile, ATR customers have called for a 90-seat aircraft that the manufacturer says it is considering. However, this is likely to be to a majority new design, rather than an ATR 72 stretch.

Series 600

With its ATR 42-600 and 72-600, the manufacturer thoroughly modernized the design. Using elements of Airbus A380 avionics architecture, it installed a state-of-the-art EFIS cockpit, featuring primary flight and multi-function displays for each pilot, plus a central engine and warning display. The cockpit also offers electronic flight bag compatibility, reducing paperwork.

The model's Armonia cabin design is more spacious and offers increased overhead bin stowage, while the PW127M powerplant can be installed with an optional reserve take-off feature, offering more power for take-off and an increase of 1000kg (2000lb) in payload from hot-and-high airports.

Operators benefit from the -600's access to the Automatic Dependent Surveillance – Broadcast (ADS-B) system via datalink, reporting the ATR's position to air traffic control, operator ground stations and other aircraft. The new models are also offered with an aircraft condition monitoring system, reporting on failures and system health so that maintenance can be planned efficiently and in advance.

Airbus A320 family (1987)

Airbus took a bold step with the A320, choosing to challenge Boeing and McDonnell Douglas in the single-aisle, short/medium-haul sector. Risking all on a high-technology design, it continues to win orders with a series of derived aircraft.

Airbus may have surprised the industry with the quality and success of its A300 and A310, but its A320 stunned it, through its combination of technology and advanced aerodynamics. A single-aisle (SA) in the class of the Boeing 737 and McDonnell Douglas DC-9 had been under consideration for the Airbus range since 1970, but national interests had complicated the case for its design. Dassault was working on the Mercure, BAC had plans for a One-Eleven development, Fokker was planning an F29 and, among other developments, Hawker Siddeley was working with Dornier and VFW-Fokker on a quiet take-off and landing design.

All these rival concepts had a degree of influence upon the subsequent Airbus design, but in particular it stemmed from the Joint European Transport (JET) programme, established by Aerospatiale, British Aerospace, Dornier and VFW-Fokker in June 1977. It schemed a 130–188 seater powered by a pair of CFM56 turbofans, although the abortive Pratt & Whitney JT10D was also considered. A March 1978 agreement between

British Airways was a reluctant A320 operator, taking the -100 model by default after it assumed responsibility for orders placed by British Caledonian.

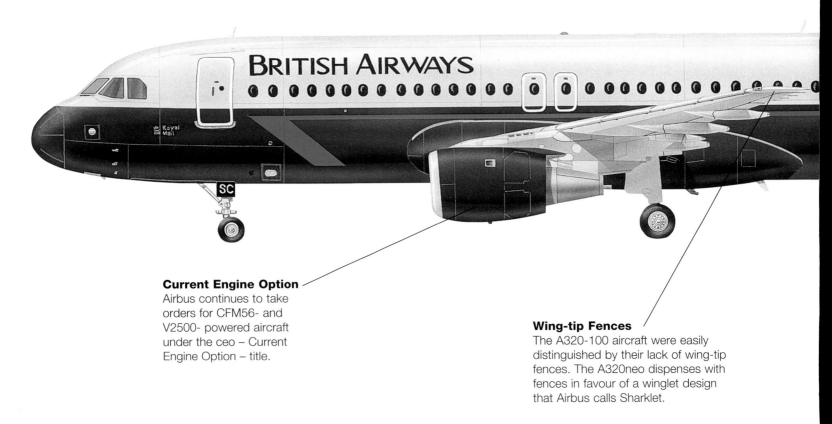

Current Engine Option
Airbus continues to take orders for CFM56- and V2500- powered aircraft under the ceo – Current Engine Option – title.

Wing-tip Fences
The A320-100 aircraft were easily distinguished by their lack of wing-tip fences. The A320neo dispenses with fences in favour of a winglet design that Airbus calls Sharklet.

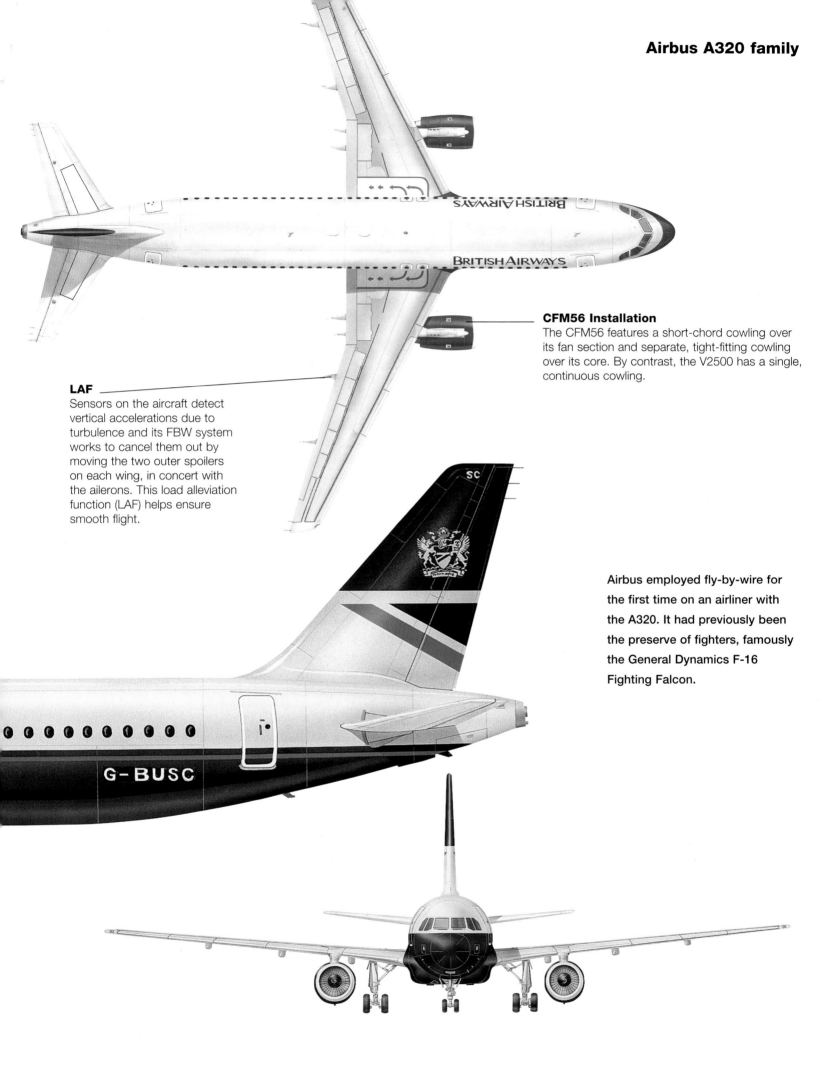

CFM56 Installation
The CFM56 features a short-chord cowling over its fan section and separate, tight-fitting cowling over its core. By contrast, the V2500 has a single, continuous cowling.

LAF
Sensors on the aircraft detect vertical accelerations due to turbulence and its FBW system works to cancel them out by moving the two outer spoilers on each wing, in concert with the ailerons. This load alleviation function (LAF) helps ensure smooth flight.

Airbus employed fly-by-wire for the first time on an airliner with the A320. It had previously been the preserve of fighters, famously the General Dynamics F-16 Fighting Falcon.

G-BUSC

Airbus A320 family

the participants confirmed their roles in A300/310 production, as well as their involvement in future JET developments.

After British Aerospace became a full member of the consortium in 1979, Airbus consolidated its JET-based plans as the SA1, SA2 and SA3 designs, the former becoming the A320 in February 1981; Airbus aimed to produce two variants, the 124-seat A320-100 and 172-seat A320-200. In June Air France signed for 16 -100s and 34 -200s, 25 of the aircraft on firm order and 25 as options. Design was far from complete, however, and with an eye to Delta's requirement for a 150-seat Boeing 727 replacement, Airbus settled on a fuselage length suitable for 150 passengers. The A320 then evolved as the short-range A320-100 and longer-ranged -200, with additional fuel in a centre-section tank, but both seating around 150 passengers. As it had with its widebody, Airbus designed the narrowbody A320 with capacity in mind. Thus its cabin width was 3.70m (12ft 1in), compared to 3.25m (10ft 8in) for the 737 and therefore, by default, also the 707, 727 and 757, the Airbus going on to replace examples of all four types in service.

Once again Airbus looked to British expertise in wing design and although there was a three-year delay while the UK government defined the level of support it would be able to offer BAe, the company produced a wing of exceptional aerodynamic qualities. The ailerons, flaps and spoilers were all controlled by the aircraft's fly-by-wire (FBW) control system, marking the first full application of the technology in a commercial design. A hardpoint under each wing mounted the pylon for the CFM56 engine, each

Specification (A320ceo with Sharklets – most powerful engine and highest weight options)

Type:	short/medium-haul airliner
Dimensions:	wing span 35.80m (117ft 5½in), length 37.57m (123ft 3in), height 11.76m (38ft 7in)
Maximum take-off weight:	78,000kg (171,960lb)
Powerplant:	two 120kN (27,000lb) thrust IAE V2500-A5 or CFM International CFM56-5B turbofan engines
Maximum operating speed:	Mach 0.82
Maximum range:	6115km (3800 miles)
Flight crew:	2
Passengers:	up to 180 in single-class accommodation

of which was controlled through a full-authority digital engine control (FADEC) unit for maximum efficiency.

As well as its pioneering FBW work, which allowed the pilots to fly with a simple side-stick controller, Airbus also introduced new levels of automation and crew awareness with the A320's six-screen EFIS, which allowed access to a tremendous amount of information, simplifying complex navigational procedures and allowing instant fault diagnosis as well as comprehensive aircraft health monitoring.

A320 Takes Off

Airbus flew the A320 for the first time from its Toulouse facility on 22 February 1987. After a remarkably speedy test and certification process for such an advanced aircraft, scheduled service with Air France and British Airways commenced in April 1988. The UK flag carrier had inherited its A320 order from British Caledonian, having been reluctant to support Airbus, but subsequently finding the A320 excellent and ordering more from the series.

These early aircraft were to A320-100 standard and although Air Inter also took the model, only 21 were built before the A320-200 became the standard model;

the -200 designation was soon dropped and the type became known simply as the A320. Since 1989 Airbus has offered A320 customers a choice of engine, adding the International Aero Engines (IAE) V2500 to its catalogue, variants of the CFM56 and V2500 also being offered on the A321 stretch and A319 'shrink'.

The 185-seat A321 flew for the first time on 11 March 1993, under V2530 power, as was the first customer A321-100, delivered to Lufthansa on 27 January 1994. Alitalia, the second A321 operator, took the first of its CFM56-5B-engined aircraft on 22 March. From 1997 the extended-range A321-200 became available, with structural reinforcement, extra fuel and seats for up to 220 passengers.

In 2010 Airbus announced its intention to offer re-engined variants of the A320, 321 and 319 under the 'neo' (New Engine Option) banner. Available with a choice of CFM's LEAP-X or Pratt & Whitney's PW1100G PurePower geared turbofan, the first of the range, the A320, should be delivered in 2015. The first A320neo, a Pratt-powered machine, completed its first flight at Toulouse on 25 September 2014.

A319 and A318

Having stretched the A320 by 6.93m (22ft 9in) to produce the A321, Airbus shortened the baseline aircraft by 3.77m (12ft 4in), creating the A319, optimized for 124 passengers over ranges up to 3700km (2300 miles). Launched against just six orders from lessor ILFC in June 1993, the A319 flew for the first time on 25 August 1995. First delivery, to Swissair, followed on 25 April 1996 and the plethora of subsequent customers includes easyJet.

Further shortened, the A318 was announced in April 1999 as Airbus's entry into the regional jet market. Offered with a choice of CFM56 or Pratt & Whitney PW6000 engines, the

107-seater was initially plagued by development problems with its P&W powerplant. The aircraft has attracted little interest, with all 79 ordered by November 2014 in service. Given its early refusal to consider Airbus equipment, it is ironic that British Airway's premier call sign, SPEEDBIRD 01, once allocated to Concorde, is now reserved for its all-business class A318 service out of London City to New York.

Airbus A340 (1991)

Airbus took the A300 and developed it into the four-engined A340 and A330 twin. The former saw its ultimate evolution in the A340-500 and -600, but ultimately lost out in the order battle to Boeing's superb 777.

With the A300 and A310, Airbus Industrie had taken a convincing step into the short/medium-haul widebody market, while the longer-ranged A310 variants allowed it to step on Boeing's long-haul toes. But it had not yet entered the long-haul market proper; it remained the preserve of the Boeing 747 and long-legged 767-200 variants, as well as the new McDonnell Douglas MD-11, while large numbers of DC-10s and Lockheed TriStars remained in service and ripe for replacement.

Several A300-based design proposals had been developed, among them the A300B9, a 330-seat twin, the A300B10, which became the A310, and the

A300B11, a four-engined, 200-seat airliner. The combined success of the A300/310 consumed much of Airbus' development capacity, but also allowed it to invest in the long-haul products required to sit alongside its medium-haul widebodies and short-haul A320 family. By 1980 the B9 and B11 had become the TA 9 and TA 11, respectively, with TA meaning 'Twin Aisle'.

Airbus released elements of their design at the Farnborough Air Show in 1982, but several changes in fuselage length, passenger capacity and range followed for both proposals before the manufacturer settled on two very similar aircraft, near identical in all but

Cockpit
The A340 and A330 were built with near-identical cockpits. The most obvious difference between them was the four throttles for the A340's engines.

Fleet Status
Air France entered 2015 with a 13-strong A340-300 fleet, each aircraft typically configured for 275 seats.

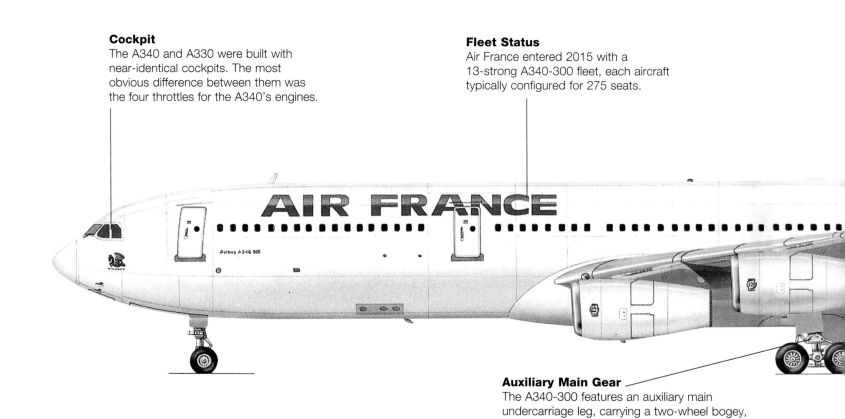

Auxiliary Main Gear
The A340-300 features an auxiliary main undercarriage leg, carrying a two-wheel bogey, under its centre fuselage.

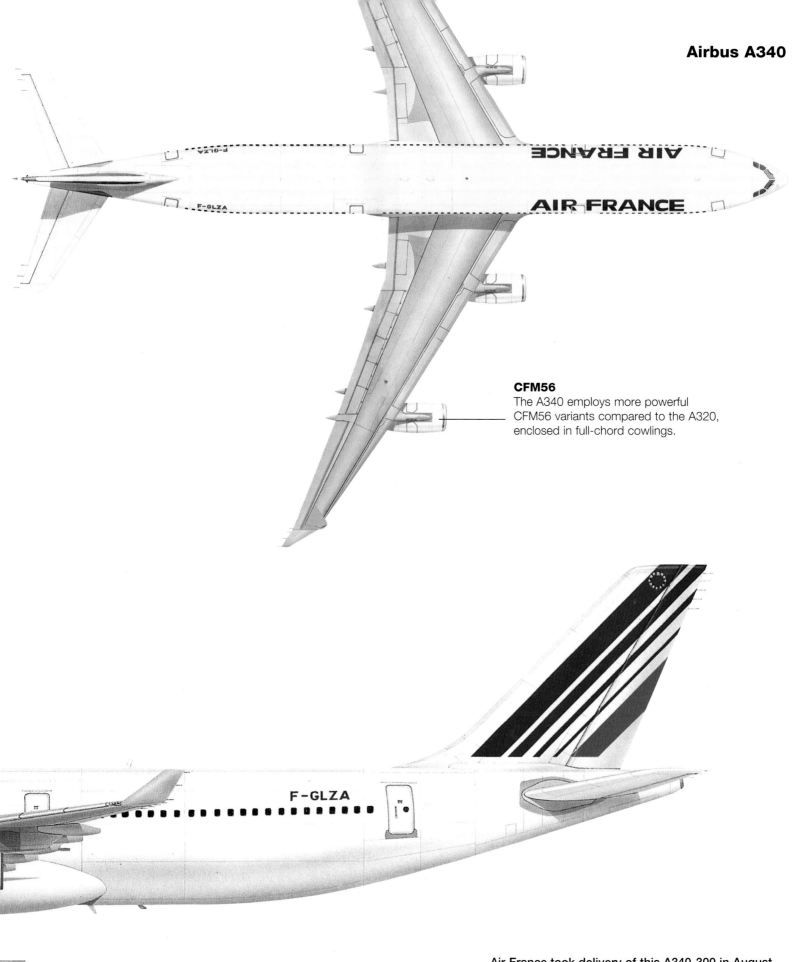

CFM56
The A340 employs more powerful CFM56 variants compared to the A320, enclosed in full-chord cowlings.

Air France took delivery of this A340-300 in August 1993. It later flew on the Spanish register for Iberia before being withdrawn from service in April 2013.

Airbus A340

powerplant, fuel capacity and weights. In essence, the TA 9 would suit medium/long-haul routes, while TA 11 would have the increased fuel capacity and additional power necessary to cover long and very long haul services.

A340 Evolves

Series designations were allocated in January 1986, TA 9 predictably becoming the A330 and TA 11 the A340. Launched prior to the Paris Air Show in June 1987, the two designs continued to evolve, but with priority on the A340, since its market included the new MD-11, while there was no new competitor in the twin's category. Airbus continued to stretched the

Specification (A340-500, optional high weight)

Type:	ultra long-haul airliner
Dimensions:	wing span 63.45m (208ft 2in), length 67.93m (222ft 10in), height 17.28m (56ft 8in)
Maximum take-off weight:	380,000kg (837,800lb)
Powerplant:	four 235.70kN (53,000lb) thrust Rolls-Royce Trent 553 turbofan engines
Maximum operating speed:	Mach 0.86
Maximum range:	16,670km (10,358 miles)
Flight crew:	2
Passengers:	up to 375 in single-class accommodation

The wings of the A330 and A340 are remarkably similar, the A330 retaining the hardpoint for the outer engine's pylon.

A340's fuselage, optimizing passenger load to market requirements and applying almost every change to the A330.

Meanwhile, British Aerospace was working on another of its exceptional wing designs in a process completed during 1987. The result was a wing suitable for either type, with minimal structural change required to mount the additional engines of the A340. For the cockpit Airbus took inspiration from the A320, installing a six-screen EFIS and sidestick controllers for a common pilot rating across the A340/330 and A320 series, albeit with 'differences' training between types.

But Airbus was struggling over powerplant choice. The A330 was close in configuration to the A300 and an obvious application for the General Electric CF6 and competing engines, but the A340 presented a range of possibilities. The CFM International CFM56 had been considered for the A340 all along, in uprated variants offering in excess of 133kN (30,000lb) thrust, although Airbus also looked at the International Aero Engines V2500 in development for the A320. Airbus had promised the airlines extreme range from the A340, but now it was concerned that the available powerplant options might not live up to those promises; it began looking at ultra-high bypass 'SuperFan' engines.

IAE was pushing a V2500-based SuperFan featuring a ducted fan geared to the existing engine core. Offering radically reduced fuel consumption, it allowed the A340 to easily match the promised range and airlines began placing orders, led by Lufthansa, with a January 1987 commitment for 15 orders and 15 options. There must have been considerable consternation in Toulouse when IAE cancelled SuperFan development work just a few months later, obliging Airbus to redesign the A340 for existing engine technology. The uprated CFM56-5C2 turbofan, an increase in wing span and the addition of winglets provided a degree of hope, and when the 151kN (34,000lb) thrust CFM56-5C4 became available, the A340's performance at last matched the brochure figures.

Airbus flew the first of the baseline model, the 375-seat A340-300, on 25 October 1991, following it with the first long-range, 263-seat A340-200 on 1 April 1992. More tweaking was required to extract the full design range, but on 2 February 1993 Lufthansa finally took delivery of the first customer A340-200. Air France took the first -300 later in the month. Subsequent variants primarily focussed on increased weights for greater range or payload, but the A340 began to make little sense economically as efficient long-haul twins – especially the Boeing 777 – reached the market. Airbus took the extreme step of re-engining the type as the A340-500 and -600, but ceased production of all variants in the second half of the 2000s after 377 had been delivered.

Ultimate A340

Airbus delivered the first A340-300X, with a 275,000kg (606,250lb) maximum take-off weight, to Singapore Airlines on 17 April 1996. Later redesignated as the A340-300E, the model introduced structural changes that were incorporated into subsequent production airframes and formed the basis of a longer-range A340-400 proposal.

The -400 was abandoned in favour of the A340-500 and A340-600, launched in December 1997 as ultra long range and high-capacity long-range airliners, respectively. Both types featured Rolls-Royce Trent power, providing sparkling performance, and the -500 was the world's longest-ranged airliner when it entered service with Emirates in 2004. Other -500 customers included Etihad

(illustrated) and Singapore Airlines. Designed to provide capacity similar to that of the Boeing 747, the A340-600 flew its first revenue services with Virgin Atlantic from 2002 and although Airbus was obliged to cure a series of teething troubles, both new variants eventually performed well.

Nevertheless, the Boeing 777-300ER soon appeared, doing everything the A340-600 could but with the economy of just two engines, while the 777-200LR matched the A340-500. Airbus offered to compensate new customers for the increased fuel burn they would incur using A340s compared to the 777, but Boeing had conclusively ended the A340's production programme.

Bombardier CRJ (1991)

Canadair created an entirely new market segment with its Regional Jet, allowing airlines to make profits with jet equipment on routes that had previously been the domain of the turboprop. Bombardier continues to sell NextGen CRJs in 2015.

The Canadian government purchased Canadian Vickers in 1944, renaming its ready-made aerospace manufacturing facility Canadair and assigning it contracts for the production of DC-4M airliners. Involvement in many aircraft production programmes and component supply chains followed after the government sold Canadair to General Dynamics, the company remaining under U.S. ownership until 1976, when the Canadian government bought it back.

In 1988 it passed from state control and merged with Bombardier, continuing to trade under the original Canadair name into the early 1990s. Among the manufacturer's key products, the Challenger business jet had flown for the first time in 1978. A T-tailed, swept-wing aircraft with rear-mounted Lycoming ALF 502 turbofan engines, the Challenger seemed ripe for stretching into a regional airliner and Bombardier had the funds to make it possible.

Conventional wisdom had it that using pure jet power over sectors shorter than 800km (500 miles) made no economic sense, but Canadair considered that the latest highly-efficient small turbofans could change the numbers sufficiently for the airlines to take note. It also recognized that given the option of taking a jet-powered aircraft over a propeller-driven machine, passengers would chose the jet every time, given the perceived obsolescence of the propeller.

Flight Deck
The CRJ700, 900 and 1000 feature six-screen Rockwell Collins Proline IV integrated avionics on the flight deck.

Regional Definition

Canadair chose to call the new aircraft the Regional Jet (quickly abbreviated to RJ), a fitting title since there had been no other. In its most basic form the RJ was a stretched Challenger, its 6.09m (20ft) of additional length allowing for a 50-seat cabin, powered by General Electric CF34-3A turbofans. Launched on 31 March 1989 against commitments including a six firm, six options agreement with West Germany's DLT, the aircraft flew for the first time as the RJ100 on 10 May 1991.

By this time, Embraer had announced its rival EMB-145, but Canadair had a healthy lead, having announced a heavier, longer-ranged Regional Jet 100ER in September 1990 and delivering its first RJ100 to Lufthansa Cityline (DLT's successor) on 19 October 1992. As the Canadair name faded from use, Bombardier

made a significant penetration into the U.S. market, Delta Connection feeder Comair taking the region's first RJ on 29 April 1993.

The even longer-legged RJ100LR (for Long Range) was announced in February 1994 and the RJ100 series continued to pick up orders until replaced in production by the CRJ200 from 1996. The letter 'C' was added to the aircraft's title to differentiate it from rival machines, especially the EMB-145, which evolved as a series of aircraft under the ERJ designation. The new CRJ variant featured uprated CF34-3B1 engines offering improved performance.

Tyrolean Airways took the first customer CRJ200 on 15 January 1996. Bombardier subsequently offered ER and LR variants, as well as hot-and-high equivalents, designated CRJ200B, CRJ200BER and CRJ200BLR,

Air Nostrum took delivery of CRJ900 EC-JZT in January 2007. It operates the type in Iberia Regional colours. The CRJ continues to sell, thanks in part to constant updating and Bombardier's willingness to listen to its customers. By late 2014 it had taken orders for 384 CRJ900s.

Go-Go Wi-Fi
In 2014 Bombardier announced the availability of line-fit Go-Go Wi-Fi on the CRJ.

Bright Cabin
Revised windows and sculpted window surrounds are among the features Bombardier introduced into the NextGen CRJ to improve passenger experience.

Common Engine
Through simple modifications, the same CF34-8C5 engine can be used on a NextGen CRJ700, 900 or 1000, allowing operators to maintain an engine pool for more efficient operations.

Bombardier CRJ

respectively. With the CRJ in service, Bombardier had examined the possibility of a further stretched CRJ-X, suited to airlines with higher-density routes as well as those whose operations had outgrown the CRJ100/200.

Yemen's Felix Airways is among many operators that have founded their business on the CRJ. It began 2015 with a four-aircraft fleet of two CRJ700s, including this aircraft, and two CRJ200s.

Specification (CRJ900 NextGen)

Type:	regional airliner
Dimensions:	wing span 24.90m (81ft 7in), length 36.20m (118ft 11in), height 7.50m (24ft 7in)
Maximum take-off weight:	36,514kg (80,500lb)
Powerplant:	two 64.50kN (14,510lb) thrust General Electric CF34-8C5 turbofan engines
Maximum cruising speed:	871km/h (541mph)
Range with 88 passengers:	1982km (1231 miles)
Maximum operating altitude:	12,497m (41,000ft)
Flight crew:	2
Passengers:	up to 90 in single-class accommodation

On 21 January 1997 the CRJ-X was launched as the CRJ700, against a four-aircraft order from Brit Air. Seating up to 70 passengers, the CRJ700's cabin was redesigned, its wings lengthened and modified for improved field performance, and its undercarriage uprated; it was powered by 56.40kN (12,670lb) thrust CF34-8C1 engines offering much reduced maintenance requirements as well as greater power. The CRJ700 flew for the first time on 28 May 1999 and Brit Air took its first example on 31 January 2001.

Not content with having successively stretched the 19-seat Challenger up to the 70-seat CRJ700, on 24 July 2000 Bombardier announced a 3.89m (12ft 8in) length increase over the CRJ700 to produce the 90-passenger CRJ900, flown for the first time as a modification of the CRJ700 prototype on 21 February 2001. Initially delivered to Mesa Airlines during January 2003, the CRJ900 was also available in ER and LR variants. Finally, Bombardier performed an ultimate stretch to produce the 104-seat CRJ1000. This last configuration flew for the first time in 2008 as the first of the upgraded NextGen CRJ series, with new cabins and other modifications, and some equipment in common with the Q400 NextGen. CRJ1000 NextGen deliveries began in 2010, the model being offered alongside similar upgrades of the CRJ700 and CRJ900.

Rising fuel costs have undeniably slowed the regional jet market and the smaller capacity machines are now much less popular, but Bombardier continues to develop and sell the NextGen CRJ, even as it begins production of the all-new CSeries.

CSeries – Replacing the CRJ

When Embraer replaced its ERJ series with the all-new, higher-capacity E-Jets, Bombardier was obliged to respond or risk losing its position in the regional jet market. It began offering its clean sheet CSeries design from 2005, but struggled to find a powerplant capable of matching the type's desired performance.

The project was therefore cancelled, only to be resurrected in 2008 with Pratt & Whitney's PW1500G geared turbofan, although orders have been difficult to secure and a subsequently challenging flight test programme, including

an on-ground uncontained engine failure, has complicated the situation. Offered in 100-seat CS100 and 130-seat CS300 variants, the CSeries nevertheless promises a step change in regional jet economics, efficiency and passenger experience.

The type's delayed first flight came on 16 September 2013, but air tests were halted for five months after the engine failure on 29 May 2014. The trial campaign resumed on 6 November and first CS100 delivery is expected later in 2015.

Airbus A330 (1992)

Airbus achieved considerably greater success with the A330 than it did with the A340. So much so, in fact, that it is developing a New Engine Option for the type, which looks set to remain in production long into the future.

In the complex process of evolution that led from the A300 to the A340/330, the A330 medium/long-haul twinjet has its origins in the A300B9 concept of the early 1970s, which by 1980 had been refined as the TA 9. Since the four-engined A300B11 (TA 11, later A340) was given design lead, various changes in configuration applied during its development, particularly in fuselage length, were reflected in the A330. It finally solidified as the A330-300, sharing a common fuselage with the A340-300.

Since it was designed for shorter ranges than the A340, the A330 was provisioned for less fuel and was lighter.

Nevertheless, its most obvious difference was in powerplant and from the outset Airbus offered A330 customers the choice of three engine options, having allowed them to select from only two on the A320, for example.

Almost inevitably, General Electric supplied the CF6-80A1, while Pratt & Whitney offered the PW4164 or more powerful PW4168, and Rolls-Royce the Trent. The aircraft was configured for a typical two-class passenger load of

Hong Kong's Cathay Pacific is a major A330 operator. It entered 2015 with a fleet of 38 -300s and five more on order.

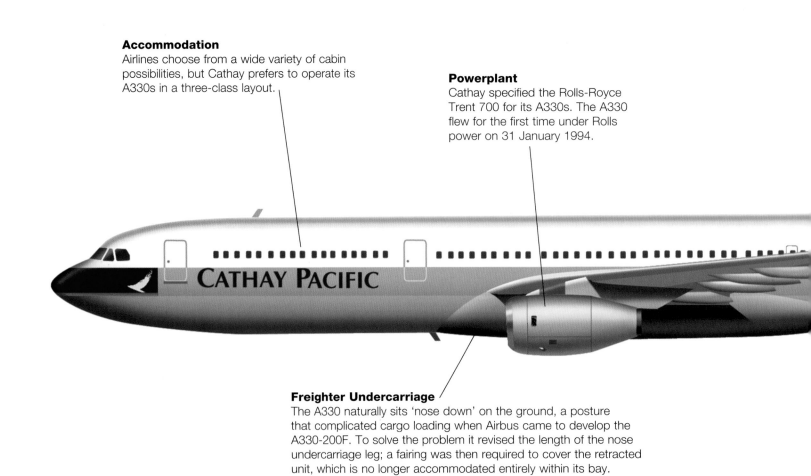

Accommodation
Airlines choose from a wide variety of cabin possibilities, but Cathay prefers to operate its A330s in a three-class layout.

Powerplant
Cathay specified the Rolls-Royce Trent 700 for its A330s. The A330 flew for the first time under Rolls power on 31 January 1994.

Freighter Undercarriage
The A330 naturally sits 'nose down' on the ground, a posture that complicated cargo loading when Airbus came to develop the A330-200F. To solve the problem it revised the length of the nose undercarriage leg; a fairing was then required to cover the retracted unit, which is no longer accommodated entirely within its bay.

335, carried over a range in the region of 8300km (5150 miles), but testing soon revealed that it was considerably lighter than expected, a weight saving easily translated into extra fuel or payload.

Such was the commonality between the types that the A330 and A340 initially shared the production line; the first A330 was the 12th airframe off the line, flying for the first time on 14 October 1992. The CF6-engined version was first into service, with Air Inter on 17 January 1994, followed by the P&W, then the Rolls. But the programme was not without trouble. A fatal crash on 30 June 1994 killed an entire test crew and resulted in cockpit modifications to prevent similar pilot error in the future. Then Cathay Pacific and Dragonair grounded their Rolls-Royce engined aircraft after three inflight shutdowns. Hispano-Suiza redesigned the gearbox and the problem never resurfaced.

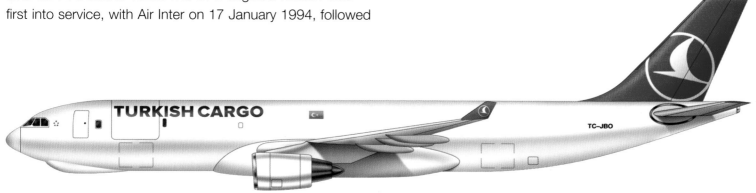

Above: As well as the A330-200 and -300, Turkish Airlines operates the A330-200F freighter, with six in service early in 2015.

Winglets
Prominent winglets are an important feature of the A330's aerodynamics. They contribute to fuel efficiency, but will be replaced by new-technology Sharklets on the A330neo.

A330-200

Airbus had used the designation A330-200 during the 1980s, eventually applying it specifically to a variant with the same fuselage length as the A340-200, but proceeding to develop and fly the longer A330-300 first. In 1995 the company announced its intention to develop the -200 with

Specification (A330-300)

Type:	medium/long-haul airliner
Dimensions:	wing span 60.30m (197ft 10in), length 63.69m (208ft 11in), height 16.83m (55ft 3in)
Maximum take-off weight:	242,000kg (529,100lb)
Powerplant:	two 303–320kN (68,000–72,000lb) thrust General Electric CF6-80E1, Pratt & Whitney PW4000 or Rolls-Royce Trent 700 turbofan engines
Maximum operating speed:	Mach 0.86
Maximum range:	11,300km (7020 miles)
Flight crew:	2
Passengers:	up to 300 in two-class accommodation

Airbus has deeply penetrated the Far Eastern market with its A320 and A330 airliners. Taiwan's China Airlines had twenty-four A330-300s in its fleet in 2015.

the shorter fuselage, reducing passenger capacity but increasing range.

Seating around 246 passengers in a typical two-class arrangement, the A330-200 was designed for services up to 11,825km (7350 miles) in length and featured an additional wing fuel tank and modified fin as standard. First flown on 13 August 1997, the first customer -200 went on lease to Canada 3000 on 30 April 1998 (it was one of 13 ordered by launch customer ILFC in March 1996). Again the CF6 option was first into service, followed by P&W and Rolls-Royce.

Orders for the A330 were initially slow in coming, but the aircraft eventually began to fair better than the A340, continuing in production as the latter faded away. Later, as Boeing struggled to mature the new-technology 787, airlines faced with delays in receiving their new Boeings looked to the A330 as a stopgap to maintain capacity and improve efficiency over their older equipment. Airbus has continuously upgraded the A330 series and in light of the resurgence of interest in the type, announced its intention to offer higher weight versions for increased payload/range.

Details of the changes were released in November 2012 and Airbus expects to introduce them on the A330-300 during 2015. It claims that combined with other modifications, it will add 50 per cent to the -300's range compared to the first aircraft into service in 1994, and reduce maintenance costs by 20 per cent. The higher-weight A330-200 is due for service entry in 2016, followed by a similar option for the A330-200F freighter.

New Engine

Airbus is also proceeding with an A330neo (New Engine Option) programme, which employs Rolls-Royce Trent 7000 engines and features cabin and aerodynamic upgrades, the latter including winglets similar to those of the A350 XWB and a longer wing span. Fuel consumption is expected to reduce by around 14 per cent per seat compared to the A330ceo. Finally, Airbus announced the A330-300 Regional during 2013. Under development for domestic markets with high demand and short stages, the aircraft will seat around 400 passengers.

A350 XWB

After its customers requested an Airbus response to Boeing's 787, the European manufacturer worked up an A350 concept based closely on the A330. The market was deeply unimpressed and the airlines, notably Qatar Airways, demanded that Airbus offer a game-changing aircraft with performance that could only be delivered by a brand new design. In 2006, Airbus therefore announced the new aircraft as the A350 XWB, for 'Xtra Wide Body', emphasizing the fact that it had bowed to industry wishes and was willing to produce a wider, more spacious cabin. Airbus makes considerable use of composites for primary A350 structures, while the Rolls-Royce Trent XWB is the sole powerplant offered.

Three variants were initially schemed, the A350-900 seating around 314 passengers, the A350-800 for 270 and the A350-1000, for 350. The -800 was scheduled for a 2012 service entry, but difficulties with the A380 programme drew resources and personnel away from the A350, causing considerable delay. First flight was eventually achieved on 13 June 2013, followed by first delivery, of an A350-900, to Qatar Airways, on 22 December 2014.

Boeing 777 (1994)

With the 777 Boeing set out to challenge the A340 and A330. In its latest developments the incredible twin offers all the performance of the first generation 747, but at a fraction of the fuel burn.

In 1986, Boeing perceived a future requirement for a widebody aircraft offering passenger capacity between that of the 767-300 and 747-400. It planned to have the new machine available from 1995 and abandoned plans for an enlarged 767 in order to concentrate resources on what it continued to call the 767-X. The aircraft was a clear challenger to the Airbus A340 and A330 then under development, and the McDonnell Douglas MD-11, when Boeing revealed it to the airlines in December 1989. A 34-firm/34-option commitment from United saw it formally launched as the 777 on 29 October 1990.

Boeing knew that in order to match the advanced technologies of its European rival it would need to develop and employ its own new technologies not only in the airframe, but in the process of its design, manufacture and testing. The company therefore turned to the new CATIA computer-aided design/computer-aided manufacturing software produced jointly by Dassault and IBM, making the 777 the first airliner completely defined and pre-assembled digitally.

Multiple design teams were created, each assigned a specific aspect of the aircraft and reporting into a

United was first into service with the 777 in June 1995. This aircraft was among its first and is shown in the carrier's contemporary livery.

Powerplant
General Electric, Pratt & Whitney and Rolls-Royce developed high-bypass turbofans of unprecedented power for the 777. United chose PW4000s for its 777-200s, but a mix of Pratt and GE power for subsequent -200ER orders.

Triple Mainwheels
Menasco/Messier-Bugatti designed the six-wheel main undercarriage bogies, holding three double sets of wheels in tandem. They distribute the aircraft's enormous weight sufficiently without recourse to a centreline gear leg.

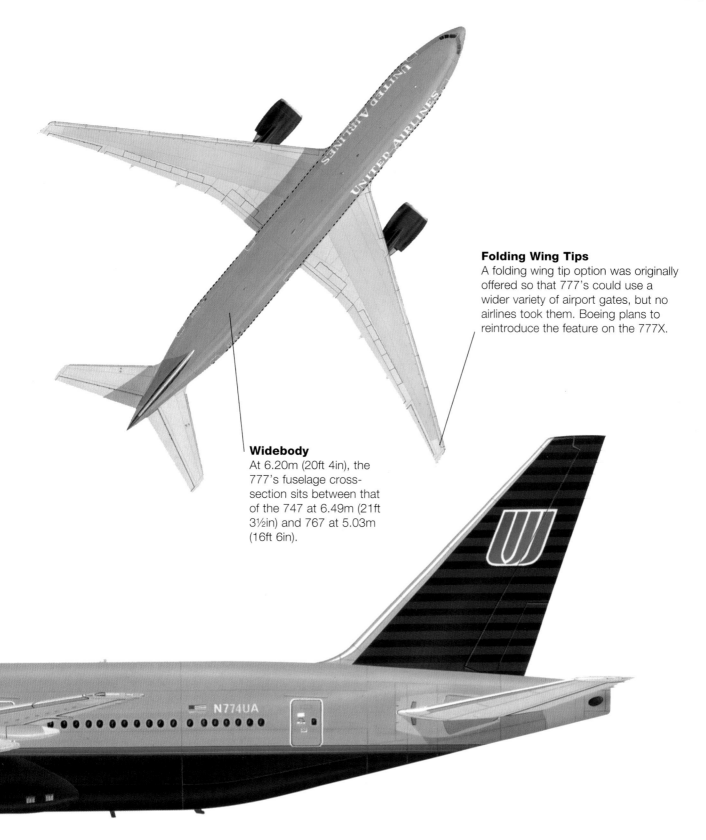

Folding Wing Tips
A folding wing tip option was originally offered so that 777's could use a wider variety of airport gates, but no airlines took them. Boeing plans to reintroduce the feature on the 777X.

Widebody
At 6.20m (20ft 4in), the 777's fuselage cross-section sits between that of the 747 at 6.49m (21ft 3½in) and 767 at 5.03m (16ft 6in).

Boeing developed a global supply chain for the 777. It included, for the first time, substantial risk sharing by foreign partners, Japanese industry taking a 20 per cent stake in the programme.

Boeing 777

common database. Boeing also called on its customer airlines, particularly United, and worked closely with them to ensure that the 777 matched their requirements and expectations and could be introduced into service with a minimum of problems.

Having adopted full fly-by-wire for the first time on the 777, Boeing tested the system on a purpose-

British Airways has been a major 777 customer. Its initial five 777-200s, including this aircraft, were followed by forty-four -200ER and six -300ER machines.

designed rig and employed nine aircraft in the flight test programme, each dedicated to unique aspects of the programme.

The three engine options offered to customers were reflected across the test fleet, so that five aircraft had Pratt & Whitney PW4000 power, two employed General Electric GE90s and the final pair Rolls-Royce Trents. Extended range overwater operations with twin-engined aircraft had increasingly become the norm with the Airbus A300-600 and A310, and longer-ranged 767s, governed by a set of regulations known as ETOPS (extended-range twin-engined operations). In-service aircraft were issued with ETOPS certification based on proven reliability, but the 777 was delivered in all three engine options, with the highest ETOPS certification. This allowed operations where the aircraft was as far as 180 minutes from the closest diversionary airport.

777 Takes Off

The 777 took its maiden flight on 12 June 1994 and thanks to the multi-aircraft test programme, United placed the type into revenue service on 7 June 1995. Regardless of the close working relationship between

Specification (777-300ER, highest weight option)

Type:	long-haul high-capacity airliner
Dimensions:	wing span 64.80m (212ft 7in), length 73.90m (242ft 4in), height 18.50m (60ft 8in)
Maximum take-off weight:	351,530kg (775,000lb)
Powerplant:	two 512kN (115,300lb) thrust General Electric GE90-115B turbofan engines
Cruising speed:	Mach 0.84
Maximum range:	14,490km (9000 miles)
Flight crew:	2
Passengers:	up to 386 in three-class accommodation

airline and manufacturer, a number of teething problems emerged, causing considerable friction between parties, but United remained faithful to the product and received its last of 80 777-200/200ER aircraft in December 2007.

Quick to exploit the 777's potential for longer range, Boeing promoted the initial 777-200 model for what it termed the 'A-market', effectively the U.S. domestic market. For the 'B-market', or transatlantic work, it offered the 777-200IGW (Increased Gross Weight) and there followed a series of confusing designations before the models settled as the 777-200 and 777-200ER (Extended Range).

With a fuselage stretch, the 777 could clearly be made to hold almost as many passengers as a 747-400 – 550 in a single-class layout. With its fuselage extended by 10m (33ft), the 777-300 was actually designed for a typical three-class configuration of 479 passengers, carried over as much as 10,805km (6710 miles), for a capacity/range combination comparable to that of the 747-100/200 variants.

And on the power of two modern high-bypass turbofans the 777-300 was considerably more economical, burning around 30 per cent less fuel.

Cathay Pacific Airways took the first customer 777-300, powered by Trent engines, in June 1998.

In 1997 Boeing had begun work on longer ranged versions of the 777-200ER and 777-300, as the 777-200X and -300X. Airbus was working on the re-engined A340-500 and -600, aimed at ultra long range and high-capacity, long range routes, respectively, and Boeing set about adapting the 777 for those same sectors, but using half as many engines. The A340-600 also posed a clear threat to the 747-400 where airlines required the type's extreme range but not its passenger capacity and the 777-300X promised to challenge for these sales too.

The two Boeings eventually emerged as the 777-200LR and 777-300ER, the former also spawning the 777F freighter. Their performance was so dramatically good that they effectively denied the market to Airbus and A340 production was closed down. In 2013, Boeing announced plans to develop the 777 even further, offering the 777X in 777-8X and -9X variants for service from around 2020. Incorporating the latest technologies, a new composite wing and General Electric GE9X engines, the 777X will challenge the A350 XWB.

777-200LR and -300ER

In February 2000, Boeing launched the 777-200LR (Longer Range), at the time named Worldliner, and 777-300ER. Both aircraft featured new raked wing tips for improved fuel efficiency and field performance, and an exclusivity deal was signed with General Electric, so that all -200LR and -300ER aircraft are GE90 powered. In its -300ER application the GE90-115B delivers an incredible 512kN (115,300lb) thrust; the LR's engines were derated to 489kN (110,100lb) thrust, but Boeing also offers the aircraft with 512kN -115BL engines and three auxiliary fuel tanks. The two models are superficially similar to the 777-200 and -300 from which

they are derived, but represent a 35 per cent redesign.

Boeing rolled the first 777-300ER out on 14 November 2002 and the model entered service, with Air France, on 29 April 2004. The 777-200LR flew for the first time on 8 March 2005 and soon became the basis for the 777F, launched in May 2005 and delivered to launch customer Air France on 19 February 2009, and subsequently to other carriers, including FedEx.

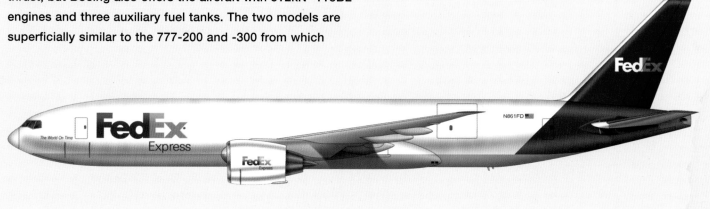

Embraer ERJ (1995)

A relative newcomer to airliner production, Embraer achieved considerable success with its first jet design. In direct competition with Bombardier and the CRJ, the Brazilian manufacturer helped establish the viability of jets in the regional market.

Aviation came to the Brazilian city of São José dos Campos after Montenegro Filho, an officer in the nation's air force, established an aerospace-dedicated educational organization there. Later in his career he headed the materials division of the Aeronautics Ministry and in 1943 he began working towards what ultimately matured as the city's Centro Técnico de Aeronáutica (CTA) and Instituto Technológico de Aeronáutica.

Teaching began at the facility in 1950 and Heinrich Focke of Focke-Wulf fame was among the experts attracted to its modern campus. A manufacturing capability was soon

under development and the possibility of creating a national aerospace company to create a turboprop transport was considered. The Empresa Brasileira de Aeronáutica – Embraer – was the direct result of these developments. Created on 19 August 1969, its first product was the turboprop transport, developed successfully as the EMB-110 Bandeirante and flown for the first time in 1972.

LOT Polish Airlines operated as many as fourteen ERJ145s. The airline remained faithful to Embraer when the time came to renew its fleet – in 2015 it had examples of the E170, E175 and E195.

CBA-123 Legacy
The ERJ's nose profile and initial cabin installation were taken from the abortive CBA-123 turboprop design.

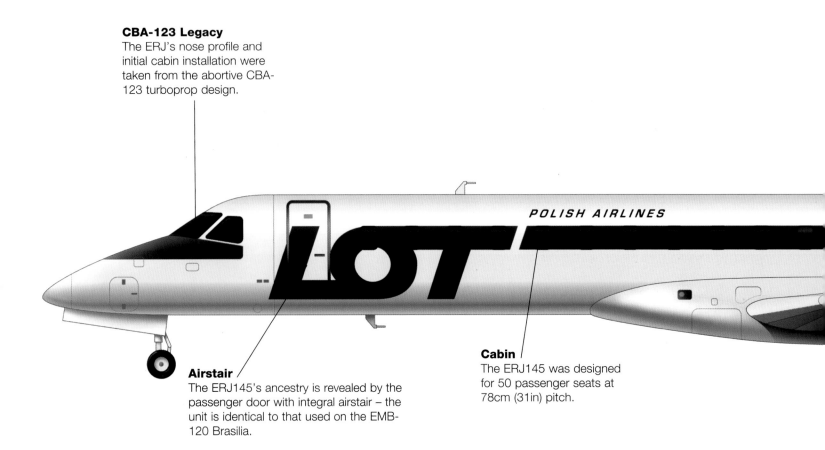

Airstair
The ERJ145's ancestry is revealed by the passenger door with integral airstair – the unit is identical to that used on the EMB-120 Brasilia.

Cabin
The ERJ145 was designed for 50 passenger seats at 78cm (31in) pitch.

POLISH AIRLINES

Seating up to 16 passengers, the EMB-110 sold well, particularly in Europe and the U.S., establishing the novice manufacturer in a difficult marketplace. With the Bandeirante and similar rival types serving U.S. feederliner routes, operators began calling for aircraft of greater capacity. Embraer considered an enlarged, pressurized EMB-110, but eventually settled on the 30-seat EMB-120 Brasilia. Flown for the first time in 1983, the EMB-120 also penetrated the U.S. market and sold well globally, cementing Embraer's reputation as a manufacturer of quality regional aircraft and laying the foundations for an ambitious new machine.

Props to Jets

Among several designs considered for production beyond the EMB-120, Embraer worked with Argentina's

Above: British Regional Airlines flew ERJ145s on behalf of the UK's national carrier British Airways.

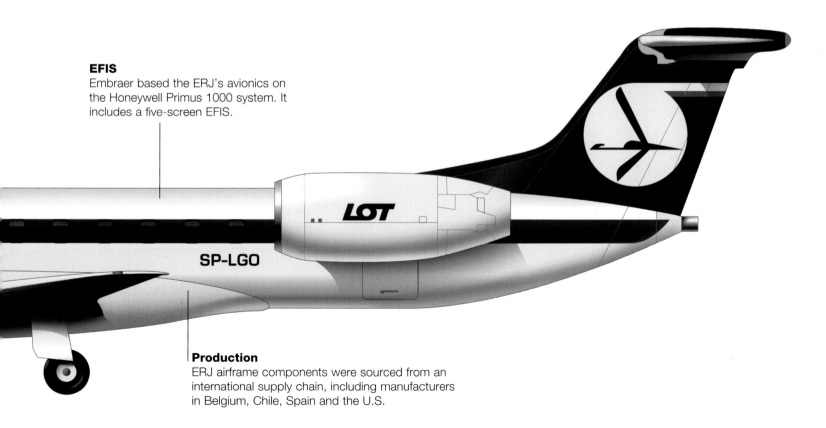

EFIS
Embraer based the ERJ's avionics on the Honeywell Primus 1000 system. It includes a five-screen EFIS.

Production
ERJ airframe components were sourced from an international supply chain, including manufacturers in Belgium, Chile, Spain and the U.S.

Embraer ERJ

PT-ZJC was the second ERJ-135 prototype. The model's forward fuselage was shortened compared to that of the ERJ145.

Specification (ERJ145ER, extended range)

Type:	short-haul/regional jet airliner
Dimensions:	wing span 20.04m (65ft 9in), length 29.87m (98ft), height 6.76m (22ft 2in)
Maximum take-off weight:	20,600kg (45,415lb)
Powerplant:	two 31.30kN (7040lb) thrust Rolls-Royce AE3007A turbofan engines
Maximum cruising speed:	833km/h (518mph)
Range with 50 passengers:	2963km (1841 miles)
Service ceiling:	11,275m (37,000ft)
Flight crew:	2
Passengers:	up to 50 in single-class accommodation

FMA on a pair of CBA-123 prototypes, producing an unusual pusher turboprop airliner that was quickly abandoned. It also created a concept for a stretched Brasilia, seating 45 passengers and powered by wing-mounted Allison GMA 3007 turbofans. Revealed at the 1989 Paris Air Show, the configuration proved suboptimal during wind tunnel testing.

Embraer therefore designed a new swept wing, mounted the engines on the rear fuselage and stretched the fuselage again, so that 50 passengers could be carried. Since it lacked the necessary funds for the predicted US$300 million development programme, the Brazilian company took on several risk-sharing partners and suppliers. The first prototype of what was by now designated EMB-145, took off for its maiden flight on 11 August 1995.

Regional Rival

Bombardier's RJ was already selling strongly by the time Embraer delivered the first EMB-145, but the aircraft went to Continental Express, demonstrating just how insatiable was the North American airlines' appetite for regional jets. Continental Express flew its first revenue service with the type on 6 April 1997, as Embraer set about creating a series of variants offering higher weight, longer range and increased power options. It also changed the aircraft's designation to ERJ-145, introducing the 'RJ' abbreviation for 'regional jet'. Later the title morphed into ERJ145.

Embraer also saw a requirement for a regional jet of smaller capacity, shortening the EMB-145 to create the 37-seat EMB-135 (ERJ135). Launched in September 1997, the EMB-135 retained the basic EMB-145 powerplant, although by now this had been redesignated as the Rolls-Royce AE3007 after the British engine manufacturer had bought Allison. The model flew for the first time on 4 July 1998 and although it entered service with Continental Express in 1999 sales were disappointing.

The relative lack of ERJ135 orders was in part due to the global downturn in air traffic following the terrorist attacks of 9/11, many airlines cutting their fleets or employing more economical equipment – in this case, 37 seats could be provided far more cost effectively in a difficult market by a turboprop. Embraer also produced the 44-seat ERJ140, designed to fit into schedules between the ERJ135 and 145, providing operators with maximum flexibility. First flown on 27 July 2000, it was subject to an American Eagle order for 130, but again sales were disappointing in the immediate aftermath of 9/11.

As a series the ERJs had easily outsold the Bandeirante, however, Embraer's previous best seller. Chinese interest in the series had led the company to establish a production line in the country, and it also used the EMB-145 as the basis of several special mission military types. The ERJ135 was relatively easily modified into the Legacy 600 business jet, quickly helping establish Embraer in one of aviation's most demanding markets.

Passenger Experience

Embraer was among the first airlines to truly embrace the concept of passenger experience. Its ERJs provided comfortable accommodation that was adequate for their regional routes, but through its market intelligence activities Embraer noticed that more and more passengers were using the Internet to share their travelling experiences.

Internet users were naming airlines for good and bad service and even picking out individual aircraft types and cabin features for comment. It used these observations to tailor its follow-on regional aircraft, the E-Jet, far more closely to passenger needs, realizing that content passengers were likely to remain loyal to E-Jet operators.

Embraer E-Jet (2002)

The E-Jets were the first in a new class of larger regional jet and continue to sell strongly. With the largest of the range Embraer takes on the smallest products from Airbus and Boeing, and has outsold them by a considerable margin.

Incredibly, Embraer had been privatized and suffered financial pressures throughout the ERJ145 development programme. While jobs were being lost and funding desperately sought, some within the company nevertheless had the foresight to look to future markets. They realized that passenger numbers on regional inter-city routes would steadily increase and that airlines would eventually require larger aircraft offering improved per-seat operating costs.

The potential for building a baseline machine larger than the ERJ145 had been examined as early as 1995 and by 1998, riding on the success of the still-new '145, Embraer had begun showing its ideas for what became the E-Jet to prospective customers. Launched at the Paris Air Show in 1999, the aircraft immediately won an order for 30 of the initial ERJ 170 from Crossair. Later the model was redesignated Embraer 170 or E170, the family of regional jets that followed becoming the E-Jets.

UK regional carrier Flybe introduced the E195 into service in 2006. Teething problems were soon rectified and the aircraft continue to prove efficient in service.

HUD
Embraer was the first commercial aircraft manufacturer to offer two head-up display (HUD) units in its aircraft. They deliver crucial information for landing in reduced visibility, allowing the pilots to keep their 'eyes out', rather than looking at the cockpit instrumentation.

Avionics
The Honeywell Primus Epic avionics suite sits at the heart of the E-Jets, presenting information on five screens. The pilots interact with the screens via cursor control panels, similar to laptop trackpads.

Embraer had brought the excellent ERJ145 to market against all the odds and sold it in large numbers, but for the E-Jet it abandoned the earlier type's configuration for a clean-sheet design. In configuration the new jet was therefore closer to a small mainline aircraft than a regional jet, with podded General Electric CF34 engines underwing. It was also designed to be inherently stretchable and Embraer always had in mind to follow the ERJ 170-100 launch model with the ERJ 170-200, in which passenger capacity increased to around 86 compared to 78 in the -100.

Stretching the E-Jet

Problems with the aircraft's advanced Honeywell avionics delayed first flight from late 2000 to 19 February 2002, so that the E170 emerged into the global slump following 9/11. An immediate effect of the downturn was Crossair's takeover of Swissair routes after the collapse of the Swiss flag carrier, creating Swiss International Air Lines. Swiss had no requirement for E-Jets and the order was cancelled.

But the E170 was an excellent aircraft and took regional services to a new level when LOT took the first delivery in March 2004, closely followed by U.S. Airways and Alitalia. With the change in model designations, the ERJ 170-200 became the E175 and entered service with Air Canada during 2005; later that year JetBlue took the first examples of the even longer E190, equipped with a taller fin, new, longer-span wing and seating as many as 106 passengers.

Fly-by-Wire
The E-Jets were designed as fly-by-wire (FBW) aircraft. Experience with the first-generation aircraft and the KC-390 tanker/transport has allowed Embraer to develop a more advanced FBW system for the E2.

Tall Fin
The lengthened fuselage of the E190 reduced lateral stability, obliging Embraer to fit a taller fin, which it retains for the E195.

G—FBJB

Cabin Configuration
Passenger seats are installed in a 2 + 2 arrangement either side of a central aisle. Embraer claims that passengers appreciate the lack of central seat, since an aisle or window seat is guaranteed.

Embraer E-Jet

The E195 is the longest member of the E-Jet family, featuring a new wing and revised tail section. This aircraft was the prototype.

Specification (E170AR)

Type:	regional/short-haul airliner
Dimensions:	wing span 28.50m (93ft 6in), length 29.67m (97ft 4in), height 7.47m (24ft 6in)
Maximum take-off weight:	38,600kg (85,098lb)
Powerplant:	two 63.15kN (14,200lb) thrust General Electric CF34-8E turbofan engines
Maximum operating speed:	Mach 0.82
Range with maximum passenger load:	3982km (2474 miles)
Service ceiling:	12,497m (41,000ft)
Flight crew:	2
Passengers:	up to 78 in single-class accommodation

With the E190, Embraer began competing with Airbus and Boeing for the first time, since it offered accommodation similar to that available in the A318 and 737-600. History records that the airlines preferred Embraer's aircraft, since neither the Airbus nor the Boeing sold well, while the Brazilians were able to launch the E195. Longer still than the E190 and taking as many as 118 passengers, the E195 entered service with Flybe in 2006.

Embraer had adopted a family approach to the E-Jets, aiming to offer airlines the ultimately in flexibility and a choice of capacities between 78 and 118 seats, allowing them to precisely match available seats to market demand, even as that demand fluctuated through the day. A common crew rating across the models allows the same crew to fly peak schedules – early morning and evening, for example – in the high-capacity E195, or off-peak services when demand is weaker, in the E170.

The manufacturer also promoted its aircraft as revenue generators to carriers operating larger equipment, suggesting than flying a full E195 rather than a two-thirds full A320 on an off-peak schedule made economic sense and might allow the exploitation of previously untenable markets. The E-Jets are offered in baseline, Long Range (LR) and Advanced Range (AR) variants, the latter suitable for long-thin routes considerably beyond what might normally be considered regional. The E170AR can cover sectors of 3982km (2474 miles) with a full passenger load, for example, while the E195AR reaches out to ranges in the region of 4448km (2764 miles) with a similar load. This performance, Embraer's careful attention to passenger appeal and incremental improvements to the range has seen the E-Jets remain extremely popular and the airframer is using the basic airframe as the basis of its E2 challenger to the Bombardier CSeries.

E2: Next Generation E-Jet

With the CSeries offering dramatically improved fuel efficiency compared to current regional jets, Embraer was forced to respond. Rather than return to the CAD screen, however, it is basing its new aircraft on the existing E-Jet series, developing two new wing configurations and employing Pratt & Whitney's PurePower geared turbofan technology. The new wings have raked tips and modified engine pylons among other changes, with different wings for the E175-E2 and E190/E195-E2; there will be no E170-E2.

The smaller aircraft will use the PW1700G engine, with PW1900Gs on the two larger models. Installation of an advanced fly-by-wire system developed from that of the first-generation E-Jets also improves efficiency, allowing smaller tail surfaces to be fitted and thereby reducing drag; it should also make for more comfortable flying in turbulence. All-new cabin interiors will be offered, along with a more comprehensive avionics suite in a revised cockpit, although crew conversion from E-Jet to E2 should take no more than three days.

Embraer aims to have the E190-E2 in service sometime in the first six months of 2018, with the E195-E2 and E175-E2 following around 2019 and 2020, respectively. For the latter model it is promising an 18 per cent reduction in fuel burn per seat compared to the E175 over 1112km (691 miles) with a two-class load of 80 passengers.

Airbus A380 (2005)

There had never been a true challenger to the Boeing 747 until Airbus conceived the considerably more capacious A380. The European 'Super Jumbo' has facilitated new levels of service and passenger comfort, but suffered a difficult and protracted gestation.

Ideas for a giant challenger to the Boeing 747 first began to bounce around the Airbus partners towards the end of the 1980s. There had never been a rival to the 747, then recently reborn as the 747-400, and Airbus intended to create an airliner offering even greater passenger capacity than the U.S. behemoth. Boeing appeared to have few plans for a 747 replacement and subsequently began promoting its thoughts on efficient point-to-point services between airports, rather than Airbus' vision of giant aircraft serving major hubs.

People living near airports were becoming less tolerant of aircraft noise as traffic increased, a fact apparently vindicating the Airbus approach, and in 1990 it embarked on the Very Large Aircraft study. In 1994 this became the Ultra High Capacity Airliner (UHCA) project, while the European manufacturer also worked with Boeing on a Very Large Commercial Aircraft, although the erstwhile partners went their separate ways again in 1996. Airbus continued with the UHCA, firming it up into a serious proposal which, by 1998, had become the A3XX. It was a remarkable

Cockpit
The A380's flight crew operates and interacts with the aircraft through an eight-screen system, using a track ball to control cursor movement between and within screens.

Operating Economics
Airbus claims that its use of composites, an advanced wing, efficient engines and other technologies allow the A380 to offer a 15 per cent per seat reduction in direct operating costs per passenger compared to the 747-8.

Brake To Vacate
A380 crews use the aircraft's Brake To Vacate function to plan the entire approach for an efficient arrival at the correct runway exit.

design, powered by four powerful turbofans and accommodating its passengers on two decks.

A minimum of 30 orders spread across five airlines was required before Airbus was willing to take the considerable risk inherent in launching the A3XX. It achieved the target during 2000, when memoranda of understanding were signed with Emirates, Air France, ILFC, Singapore Airlines, QANTAS and Virgin Atlantic, covering 50 orders and 42 options. The new airliner, soon dubbed the 'Super Jumbo' by the press, was launched as the A380 on 19 December 2000.

Two engine types in the 311–338kN (70,000–76,000lb) thrust class were offered, the Engine Alliance GP7200 and Rolls-Royce Trent 900. Both were

designed for the aircraft, the Trent 900 as an extension of the existing Trent line and the GP7200 by a new General Electric/Pratt & Whitney joint venture. In the event, the Trent was cleared up to 355kN (80,000lb) thrust, having run for the first time in March 2003, while the GP7200 flew for the first time in December 2004.

Jumbo Variations

The initial A380-100 variant was planned for 555 passengers and soon redesignated A380-800. It formed the basis of the A380-800F freighter, offering a 150-tonne payload and subsequently cancelled, and the shorter, 480-seat A380-700, also abandoned. This left the final potential variant as the stretched A380-900,

This aircraft flew the first ever A380 revenue service, between Singapore and Sydney, Australia, on 25 October 2007. Having entered service in 2007, by the time the A380 breaks even it will be almost a decade old. Airbus is considering an upgrade to keep the 'Super Jumbo' at the top of its game well into the future.

Main Undercarriage
Four giant main undercarriage legs distribute the A380's weight, helping avoid damage to airport surfaces. The two inner legs each mount a six-wheel bogey, with four wheels on each of the outer legs.

Airbus A380

but this too failed to progress. Airbus expected to fly the first A380 in 2004 and to place it in service around two years later.

In the event, the first aircraft was rolled out at Toulouse on 18 January 2005 and another two months'

Specification (A380-800, highest weight option)

Type:	long-haul, high-capacity airliner
Dimensions:	wing span 79.75m (261ft 8in), length 72.72m (238ft 7in), height 24.09m (79ft 1in)
Maximum take-off weight:	560,000kg (1,268,000lb)
Powerplant:	four 311kN (70,000lb) thrust Engine Alliance GP7200 or Rolls-Royce Trent 900 turbofan engines
Maximum operating speed:	Mach 0.89
Maximum range:	15,700km (9756 miles)
Flight crew:	2
Passengers:	up to 853 in single-class accommodation

Lufthansa flew its first Airbus A380 service, to New York, on 28 February 2011.

work was required before it was ready for its maiden flight on 27 April. Airbus used a five-jet fleet for the test and certification programme, while a dedicated airframe was fatigue-tested over a period of 27 months and stressed to the equivalent of 47,500 cycles. Four of the test aircraft were Rolls-Royce powered, the GP7200-engined machine flying for the first time on 25 August 2006.

A major crisis had loomed in June 2005, however, with the aircraft's many miles of cabling, especially in the wings. Subsequent remedial work was slow and difficult, and Airbus undertook considerable redesign to fully 'productionize' the wiring installations, and valuable time had been lost.

Other potential problems were more easily addressed. Operators and regulators had been concerned that evacuating a full passenger load from a stricken A380 might prove difficult, but in March 2006, 20 crew and 853 people acting as passengers evacuated safely in 78 seconds through only eight of the aircraft's 16 exits, proving the case for its safe evacuation.

On 15 October 2007, considerably later than planned, Airbus delivered the first A380 to Singapore Airlines.

It was Trent engined, and certification for the GP7200 option was not achieved until 14 December 2007. Singapore Airlines flew its first revenue service on 25 October and the passenger appeal of the A380 was immediately obvious. Soon the type was also in service with Emirates and Qantas, Airbus working hard to iron out teething problems with the electrical systems.

The A380 is an immensely complex machine and subsequent issues with the fuel system, sensors and noisy doors have been rectified, as have two more serious problems. In November 2010, a Qantas A380 suffered an uncontained failure of one of its Trent engines. The aircraft made a safe landing and the fault was traced to a manufacturing error – all of the Trent-engined A380s in service were then grounded for checks.

Subsequent problems with tiny cracks in the 'feet' connecting the wing ribs to the aircraft's outer skin were also identified and fixed, but not without considerable expense. Problems aside, the A380 is regarded as a flagship by all its operators and deeply appreciated by passengers. But orders have not been as forthcoming as Airbus had hoped. In late 2014, company executives commented that the programme was expected to break even in 2015, with few sales through into 2018. With 318 aircraft ordered and 147 delivered, Airbus was considering whether to upgrade or discontinue the A380.

Passenger Experience

The A380's capacious cabin space has allowed operators to explore new concepts in passenger experience, especially at the first and super first class levels. Emirates was first with showers for its premium passengers, for example, while Etihad introduced Residence suites alongside First Apartments when it began A380 services in December 2014. Only one Residence suite is fitted per aircraft. The Residence is a suite of three rooms – lounge, double bedroom and shower room – for a single passenger or two travelling together. It includes the dedicated services of a butler and comprehensive inflight entertainment options.

Boeing 787 Dreamliner (2009)

With the 787 Dreamliner, Boeing produced perhaps one of the most ambitious and technologically advanced airliners ever. Like Airbus with the A380, it struggled to bring the high-tech 787 to market, but it is now proving itself in service.

Airbus designed the A380 to deliver large passenger loads into primary airport hubs, from where smaller aircraft would take them on to their final destinations. This traditional approach to operations had begun to evolve soon after the first big jets entered service and the A380 was intended to reduce the number of large aircraft movements into the hubs.

Having found little market interest in a stretched new-technology 747, Boeing embarked on multiple studies and arrived at a different solution to the problems of congestion and noise surrounding the inexorable rise in airline traffic. It proposed highly efficient mid-sized aircraft capable of directly connecting more city pairs over long ranges. Taking on what might once have been niche, long, thin routes, a new Boeing would serve cities with smaller airports direct, relieving the pressure on the hubs and reducing the need for regional connections.

In 2001 Boeing revealed considerable detail on one of its more radical ideas. Seating a maximum of 250 passengers over ranges as long as 16,660km (10,350 miles), the Sonic Cruiser was designed for a Mach 0.98

Qatar Airways flew its first 787-8 service on 13 December 2012. The airline ordered thirty 787-8s on 5 April 2007.

Composites
Boeing employs composite construction on a massive scale with the 787. Around 50 per cent of the aircraft's structure by weight is in composite materials.

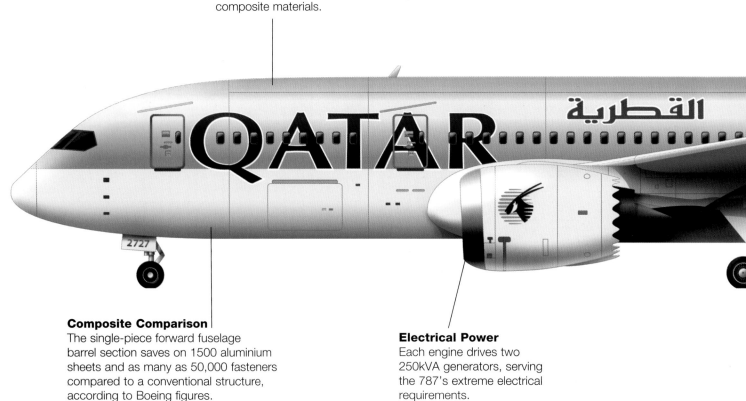

Composite Comparison
The single-piece forward fuselage barrel section saves on 1500 aluminium sheets and as many as 50,000 fasteners compared to a conventional structure, according to Boeing figures.

Electrical Power
Each engine drives two 250kVA generators, serving the 787's extreme electrical requirements.

cruising speed, considerably faster than all in-service airliners with the exception of Concorde. Flying at high subsonic speed the aircraft avoided the problems of excessive fuel consumption and sonic boom that accompany supersonic flight, but managed to return a significant saving in travel time. Once projected for service from 2008, the Sonic Cruiser failed to gain airline approval in the post-9/11 world, where efficiency in operation was more important than speed.

With little interest from its customers, Boeing abandoned the Sonic Cruiser in 2002, instead concentrating on the 7E7, an extremely ambitious aircraft designed to exploit technology yet to be developed and planned to operate with lower fuel burn over medium/

Above: All Nippon Airways were the first airliner to operate the Boeing 787-8, which first flew commercially in October 2011. The 787-8 is the base model of the 787 family, with a length of 57m (186ft) and a wingspan of 60m (197ft).

Passenger Experience
Among the 787's many cabin features, its automatically dimming cabin windows and LED mood lighting have been particularly well accepted.

Efficiency
Customers appreciate the 787's 20 per cent reduction in fuel burn compared to other types over similar routes, but it also produces 20 per cent lower emissions.

Boeing 787 Dreamliner

The 787 is equipped for the latest navigational procedures and optimum crew efficiency. It also retains commonality with the 777.

Specification (787-9 Dreamliner)

Type:	medium/long-haul airliner
Dimensions:	wing span 60m (197ft), length 63m (206ft), height 17m (56ft)
Maximum take-off weight:	252,651kg (557,000lb)
Powerplant:	two 320kN (71,000lb) thrust Rolls-Royce Trent 1000 or General Electric GEnx turbofan engines
Cruising speed:	Mach 0.85
Range:	15,372km (9552 miles)
Service ceiling:	13,106m (43,000ft)
Flight crew:	2
Passengers:	up to 280 in single-class accommodation

long-haul routes than any aircraft before or then in development. It would require new engines compatible with Boeing's vision of turning to 'all electric' systems rather than relying on bleed air from the engines, as in previous designs. It would also use weight-saving composites on an unprecedented scale and revolutionize the passenger experience.

The sheer ambition of the project combined with increasing employee welfare costs to convince Boeing's executives that they should seek a network of risk sharing partners and establish a global supply chain. Ultimately, more than 40 aerospace companies became involved, supplying components from locations spread across the world. By the time it launched the 7E7 as a production programme in April 2004, Boeing had designated the type 787 and subsequently named it the Dreamliner.

Dreamliner Defined

With the Dreamliner Boeing not only pushed existing technology to the limit, but, in close cooperation with its partners, developed extreme new technologies. The fuselage, for example, is built from a series of single-piece composite barrels, the complete structure weighing approximately 4536kg (10,000lb) less than if it were in conventional aluminium alloys. The wings also employ a high degree of composite construction and include raked wing tips for optimum efficiency.

Boeing itself notes that the major fuel-saving technology is in the 787's powerplant. Both the Rolls-Royce Trent 1000 and General Electric GEnx were specially developed for the 787 to support the aircraft's electric architecture. Rolls-Royce based the Trent 1000 on elements of the A380's Trent 900, while GE exploited GE90 technology in the GEnx. Both engines are installed in nacelles featuring scalloped trailing edges, a noise reducing feature that also appears on the GEnx-engined 747-8.

The first Dreamliner was rolled out on 8 July 2007, but hopes of an imminent first flight were soon dashed. Such had been the demand on the supply chain that much of the internal work on major components in that first aircraft was incomplete. Wiring runs and other crucial construction items had to be completed retrospectively in a painstaking process that Boeing completed while also knocking its supply chain into shape. The company's entire product line was then hit by industrial action, a 58-day strike further delaying Dreamliner development,

but the aircraft was finally moved to the flightline on 3 May 2009. Now Boeing discovered that it needed to reinforce the structure in the area of the wing–fuselage joint, work that delayed first flight again, this time to 15 December, when the aircraft finally lifted off.

Eight machines flew the 787 test and certification programme, allowing first delivery, to All Nippon Airways (ANA), on 25 September 2011. The aircraft's efficiency and passenger appeal was immediately obvious, but problems remained. In January 2013 a Japan Airlines (JAL) jet suffered a fuel leak on the ground and later that month both ANA and JAL suffered fires connected with the 787's high-tech lithium-ion batteries. There followed a three-month grounding while Boeing redesigned the battery installation, but the fleet began returning to the air from late April.

A subsequent fire on an Ethiopian Airlines 787 in July 2013 was traced to the batteries of an emergency locator beacon, but Boeing has worked tirelessly to find fixes for all these issues and by the beginning of 2014 the aircraft was beginning to mature. In June the first of the 290-seat 787-9 joined the 250-seat -8 in service, when Air New Zealand took the first example.

787 Variants

The Boeing 787-8 is the base model Dreamliner, as shown here. Carrying up to 250 passengers over routes as long as 14,500km (9010 miles), it is the successor to the 767-200ER/300ER. Next into service was the 787-9, hauling a maximum of 280 passengers over 15,372km (9552 miles)

as an efficient alternative to the A340-300 and 777-200ER. Finally, the 787-10 is scheduled for delivery from 2018. Optimized for a maximum range of 12,964km (8055 miles) with up to 330 passengers, it will be a direct competitor to the A350-1000.

Index

Page numbers in *italics* refer to illustration captions.

Index

Index